Protocol for Profit

OTHER BOOKS BY CARL NELSON

Your Own Import–Export Business:
Winning the Trade Game

Import/Export: How to Get Started in
International Trade

Global Success: International Business
Tactics for the 1990s

Managing Globally: A Complete Guide to
Competing Worldwide

■ GLOBAL MANAGER SERIES ■

Protocol for Profit

A Manager's Guide to Competing Worldwide

Carl A Nelson

INTERNATIONAL THOMSON BUSINESS PRESS
I(T)P® An International Thomson Publishing Company

London • Bonn • Johannesburg • Madrid • Melbourne • Mexico City • New York • Paris
Singapore • Tokyo • Toronto • Albany, NY • Belmont, CA • Cincinnati, OH • Detroit, MI

Protocol for Profit

British Library Cataloguing-in-Publication Data
A catalogue record for this book is available from the British Library

First published 1998 by International Business Press

Typeset by J&L Composition Ltd, Filey, North Yorkshire
Printed in the UK by TJ International, Padstow, Cornwall

ISBN 1–86152–314–9

International Thomson Business Press
Berkshire House
168–173 High Holborn
London WCIV 7AA
UK

http://www.itbp.com

DEDICATION

To grandchildren Jocelyn, Justin, Kristina, and Andrei,
and to
Dr. Dorothy Lipp Harris, Ph.D.,
a professional woman leader who made a difference

Contents

Preface

Since World War II the proportion of international trade as a share of global income has risen from 7 percent to 21 percent. Today the trend marches on and is the primary driver of world growth.

Renato Ruggiero, the Director-General of the World Trade Organization, said it best: "Globalism is a reality of our time." And unless mankind resorts to Luddite practices or enters into another mass madness like World Wars I and II globalism will remain an irreversible process which thrusts businesses of every nation into the transnational marketplace. Cultural lines are being crossed every day. Even the smallest of businesses must compete in the shrinking global village, where understanding cultural contexts can make or break sales and marketing efforts. Something as simple as a greeting can be misunderstood. Comprehension and heeding cultural variables are critical to success in the ever-growing international marketplace.

Protocol has been a part of life for thousands of years. Scenes painted in Egyptian tombs and writings of early times tell of the strict rules that applied to various phases of life, and even death. Even the term "protocol" comes from the Greek words meaning "the first glue," and indeed it may be said that protocol is the glue which holds official life in our global society together. It represents a body of social discipline which brings to meetings of business leaders a mixture of good manners and common sense that makes effective communications possible.

Lack of familiarity with foreign business protocol, practices and social customs can weaken a company's position in the market and ultimately lead to failure. Some of the cultural differences include distinctions in business styles, attitudes toward punctuality, and such things as gift giving, titles, and gestures.

Personnel from these firms, be they Polish, French, Japanese, or American, need a ready reference to prepare them at least minimally for their international business dealings. The purpose of *Protocol for Profit* is to present such a practical guide. It offers an extensive universal understanding of key global behaviors coupled with a synopsis of business conditions for most of the nations of the world, with special emphasis on emerging markets such as New Europe, China, Mexico, Russia, and Vietnam.

The theme of *Protocol for Profit* is that it is essential to prepare before traveling to a foreign country to do business—disaster awaits those who have not done their homework.

Enjoy this book and take away the optimistic view that the twenty-first century will be a good time—when global business, tourism, and recreation will be a pleasurable experience—a world in which you will want to participate by traveling to foreign places and tasting their richness.

Acknowledgments

I am deeply indebted to the following people who took time to read and critique the draft manuscript and contribute to its authenticity: Carol Ding (China), Huong Yen Duong (Vietnam), Charles Fordjour (Ghana), Vicente Hernandez (Mexico), Xing Wei Liang (China), Aswin Pranata (Indonesia), Roberto Sainz (Mexico), Tanya Wrage (Germany), Kun Yang (China), Frank J. Catterson (International banker), Captain Duane Heisinger, U.S. Navy (retired), Captain Rudy Daus U.S. Navy (retired), Dr. Michael McManus, Ph.D. (President, International School of Management), Julian Thomas (Publishing Manager, ITBP Europe), So-Shan Au (Editor, ITBP), Lisa Williams (copy-editor), Jacqui Baldwin (Marketing Manager, ITP), and Rebecca George (Marketing Executive, ITP).

A special acknowledgement also for minor segments of Chapters 3 and 4 printed with permission of the McGraw-Hill Companies, New York, NY, from my book *Import/Export: How to Get Started in International Trade*.

About the author

Carl Nelson is well qualified to write this book. Over a thirty-year naval career rising, by way of the United States Naval Academy at Annapolis, Maryland, to Captain in the U.S. Navy and command of guided-missile cruisers, destroyers, and combat in South-east Asia, he met and entertained diplomats as well as business people in most countries of the world.

In his sixteen-year second career he has concentrated on the field of international business as an educator, lecturer, trainer, and writer. He is a recognized specialist in global business strategy, and is listed in *Who's Who in California* and *Who's Who in the World*.

Dr. Nelson is Professor of International Business at the School of International Management (ISM), San Diego, California, where he teaches graduate-level courses. He previously served on the faculties of the U.S. Military Academy at West Point and the U.S. Naval Academy at Annapolis, Maryland.

He is also president of Global Business Systems (GBS), an international business consulting and training company. He has more than forty years of global experience in government and private business, and has traveled to most countries of the world. He lived for two years in Japan, one year in South Vietnam, and is intimately knowledgeable about the Western Pacific and the Indian Ocean area. His experience includes third-world economic development under the Agency for International Development (USAID) and Mexican *maquiladora* operations. He specializes in presenting seminars and workshops on the basics and advanced business applications of global trade. He has given these seminars to Asian, American, Mexican, and Russian business people.

As a professional writer he has published both fiction and non-fiction. He is the author of: *Your Own Import–Export Business: Winning the Trade Game* (Global Business and Trade Communications, 1988); *Global Success: International Business Tactics of the 1990s* (TAB-McGraw-Hill, 1990); *Managing Globally: A Complete Guide to Competing Worldwide* (Irwin Professional Publishing, 1993), and *Import/Export: How to Get Started in International Trade*, 2nd edition (McGraw-Hill, 1995). His articles on international business matters have been published in

The World & I, Global Trade Executive, Twin Plant News, and the *Daily Transcript* (a local San Diego business newspaper). Technical papers authored by him have been published by the Association of Global Business. He has won awards for both fiction and non-fiction, and is president of the San Diego Writers'/Editors' Guild.

His international experience is complemented by his academic training. He earned his Doctorate in Business Administration (D.B.A.), Finance (emphasis on international finance and trade), from the United States International University (ISIU) in San Diego, California. His doctoral dissertation, *The Relationship of Export Obstacles to the Export Trading Company Act of 1982,* focused on U.S. small business export problems. He was recognized by USIU with its 1989 outstanding alumni award. Dr. Nelson is also a graduate of the Naval War College, holds a Master of Science degree in Management (Economics/Systems Analysis) from the Naval Post Graduate School in Monterey, California, and an engineering degree from the U.S. Naval Academy at Annapolis, Maryland.

PART ONE

Understanding global protocol

This part of the book presents the underpinning matters of global protocol. That is, it discusses why it is important that we leave our own borders to do business and gives the key elements of protocol. It explains how our cultural roots determine protocol, and then offers several chapters that are designed to assist you practically in your work.

Introduction

The globalization of international finance has created a renaissance in culture, language, and social customs. And those individuals and corporations that pursue international discussions and negotiations with assurance and skill ... and without avoidable blunders due to unfamiliarity of cultural differences ... will succeed where others wonder what went wrong!

John Nesbitt

So you're off to Japan, then to Russia, then to Indonesia, then to Mexico, then to ... and you want to do a lot of business, but don't have time to do exhaustive research. To transform global challenges into profitable reality you need a guide book that gives you quick answers, one that makes certain you will not offend anyone and mess up the business deals. *Protocol for Profit* is the book for you.

Why can't they be more like us?

Some say that the enormous changes in communications—satellites, television, and interlinked computers—are causing cultures to merge. If that is happening you can wager profitably that the merger will not take place overnight—cultural change just does not happen that way. A complete homogenization of earth may never occur; on the other hand, if it ever does the time frame for that change will be more like 5,000 years from now rather than fifty or 500. Until then, "they" won't be exactly like "us."

Why worry about protocol?

Businesses are going global.

No!

Businesses *have* gone global and they are playing an ever-expanding role in world affairs. Globalism is an irreversible process that has thrust businesses of every nation into the transnational marketplace. Products and services, as well as the people who represent them in the global trade arena, must be world class. People are also traveling more—we vacation wherever the venue is exciting and interesting. Yet accommodating different behaviors seems to confound many of us.

In this era of intensifying global competition and unprecedented complexity of doing business across national borders the challenges for the traveling global manager can be overwhelming. Too many lucrative deals and opportunities have been lost because the players lacked sensitivity to protocol. What is appropriate in one country may be inappropriate in another. Gift giving can be tricky—it can be intended as a thoughtful gesture or considered a bribe. It is imperative to understand culture, customs, and business practices. You must have practical, effective protocol skills for establishing important relationships, for negotiating critical contracts, and for incorporating key cultural differences into product design and marketing.

For you to succeed, new disciplines are needed. Doing your homework before undertaking a trip to a foreign country will be your best investment toward enjoyment and success or unhappiness and failure.

Viva la différence!

One of the most interesting things about global travel is that "they" are not like "us"—"they" are foreigners. "Those" people are attractive and enticing; "they" make "us" want to travel. There is great diversity in the world, even within nations, and when we travel across borders variety enlarges. If you only wish to view people as if they were in a fish bowl this book is not necessary. But if you wish to have interchange—that is, do business, discuss life and issues, and enjoy the benefits of diversity—then this book offers some short cuts and ideas that will smooth the road and endear you to "those" people.

What the book is designed to do

All too often business people think culture will take care of itself after technical business studies and analyses are complete, but maintaining competitiveness means changing your viewpoint and adjusting strategy to the demands imposed by the new world environment of globalism and interdependence. To cope and compete in international markets one must factor foreign cultures into business strategies, and this book is designed to do just that.

The approach of this book is to present a practical guide to key global behaviors and a snapshot of business conditions for about 135 countries, with emphasis on the major trading nations as well as such emerging traders as New Europe, Mexico, China, Russia, and Vietnam.

This professional "how-to" book offers a small amount of theory with large portions of practical information in a country-by-country format.

The origin of the book

Protocol for Profit is the product of my own global travels during a thirty-year naval career, in which I met, entertained, and conducted business with diplomats as well as commercial people. Some material was collected while attending several very excellent military training courses in preparation for overseas duty in Vietnam and Japan. Even more was gathered while traveling during my more than sixteen-year (thus far) second career in international business. Still more was gained through primary research. I personally interviewed people from many countries and sought the advice and criticism of natives of every country listed in this book.

To make it even better, I continue to seek advice. It is intended that no reader should find an offensive word or sentence or a single inaccuracy about his or her country. Should that happen I would appreciate a note. Explain for me how it could be better done.

What sets this book apart

This is a practical book, the key elements of which are the discussions of each of the major elements of behavior, culture, and the country-by-country protocol information.

The things that set this book apart from others are its practical approach and universal viewpoint. It offers an easy reference (snapshot) to business conditions and protocols for 135 countries, organized by regional groups. Equally important is its global viewpoint—people from all countries will find this book useful.

In addition, the book explains:

- the eight key elements of protocol;
- advance preparations;
- gender tips;
- time value;
- communications;
- travel tips;
- body language;
- about jokes;
- gift giving;
- culture shock;
- negotiations;
- commercial holidays.

Audience

Protocol for Profit is for ordinary international business people as well as general travelers who must think critically about the correctness of their dealings in other cultures. The world is shrinking, but the need to observe the cultures of other countries is more important than ever. There is no excuse for ignorance and *Protocol for Profit* will help you avoid common faux pas.

What this book explains

Protocol for Profit not only explains why we must be concerned about human relations when in another culture, but also offers the key practical protocols for each of 135 countries where we might travel to do business. It does so in two parts: "Understanding global protocol" and "Tips and traps: country-by-country business conditions and Protocols." The first part presents the underpinning matters of global protocol. That is, it discusses why it is important that we leave our own borders to do business and gives the key elements of protocol. It explains how cultural roots determine protocol, and then offers several chapters that are designed to assist you in your work. The second part provides an easy reference to business conditions and specific, practical country-by-country protocols by region.

How to use this book

Preparation is half the battle. Even a little homework will be appreciated by the people of the place you are visiting. The best way to use *Protocol for Profit* is to review the appropriate sections prior to visiting a new country. You should carry the book with you in your travels and refer to it often. Obviously a book such as this cannot explain every nuance of protocol. How much do you need to know? Enough so that you do not unwittingly offend. Enough so that you do not lose business. Enough so that you avoid costly mistakes. Enough so that you convey an image of a professional with a positive business intention.

Remember, there are no ugly Americans or Frenchmen, or Japanese, there are only thoughtless individuals who assume erroneously that there is a hierarchy of cultures and theirs is the best.

The next chapter discusses the global economic conditions that explain why the people of the world are doing so much business across borders.

■ Hot tip

There is one universal tip to enjoying the people of the world and that is "smile." When all else fails, raise your eyebrows, show your teeth and be of good humor— it works everywhere and may supplant everything else that is written.

For instance, we know that when entering any country the order is: (1) pass through immigration, then, if they decide to let you in, (2) you may go through customs. It happens that way at every port of entry, everywhere in the world. Now, the people who guard the immigration and customs gates are hard-working patriots of the highest order. They know it is their duty to protect their country and they often have long irritable days carrying out that responsibility. So, you come along and they ask you to *open* your luggage so they can quickly examine the contents and you say, "Again? Can't any of you guys get it straight? I just did this in thus and so county and nothing has changed. Besides don't you know we (nationality) are honest people? This is stupid." And the guard points to a table against the wall and says, with a wrinkled brow, "Please empty everything out of every piece of your luggage and lay the clothes over there." Pointing to another table he or she says, "Lay all other articles over there and when I have time I will look at what you have done." And you begin to say—but before you say it you remember the word "smile." And you do what he or she asks and say to yourself, "Why didn't I do that in the first place?"

CHAPTER ONE

Why do business across borders?

As we enter the 21st century, I believe that globalization will progress
to a point much further than any of us can foresee.
Jong-Hyon Chey, Chairman of the Sunkyong Group

The primary reason people from all nations want to do business in other
countries as well as their own is that in the twenty-first century markets
will be worldwide.

Think about it.

As late as the 1930s, limited to cross-country rail travel, most businesses still served only local or regional markets. It wasn't until the late
1940s that masses of firms in Europe as well as the United States
expanded nationally. It was only after the development of paved highways supported by gas stations serving cars and trucks that smaller firms
began to expand geographically.

In the 1980s and 1990s national expansion finally approached its natural limits, and competing in other national markets became the next
target. Businesses all over the world began looking beyond their own borders to sell products previously sold only in their own country. At the
same time, governments began to realize that trade was the new means
to grow economically. Nations without an abundance of natural
resources and without high per capita incomes began selling their products in countries where people had higher incomes and could afford their
products.

Global wealth

As recently as the seventeenth century humankind looked about and saw
a life which was short and brutish, and the outlook was that it would
likely remain so. However, over the subsequent centuries things have
improved, certainly for the people of the richest nations, who see significantly longer, healthier, and more enjoyable lives.

But now, for the first time, there is credible opportunity for all of humankind. Why? Because the world is experiencing its era of greatest wealth.

What is driving the incredible growth of global wealth? The evidence is clear. The engine is free enterprise, free markets, and, above all, globalization, which has been brought about by the technology that opened worldwide financial and product markets.

Trade the wealth driver

The emergence of globalization, which ushered in an era of unprecedented economic growth, is characterized by a reduction in trade barriers, rapid technological developments, and a decline in transportation costs. This permits producers to separate production functions that were once integrated within the firm. For each production process companies now seek the most cost-effective locations throughout the world. Because of the emergence of new market economies in Asia as well as Central and Eastern Europe, the number of potential locations where these processes can be executed is increasing.

Gross global trade (GGT)

The curve of GGT was essentially flat until the late 1800s, when the development of clipper ships began to change the slope. The curve sprang to life about the turn of the twentieth century and took a dynamic upward turn as the technological revolution heated up. But the real explosion of globalism did not begin until 1965–70, about twenty years after World War II, when, like the arrival of spring, all over the globe economies awakened from a sleep caused by the ravages of death and destruction. The boom came after production capability had been restored and when people worldwide wanted more of everything.

Figure 1 shows the incredible twenty-year growth of world exports (expressed in U.S. dollars) between about 1950 and 1970 and projects the trend line into the future.

According to the World Bank, global trade prospects were never brighter. Merchandise trade will average more than 6% into the foreseeable future, and a number of developing countries, especially in East and South Asia, will post even bigger gains. Increased opening of markets and concomitant competition are holding inflation down, thus providing the conditions needed to sustain long term growth.

Evidence of wealth

For fifty years, since the end of World War II, the governments of the world have been working at freeing trade, and the evidence of their success is that tariff levels among the industrial nations have been reduced

Figure 1 Growth of international trade

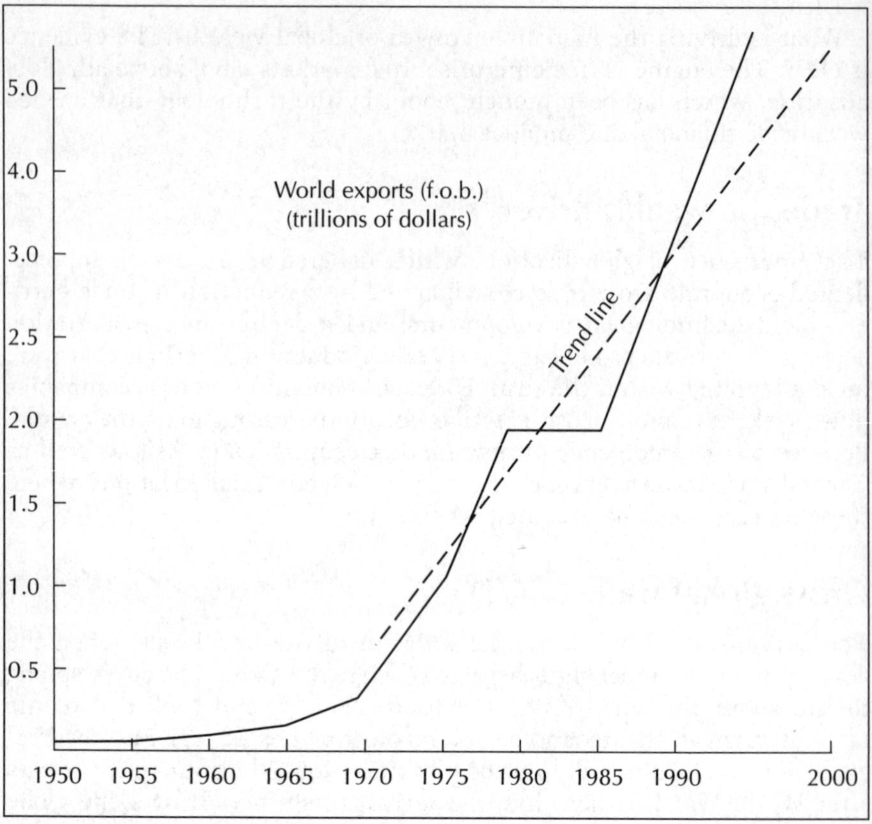

Source: Constructed by the author from United Nations annual reports, 1983–9 and International Monetary Fund statistics 1948–89. *Note*: Not adjusted for real dollars.

from about 40 percent to about 5 percent, world trade has grown by fourteen times, and global output has soared sixfold since 1950.

Deterrence to growth

Recognizing the danger of projections based on trends, the future could look totally different from the optimistic view hypothesized here. By closing borders and sheltering its industries trade could come to a dead stop, as it did during the late 1920s and early 1930s. However, that would happen only if there was another mass war like World War I and II or if the nations of the world regressed to ultra-nationalism. It is unlikely that business people of the world, having experienced the wealth international trade produces, will permit political forces to reverse global progress.

Boundless opportunity

Given the consumption possibilities that result from the incredible growth of global wealth, what are the opportunities?

North America

The United States is the wealthiest consumer market in the world, having more than 270 million people (1996 census), with about $25,000 per capita incomes. Canada is an equally excellent market.

Emerging markets

Businesses worldwide have entered emerging markets such as Latin America, South-east Asia, and Eastern Europe, where growth is expected to be as high as double the levels found in industrialized nations.

Asia

Despite the currency setbacks of the late 1990s, the fastest growing region of the world today will continue to be East Asia, where expansion is as much as 8–10 percent in such nations as China and Malaysia. This represents business opportunity and untold wealth for those who sell in these markets.

New Europe

With the fall of the Berlin Wall in 1989 and the disintegration of the former Soviet Union a year or two later, a new Europe came into being—a place of increasing free enterprise. Naturally, these former communist states are racing to catch up with a West that had a five-decade advantage to prosper in an environment of free markets and competition. Businesses in these newly independent nations seek trading partners for products previously not marketed to their people.

Trade blocs

For many years a creative Europe, step by step, harmonized first its customs regulations then its transportation laws, until now it is, some believe, on the verge of a complete economic and political union that will look and act much like the United States of America. The European trade bloc consists of the fifteen nations of the European Community plus a growing number of other European countries.

As if in competition with the European Union, the United States, Canada, and Mexico formed their own bloc, the North American Free-

Trade Agreement (NAFTA), which is in the process of harmonizing its internal barriers to trade.

Simultaneously, talks have begun on the early developmental stages of a similar Asian bloc, the Asian-Pacific Economic Cooperation (APEC).

The formation of these blocs has resulted in a reduction in barriers and the freeing of trade, which has contributed to the growing wealth of the world. They represent increasing trade opportunities never before available to businesses.

The World Trade Organization (WTO)

The major reason for the growth of international trade has been general agreement among the nations that freeing trade is good for the world. During the last half of the twentieth century this consensus manifested itself in trade-rule negotiations ("rounds") between the members of the General Agreement on Tariffs and Trade (GATT). Each periodic meeting resulted in an incremental increase in the number of nations that participated and a reduction in tariffs. Each round has leveraged on the last, thus moving toward ever-increasing commercial freedom. Each round thus brought freer world trade and an uplifting of global wealth. The most recent round, the Uruguay round, made historic progress by its adoption of the new organizational name World Trade Organization (WTO), with stronger refereeing powers, thus strengthening its position as a supranational organization that ranks in equal importance with the World Bank and the International Monetary Fund (IMF).

Future economic strategies

The reduction of tariffs and the success of trade preference regimes such as NAFTA and the European Union have sparked a number of proposals which would further expand global business opportunity. One option would expand NAFTA, another would form a North Atlantic free-trade arrangement by merging European free trade with NAFTA.

Taking action

Of course, if you are waiting for your phone to ring from someone asking you to sell your products across national borders you should expect a long delay. The choice has already been made for you by the marketplace. Your telephone will not ring because your competitors are already selling in your markets and your firm could be out of business in the twenty-first century if it does not compete.

This means executives and managers at all levels of small, medium-sized, and large firms must travel in order to:

■ take advantage of opportunities;
■ minimize the risks of operating across borders;
■ close deals;
■ cement relationships;
■ reduce inherent mistrust;
■ enjoy the magnificent diversity of the world.

Why worry about protocol?

To take advantage of global opportunities, like it or not, business people worldwide must travel. Simple mistakes in protocol could be the cause of lost sales and "oops," there goes another promising and otherwise successful career.

It's about sales

Selling is, simply put, about finding decision-makers, those who have the authority to say yes, and then convincing them to do so. Much of that process is behavioral. Of course, you must have a salable product and there must be a market, but competition today is so fierce that the selection of your product over another is often based on your ability to connect with the decision-maker.

It's about relationships

Of course, contacts are important, but more important are the relationships that can be lost on one mistake of protocol.

It's your career

Another reason to worry about protocol is the fact that how you deal with others is the key to a successful career. However, most careers are not subject to the "fish-bowl" environment of global business. Your career in international business depends on several things:

■ your understanding of business protocol;
■ your desire and ability to sell;
■ your enjoyment of travel;
■ your desire to deal with a foreign environment and language;
■ your ability to adapt to other cultures;
■ a track record or at least the display of behavioral instincts for the bottom line;
■ your ability to close;
■ your ability to bounce back, to regroup and deal with rejection.

Of course, your understanding and sensitivity to protocol are major factors in achieving each of these characteristics.

The next chapter describes the eight elements of international protocol which will aid you in achieving your international business objectives.

CHAPTER TWO

Eight common elements of international protocol

Protocol: a Code prescribing strict adherence to correct etiquette and procedures.

Webster's Dictionary

There are eight common protocol elements or categories which permit you to do business successfully in any culture. Ranked by importance, they are:

- names;
- rank and title;
- time;
- dress;
- behavior;
- communications;
- gift giving;
- food and drink.

The purpose of this chapter is to provide the meanings of the eight protocol elements so you can better understand their importance and use them, along with the discussions in the following chapters, to do your homework for your next cross-border trip.

Names

Names are our most precious asset. Names set us apart—they are what makes us different from others. Of course, remembering names and using them in addressing others is one of the most important yet difficult elements of protocol. One of the most sticky aspects is which name to use and when to use it. A general rule is to adopt a conservative approach by addressing a person by their title followed by their last or family name. Only after the relationship has progressed and the other has given permission would you address them in the more familiar way, using their first or given name. It sounds easy, but in some cases it is very troublesome because different cultures arrange their names differently and it is not always easy to discern the given from the family name. For instance, in Asia the surname precedes the personal name, and in many Hispanic cultures the person's family name is followed by the mother's family name and it is not always clear which is to be used and when.

Rank and title

Notwithstanding powerful ideas about democracy and individual equality, most of the societies of the world still prize rank and titles highly. This is as true in business as it is in the diplomatic relations between nations. In other words, the world is still rank-conscious and in order to be successful you must be able to sort juniors from seniors. Failure to understand who has influence may close doors instead of opening them.

By rank, we mean those who have a higher status among the hierarchy of their organization, not necessarily in the world at large. There are no worldwide rules and, unlike military officers or the police, business people do not wear uniforms that show their rank. In the business world the only way we know relative rank is through research or by what is shown on our business cards. Very high-ranking people, if they have cards at all, often have only name cards—their point is, it is your job to research who they are and it is unlikely they want to do business with you if you don't.

Titles vary in their usage. Mister (Mr.), miss, Ms., missus (Mrs.), doctor (Dr.), colonel (Col.), licencia (Lic.), mean essentially what they say. But president, vice-president, manager, or director may mean different things in different companies and countries. Be sure your research leads you to understand the rank of your foreign business partners. (See Appendix C for more information.)

Time

Time is one of the main variables among national cultures. In some countries the day seems to fly by with little opportunity to get everything done. Yet in others time seems to stand still, as those things that have to be done get done and others never do and no one cares. Americans often say "time is money," but, in truth, the careful use of time is more a determinate of lifestyle and that varies among culture segments within nations as well as among them.

Timeliness or punctuality is one of those variables. In most countries it is a gross discourtesy to be late for an appointment. In others, particularly those of Latin origin, being late by as much as a half-hour is quite acceptable and mannerly.

The duration of your stay is also a variable. In some countries the longer you stay, the more you convey closeness and trust. In others it is appropriate to gage your departure in very precise terms—per the invitation. (See Appendix D for rough rules of thumb.)

■ Hot tip	lingering hostility. Frank
Don't disrespect: Frank had an appointment to meet Isuko at 11.30 in the morning, but he arrived at 12 o'clock. Their conversation was friendly but Isuko harbored a	unconsciously communicated his disrespect by thinking the appointment was not very important or that Isuko was a person who didn't need to be treated with respect.

Dress

Do first impressions matter? You bet they do, and the clothes you wear often provide that first impression. It is always safe to project a conservative image. That is, for men: a dark suit, white shirt, and conservative tie; for women: a knee-length dress, high-cut blouse and comfortable shoes. Of course, weather and culture may dictate that on certain occasions non-Western dress may be appropriate. For instance, in the Philippines a Barong Tagolog shirt is always appropriate. Light clothes in particularly sultry climates may also make sense. On all matters related to dress don't hesitate to ask your host or business partner for advice and follow the country culture.

Behavior

Our personal behavior conveys how serious we are about doing business and can reap the greatest payoff in cross-border dealings.

Concern for others

We extend our sincerity by displaying constancy of concern for others. Good manners are valued by every society—and manners are rooted conceptually in acts which do not offend. Of course, understanding and appreciating the problems of others tightens the bonds of trust so important to doing international business.

Tact and discretion

Not to criticize and to avoid criticism are the foundations of civil behavior and they apply on a global basis. Being tactful and discreet applies to that behavior which conveys a lower level of emotion and contributes to confidence and good faith.

Manners

Manners are universally taught in every country by fathers, mothers and grandparents, and of course they are reinforced in schools. Don't get caught in the trap of believing that the manners you were taught are universal. What constitutes good manners in one country may not in another.

Ethics

Among people of different countries and cultures one often hears arguments that ethics differ from nation to nation. However, when pinned down to specifics it is not unusual to learn that, worldwide, there is a general understanding of what is right and what is wrong. Don't be quick to judge an entire people on the basis of a few. Ethics have never been more important than in today's global marketplace, because ethics are the foundation of mutual trust.

Communications

We communicate in many ways—written and oral—and often our communications give the first and lasting impression. Our speech conveys ideas, but our eyes, hands, shoulders, and, yes, even our feet sometimes tell a different story. The key to good communication in all cultures is the ability to convey openness and trust. A simple greeting in "their" language is flattering and is often the only signal necessary to let them know you are willing to do business on mutual grounds.

Letters/fax/the Internet/the telephone

The beauty of letters, faxes, and the Internet is that we have the benefit of thinking before sending the hard copy. That is, there is plenty of opportunity to rewrite what we intend to say before we send it—even to let it be read by another pair of eyes. The telephone is a different matter, and what we say when we open our mouth before contemplating can cost us business or gain us riches.

■ Hot tip

There is an old saying, 'You'll never get a second chance to make a first impression," and it is never more true than in the international marketplace.

Language

Because English has become the universal connector in most business dealings, it is now taught in most schools throughout the world as a second language. But don't rely on the other person's mastery. Be prepared to use some of their first language even if it is only a few of their local phrases—it is courteous to do so and establishes a bond of willingness on your part to meet the other halfway. When it becomes clear that the exchange of information will be difficult, always get a translator. Of course, you must be careful of foul, improper, or inappropriate language. Don't allow yourself to be drawn into the trap of off-color jokes. Too often they backfire and destroy the image you wish to project.

Body language

Body language is sometimes called the "silent language"—the subtle power of non-verbal communication. It is the first form of communication we learn, and we use it every day to tell other people how we feel about ourselves and them. Body language is learned the same way we learned spoken language—by observing and imitating the people around us when we were growing up. We learned gender signals appropriate to our sex by imitating our mother and father and other adults.

People communicate a great deal by their gestures, facial expressions, posture, and even their walk. Can body language affect your business dealings? Of course it can!

Body language includes the way we walk, the treatment of time, material things, and space. People are very sensitive to any intrusion into their spatial "bubble." The American bubble of psychological distance or space is about 18 inches—very wide compared to that of other cultures. If someone stands too close to an American the American backs up or leans away, or tenses his or her muscles. Watch them as they try to adjust their space in such a way that they feel comfortable. Some protect themselves with a purse, or an umbrella. Others move away to another spot behind a desk or a chair.

Eye contact

The language of the eyes is another age-old way people exchange feelings. We look away from someone who uses their eyes in a way we are not accustomed to. Yet the use of eyes varies worldwide by class, generation, region, ethnicity, and national differences. Think about it. Eye contact between men and women is measured in seconds and micro-seconds. In some cultures it is believed that only prostitutes look at a man for longer than a micro-second. In other cultures, like Saudi Arabia, it is taboo to look at women at all. The wink of an eye means one thing in some countries, but something entirely different in another. People of some castes or ranks show subservience by keeping their eyes down and unfocused while conversing with a person of a higher rank or order.

Feet and legs

Patterns of body language vary widely from one culture to another. American women sit with their legs crossed at the knee, or they may cross their ankles. Young Latin males, in their machismo, sit on the base of their spine, with their legs and feet spread wide apart. For Asians and some Arabs the soles of feet are taboo.

Hand gestures

Palms up can mean one thing, palms down another. When we call the waiter in the Mediterranean we motion with our fingers and palms down; to do otherwise might court disaster by delaying our food or maybe stopping delivery at all. Fingers are another thing about which we must be careful. The finger(s)-up sign is universally bad, but even pointing with our fingers should be avoided in some countries. Most cultures favor the use of the right hand over the left, the left being the toilet hand. Gifts are given and received in certain ways in different countries. Most offer and receive with both hands, while some extend the gift only with the right, the left hand resting on the forearm of the right.

Touching

In countries like Vietnam and Italy male friends often hold hands when they are walking. Hugs are ritual among men in Mexico. A male friend in Asia may place his hand on the leg or arm of another. All this touching is differentiated from sexuality, but might be falsely construed as such in a society like that of the United States.

Bowing

Bowing is another form of body language that exists primarily in Asia, and is appropriate behavior for people of other countries to use when visiting. The tip for successful bowing is always to out-bow the other person. That is, bend lower and you can't go wrong.

Business cards

Business cards have become the universal silent method of communicating such things as rank and position. Your company name and the title of your position should be on the card. Many have the same information in a second language on the back of the card. Business cards are often the first form of communication between business people and the body language of the exchange is important. In Asia and the Middle East extending the card with the right hand while bowing slightly is the standard method of presentation; however, in some Asian nations two hands are used.

Conversation

The art of conversation is often described as the art of knowing when to listen and when to talk. Strangely, listening is the most difficult part of conversation, yet it is this which gives the greatest return. It is not unusual to hear someone comment about a good conversationalist who in fact didn't talk at all, yet by body language and the appearance of attention conveyed enthusiastic, interested two-way participation. Even the way we listen has a silent language of its own. You know immediately whether or not the person you're talking to is "tuned in." If a person is listening the head will nod, and occasionally the "hmm" sound will be made. Speaker will know listeners want to terminate the conversation when they fidget and begin to look either at their watch or gaze about the room.

What we talk about

Of course, there are right things to say. The wrong things can cost you a contract and friends. Some call it being "politically correct," while others explain it as just engaging the brain before unlocking the jaw. It makes sense to know as much as possible about the country and people you will be visiting in terms of what is correct and polite. What to talk about and what to avoid are equally important. Religion and politics are usually not on the table for discussion, but sports, art, literature, and family are.

Gift giving and receiving

We seldom can go wrong when we give a gift to others. In general people love to give and receive gifts. In most societies adults, although they may not show it among company, are as enthusiastic as children when given a gift, even though in many cultures the gifts aren't opened in front of the giver. They are often reminders of pleasant times and friendships. Years later, people look at an object and say, "That was given to me by _____ on the occasion of _____." Women must be careful of the message that a gift could convey in some cultures, but in general gift giving shows our interest and respect. It is better often to bestow several inexpensive, well-thought-out gifts instead of lavish expenditures. The later may apply if you have developed a long-term relationship. Often the best gift is one representative of your country, something crafted only where you come from. When presenting gifts to a group, give things of equal value, but be certain the person at the top of the rank structure receives his or hers first. On the other hand, the kind of gift we give can get us in a whole lot of trouble.

Bribes

Be certain you don't mix up gift giving with bribery, which is commonplace in many countries as a method of facilitating certain things that otherwise would be done as a routine function of employment. Called *baksheesh* in Eastern countries, *mordida* (a little bite) in Spain and Mexico, *jeito* in Brazil, grease in the U.S.A., dash in Africa, *kumshaw* in South-east Asia, these payments can become a habit and in no way equate to a friendship gift.

Cost

In general your gifts should be modest in cost yet convey the sincerity of the act. If your gift is too expensive it might be construed as naive bribery; if it is too inexpensive it might give the impression that it is given artlessly.

Use

To be on the safe side, gifts should either have utility, or stimulate conversation about your culture and country. CDs, cologne for a woman, a favorite book, or imported liquor are in the category of safe gifts. Handcrafted gifts are better than mass-produced gifts.

Food and drink

Much of the world's business is done while enjoying social events rather than in a bland office environment. We go to restaurants and bars, where inhibitions are reduced and friendships are formed.

Dining out

In most countries, to be invited into the home for entertainment is the highest form of esteem. This is especially true in those places where women are typically not a part of the business culture.

Seating

As a general rule seating at most functions is by rank. In the business world even though there are no markings on sleeves or collars rank is well understood. Take your cue from your host and don't be in a hurry to sit down.

The utensils

Try the utensils of another land. Using eating sticks (chopsticks), as they are known in Asia, although awkward to the European, can be fun and will endear you to your foreign companions.

Of course it would be impossible to cover in one book every item of protocol difference for every country. Therefore, the next chapter explains how to do additional homework.

CHAPTER THREE

Culture
The roots of protocol

Understanding the various nuances of protocol can determine the success or failure of a venture from the very first greeting.
personal correspondence between the author and
Ms. Marie Betts-Johnson, March 21, 1998

Modern aviation dominates global transportation and makes the world
seem much smaller. Economies have become increasingly open to foreign competition. Market barriers have been reduced and competitors
have made significant market-share gains. The manufacturing base has
changed from smokestack to high tech, and national survival as well as
business survival increasingly depends on reaching out to the people and
cultures of the world to sell goods.

Caution!

To be effective in international dealings it is essential that you be prepared. You must do your homework before you interact in a foreign country. This book is designed to help you prepare. However, it would be
impossible to express all the answers to cultural differences in one book;
therefore, you should do some additional research into the specifics of
the cultural differences of the countries you will be visiting. Use the
checklist shown in Table 3.1.

There's an old saying that the best way to appreciate the behavior of
people is to "walk in the other fellow's shoes," that is, to live where he
or she lives and get a feel for the similarities and differences. Short of
being able to walk in the other's shoes, this chapter is the next best thing,
because its purpose is to help you break through behavior barriers so you
can appreciate the concepts which rule behavior in another place, then
get on with enjoying that place.

Overcoming fears and ethnocentricity

The very thought of doing business in a foreign culture can be a major
barrier to negotiations, but it shouldn't be. After all, historically, world

Table 3.1   Protocol/travel checklist

For _____ (country) make notes on the following:

History/geography/demographics

Culture(s)

Language(s)

Religion

Values and attitudes

Laws and legal environment

Education

Technology

Social organization

Family

Political environment

Transport/travel

Economy

Health

Medical requirements

Food

Time

Communications

Attitudes

Business differences

Cost of living

Where are my missions/embassies?

Do I need a visa?

Holidays

traders have been known for their spirit of curiousity, inquisitiveness, and risk-taking.

It's not that people don't periodically kick around the idea of going overseas; they do. But all too often the prospect is dismissed as too risky, or the market too complicated, when the underlying reason is really fear of the unknown, fear of things that are strange. Sometimes it is the myth that other languages are unintelligible and the people are different— "they" can't be trusted.

Can one culture be superior to another? The answer is *No*! Political systems, armies, navies, and even economic systems may be superior, but cultures are not.

What are people really like?

A lack of understanding of another's behavior begets mistrust. As a result, some people become intimidated and consequently develop an irrational xenophobia, an anxiety or, in the worst case, a hatred of things foreign. National boundaries are "safe," even when sales and profit yields indicate otherwise.

Does understanding foreign behaviors really make a difference? You bet it does!

One man who traveled overseas regularly and made friends in many countries, said, "They are more like us than they're different." He meant that "they" like children, "they" want them to be educated, "they" want to do business, and "they" work hard. What he didn't say was that the differences are what affect attitudes, so much at times that some people refuse to travel and some managers won't even consider entering the market to do business with "them."

Top executives acknowledge the problem. Most feel strongly that living and traveling, as well as having an appreciation of the many factors of culture and language, make a difference to their decision or ability to enter the international market. Most agree that the first step for an international manager is to put aside cultural blinders and become more cosmopolitan.

One executive of a major American manufacturing company stated, "It routinely takes us as much as sixty hours of preparation for a fifteen-minute business meeting." He questions his staff to make certain that they are totally familiar with the customs and history of the country, and with the company and even mid-level government officials they may deal with.

Rooted in culture

Culture is a set of shared meanings or orientations for a given society, or social setting. It's a complex concept because there are often many cultures within a given nation. For an international business person the definition is more difficult because a country's business culture is often different from its general culture. Thus the environment of international business is composed of language, religion, values and attitudes, law, education, politics, technology, and social organizations which are all different.

Let's get the word "culture" straight in our minds. Most dictionaries give three definitions. In the first instance it is thought of as the act of developing the intellectual and moral faculties; enlightenment and excellence of taste acquired by intellectual and aesthetic training; acquaintance with and taste for fine arts, humanities, and broad aspects of science, as distinguished from ordinary trade and craft pursuits. That's a good definition, but not what we refer to in this chapter.

A second definition refers to culture as the integrated pattern of human knowledge, belief and behavior that depends on human knowledge and the capacity to pass on that knowledge to succeeding generations. That's not what were are referring to either.

The definition that interests us from a traveling manager's point of view is that which has to do with diverse groups of people—the customary beliefs, social forms, and material traits of a racial, religious, or social group.

Culture gives us a set of codes to deal with phenomena found in a social environment. It sets priorities among the codes, and it justifies the need for the culture, usually by means of its association with a religion which oftentimes is an integral part of the existing culture, be it Christian, Muslim, or whatever.

Whatever a nation's culture is, it works for them. In order to function within it, it is you who must get on the bandwagon.

The Japanese do this very well. They learn how to penetrate foreign markets by sending their managers to live and study in "the other fellow's shoes." Their mission is to develop relationships with contemporaries that will last for years. The Japanese don't try to change the way of life in the other country; they learn about it. When they go home they are specialists in marketing and production in the country which they researched.

It is a country's culture that regulates such things as sexuality, child-raising, acquisition of food and clothing, and the incentives that motivate people to work and buy products. All of these things are, of course, major factors in marketing products. Business culture is secondary to a country's general culture, but provides the rules of the business game and explains the differences and the priorities.

Country culture

The process of taking the baggage of one's own culture into another is commonly called "cross-cultural communication." The ability to be successful in another culture requires an appreciation of theory, time, some practical rules, and an accommodating attitude.

Let's look first at the theory.

History, geography, and demographics

The way people behave correlates with their history and experiences, and many times those experiences have been passed along by word of mouth from generation to generation. Often understanding the reasons for historical, demographic, and geographical changes can explain the evolution of a country's culture. A study of the key periods of a country's history may provide just the right information to close a deal or avoid a mistake.

Relationships

Relationships developed over a long period of time reduce mistrust. To meet this challenge you need to understand the countries, their people, and the cultures where you intend to visit or do business.

Language

Ask a Japanese businessman what language he speaks and he will say the language of the customer.

Language is the thing that sets humans apart from other forms of life. It is the way we tell others about our history, and our intentions for the future. Language is the means of communicating within a culture.

For people in a given culture their language defines their socialization. Sometimes, based on the substance of information, it is possible to tell immediately the origin of the speaker. For instance, consider this person. What is the country of origin?"If y'all play ball –we can interface the system architecture, put on a dog-and-pony show, then split some knock-out profits."

There are more than 3,000 languages in the world today and probably as many as 10,000 dialects. Obviously, since there are only about 200 nations on earth many countries have more than one language and culture. Some of the languages within a country have priority. Some are used for business; others are used for training and education. In order to proceed with such everyday practices as contract definition, you need to have an appreciation that there are language hierarchies within nations, and that the multiplicity of languages and the accompanying cultures is having a dynamic effect on global trade. Every time a cultural barrier is crossed there is a potential communication problem, and international trade depends on communications.

■ Hot tip

The cardinal rule of international travel and trade is: when possible, speak in the customer's language.

Probably nothing deserves your attention more than the possibility of language confusion and misunderstanding. It is not uncommon for foreign travel and business to be stifled simply because one or both parties to the relationship misinterpreted the meaning of a simple sentence. For instance, when Coca-Cola first introduced its soda to the Asian market the name was translated with Chinese characters that sounded like "Coca-Cola" but read as "bite the wax tadpole." Obviously, on a practical basis, persuasive communications requires accurate translation for advertisement, packages, and labels. A company whose work is poorly translated runs the risk of being laughed at, offending a customer, and in the end losing the business deal.

English

Some languages have become more dominant than others. On a global basis it is generally agreed that English is the world's major language. Because of its extensive vocabulary (1,000 words are added each year) it is not easy to learn, yet it is estimated that more than a billion people speak English. Therefore those who can use it often have an advantage. Because of its dominant role English has become the most useful second language for people of other countries to learn. A Dane can sell his cheese to an Egyptian because they both know enough English to communicate and come to contract. Employees within a transnational firm communicate among global subsidiaries using English as the common language. For instance, Daihatsu, a Japanese-based company, uses what some call broken English or foreigner talk to get around complicated technical problems. For them it is pragmatic English or "praglish"—whatever works to get the job done.

The reason English has become so popular is that it follows markets. For instance, as soon as Vietnam dipped into capitalism it dropped French and took up English. More than 80 percent of teenagers worldwide are studying it because it will be needed to do business in the twenty-first century.

Other dominant languages

Although it is not growing in popularity, French is probably the second most useful language in the world. Of course, Spanish is essential to do business in Central and Latin America. Languages such as Japanese and Chinese are also growing in importance as these nations grow economically.

Cyberspace language

As the World Wide Web grows in importance to the global market so does the need for mutually understandable communications skills.

Cyberspace hackers are using a "praglish" of their own, composed of whatever English they learned in the classroom, reinforced by what they hear on satellite broadcasts such as CNN. In other words, English no longer has cultural baggage. As more and more non-native speakers use it the language is changing to suit the medium.

Body language

The only language used throughout most of the history of humanity (in evolutionary terms, vocal communication is relatively recent), body language is the first form of communication people of any country learn. This non-verbal language includes our posture, gestures, facial expressions, national dress, the way we walk, even the treatment of time, material things, and space. All people communicate on several different levels at the same time, but they are usually aware of only the dialog and don't realize that they respond to non-verbal messages. But when a person says one thing and really believes something else, the discrepancy between the two can usually be sensed. Non-verbal communications systems are much less subject to conscious deception than often occurs in verbal systems. Sometimes we find ourselves asking, "What is it about that person that I don't like? He or she doesn't seem sincere." It's probably the lack of congruity between the person's words and behavior.

Why has man developed all these different ways of communicating messages without words? One reason is that people don't like to spell out certain kinds of messages. We prefer to find other ways to show our feelings.

■ Hot tip

Adapt: It was important that José Arriba and Bill Martin develop a cordial relationship for business reasons. At a party, José, in Latin fashion, moved closer and closer to Bill as they spoke. Bill, interpreting this as an invasion of his space or a pushiness on the part of José, backed away. José interpreted this as a coldness. Body language, sometimes called the "sounds of silence," spoke again.

A very basic difference between people of different ethnic backgrounds is their sense of territoriality and how they handle space. This is the silent communication, or miscommunication, that caused discomfort on the part of Bill Martin and José Arriba in the above example. People of Northern Europe—England, Scandinavia, Switzerland or Germany—tend to avoid contact. Those of Italian, Greek, French, Spanish, Russian, Latin American or Middle Eastern origin like close personal contact. Touch is also an important part of the stream of communications that takes place between people. A light touch, a firm touch, a blow, a caress are all forms of communications.

As it turns out, perceived space and distances are not set by vision alone but by all the senses. Auditory space is perceived with the ears, thermal space with the skin, kinesthetic space with the muscles of the body, and olfactory space with the nose. One's culture determines how these are programmed—which sensory information ranks highest and which lowest. The important thing to remember is that culture is very persistent—culture lasts generations even when it is in prolonged contact with people of very different cultural heritages.

All over the world people not only walk in their own characteristic way, but have walks that communicate the nature of their involvement with whatever it is they are doing. The purposeful walk of North Europeans is an important component of proper behavior on the job. The quick shuffle of servants in the Far East in the old days was a show of respect. In some places the inhabitants even have a name for the special walk that one uses in the presence of a chief—that of appearing humble and respectful.

The notion that people communicate volumes by their gestures, facial expressions, posture, and walk is not new. Actors, dancers, writers, and psychologists have long been aware of it. Scientists have begun to make systematic observations of body motions, looking for the slightest movement that conveys certain messages.

Religion

Nothing destroys the development of relationships more than stereotypes of religious attitudes. Religion plays a major part in the cultural similarities and differences of nations. In itself, religion can be a basis of mistrust and a barrier to trade. Both Eastman Kodak and General Motors have been the target of organized religious movements in other countries because of management decisions.

Religion is often the dominant influence for the consumer of products. Such things as religious holidays determine buying and consumption patterns. Knowing what is forbidden and what a society expects as a result of its various religions affects market strategy.

Values and attitudes

The role of values and attitudes in international business is difficult to measure but vital to success. Work ethic and motivation are the intangibles that affect economic performance. For instance, values affect how we view time. The saying is: "the clock runs in English and walks in Spanish and French." One international traveler said: "The only time the Spanish are on time is for the bull fight."

In modern societies time has become a commodity, i.e. "time is money." As an example, the time horizon of many American firms is measured in quarterly profits, yet for most Asian business cultures the time horizon is measured in terms of twenty-five, fifty or even 100 years. The building of international business and trade across national borders just doesn't happen at big-city pace. In countries that have older, more traditional values time is often measured by the movement of the sun, by the phases of the moon, or relative to planting seasons.

The values of a society determine its attitudes toward wealth, consumption, achievement, technology, and change, and you must evaluate things in terms of the host culture. Researching attitudes about openness and the receptiveness to new technology are the essentials of marketing America's changing products.

Laws and the legal environment

The laws of a society are another dimension of its culture. They are the rules established by authority and society. On the one hand, laws provide an opportunity to handle the mistrust of doing business across international boundaries, and on the other, they can become barriers and constraints to operations. The laws of different nations are often vastly different. The fact that most of the world's legal systems can be classified under the two headings of code law and common law does not mean the identity of laws under those two headings, any more than it means that those are the only two systems. About half of the nations of the world are under a form of either code or common law, but the other half are under indigenous national enforcement such as canon (communist) or religious (Muslim) laws. In most cases the world's legal systems are not pure. Each nation has its own unique laws; nevertheless, one can find more and more similarities and mixtures within each classification.

Complications between national legal systems could drive the feint heart from international trade, but international law is growing and a set of adjudication practices has developed over the years. International law is the derived law that in effect minimizes the range of differences among national laws. In the interdependent world of today international law is the growth area in the legal environment. There is no international legislative body that makes international laws. What does exist is a set of agreements, treaties, and conventions between two or more nations that represents the dampening of intercultural conflict.

For most dealings you will be most interested in the law as it relates to contracts, but you should always consider litigation as a last resort. Settle disputes in other ways if possible. Litigation is only for the stupid and the rich, because it usually involves long delays, during which inventories are tied up and trade halted. Lawsuits are costly, not just because of the money, but also because of the broken relationships that result. Most international commercial disputes can be solved by conciliation, mediation, and arbitration. The International Chamber of Commerce provides an arbitration service that can often be written right into a sales contract for use should the unspeakable happen.

Education

Culture shapes our thoughts and emotions. Your motivation is influenced by your education as well as other things such as values and religion, which we have already discussed. The biggest international difference is the educational attainment of the populace. The next biggest difference is the educational mix. In Europe and the United States there is little difference in the mix. Practically all children are educated from kindergarten (age 5) through twelfth grade (age 17). In industrialized countries education is no longer a function of wealth, but this is not so in many other countries. It is not unusual to find only the elite of some nations educated to the levels Europeans and Americans assume for all people. The impact of education is therefore profound for marketing products as well as establishing relationships, because good communications are often based on relative education capacities and standards.

Technology

The most recent change in technology is our growing control over energy and information. The word "technology" begets concepts such as science, development, invention, and innovation. Some older languages don't even have words to express these concepts. Understanding the technological gaps between nations is an essential element to exporting products across borders. Wide gaps exist between the most advanced nations and those that are still what we call "traditional societies." The implications for us are that such things as training needs for technology transfer and the impact of that transfer on social environments must be considered. We should always look at technology from the importing country's point of view.

Social organization

International trade cannot be conducted without involvement in foreign social relationships. In order to develop market segmentation and target markets, the social organizations of a country must be studied. Insensitivity to the customs of the consumer country will not only result in misinformed decisions but also precipitate resentment and in some cases recrimination.

Nothing is universal in business organizations. There are no universal theories of motivation, leadership style, or consumer behavior. Such theories are myths of American business schools and do not stand up well in practice, nor do they export well. The truth is that humans have invented an amazing diversity of institutions.

Social stratification is the hierarchy of classes within a society—the relative power, social priorities, privilege, and income of those classes. Each class within a system has somewhat different and distinct tastes, political views, and consumption patterns. Many countries have a socio-religious ideology that allows rank to be intrinsic and inherited by birth. This implies that different categories of humans are culturally defined as consisting of different worth and potential for performance. Regardless of how you react to such non-competitive socialization, such ideas are predictable in some countries. Faced with such a system of socio-religious rank it is essential that we learn how to deal with it—not attempt to change it.

The next chapter deals with a special set of tips and traps, the things that can sink a relationship or prevent a lucrative contract being signed.

CHAPTER FOUR

Special tips and traps

If it be appropriate to kiss the Pope's slipper, by all means do so.
Lord Chesterfield

The intention of this chapter is to focus on several areas that can manifest special problems and to offer several ways to avoid these traps. Here are some ideas that will help you make a good impression no matter where you are.

When just visiting

Most business or recreational trips are short term and there is a tendency to believe that on a quick in-and-out junket you have nothing to fear. Don't make this mistake! When just visiting it *is* important to understand as much of the culture of a country as possible.

Saving face

Saving face is not just an Asian concept, although it is particularly important in those countries—Asians seem more sensitive. However, avoiding embarrassment to others, particularly ranking persons, is essential wherever you are in the world.

First impressions

First impressions do count, and the trap of an unfavorable first impression can stop your business deal in its tracks. Bad first impressions are all but impossible to overcome.

The greeting smile

Smiling is the universal language and saves many problems, but smile in the right way. The smile in which the lips are parted in a sort of ellipse around the teeth comes across as phony and dishonest. Smile easy, the kind where the full teeth are exposed and the corners of the mouth are pulled up. This kind of smile says, "Hi, I'm sure pleased to meet you!"

Grooming

Grooming is important all over the world. Studies indicate that most people are more attracted to others who are neat, well groomed, and dress crisply.

Body language

Flash your eyebrows. In most cultures raising the eyebrows almost instinctively in a rapid movement and keeping them raised for about a half-second is an unspoken signal of friendliness and approval.

Lean forward. Liking is produced by leaning forward.

Look for similarities. People tend to like others who are like them, so common experiences and interests are often a starting point for producing liking.

Nod your head. People like other people who agree with them and are attentive to what they are saying.

Open up. A position in which your arms are crossed in front of your chest may project the impression that you're resisting the other person's ideas. Open, frequently outstretched arms and open palms project the opposite.

Conversation

People of any country like to talk about their own land and people. If you ask questions which show genuine interest it will cultivate their respect towards you. But no one likes critical questions such as: "Why don't you do it this way?" or "How come you do it that way?" Above all, they don't want to hear how much better it is where you come from.

Gender issues

Around the world, like it or not, it's the same old *vive la différence*. Even today women are forbidden to drive cars or ride bicycles in Saudi Arabia. In Japan the regard for women is still many years behind that in other countries. Even though a few have broken into middle management, general acceptance is still in the 1950s.

Obstacles confronting women in the many domestic marketplaces are still substantial, and this bias requires them to overcome more hurdles than men. It is not surprising that there is a diversity of views about female participation in the still overwhelmingly male-dominated business worlds of other countries.

Recently greater numbers of women have begun starting up or running their own businesses. As the number has increased, the number involved in international business has proportionately increased. Women are slowly remaking companies, society, and themselves, but in each country they have achieved different things, fought different battles, and are making different sacrifices.

In the battle of the sexes American women are way ahead. There's more opportunity and freedom for women in business in the U.S.A. than in almost any other country in the world. More than 5 million women own businesses—30 percent of all entrepreneurial firms—grossing more than $800 billion annually. As against 46 in 1977, today some 570 women serve on corporate boards of the Fortune 500 companies.

Much of the biases stem from acceptance of age-old gender rules—even women themselves are part of that problem. A 1992 poll of 1,000 Japanese women showed that 56 percent of Japanese women believe that the husband should be the breadwinner and the wife should stay home. Just 13 percent of Swedish women thought women should stay home, 20 percent of British women, 22 percent of French women, 24 percent of American women, and 25 percent of German women.

For the most part, those women who enter international business figure out ways to overcome the obstacles by simply end-running the problem and going to more receptive markets. Women doing business in most Middle Eastern countries often arrange for men to handle their direct negotiations with Arab businessmen. One woman, on arrival in Egypt, moves directly into a hotel room and from there directs the negotiations of her Egyptian associate. She meets the principals involved only when the deal is essentially complete. Despite the difficulties, there are many success stories, and women in the international marketplace are encouraging other women to join them.

One former U.S. Commerce official said that it is certainly more difficult for women and that by far the most common path for enterprising women to enter the international market is through retailing. Typically a woman starts by importing products for sale in her own shop. As the business grows and she travels more extensively, she begins to see opportunities for selling American products abroad and soon she is an exporter.

One woman in the private sector, the president of a bank export trading company (ETC), reports that there is a lot more opportunity than people were aware of, especially to do business in the People's Republic of China. She finds that in some markets having a male associate with extensive exporting experience who introduces her as president of the company opens doors. It gives her more stature and credibility. Another international business manager says not to let being a woman hinder you. She suggests signing mail and telexes with your initials and last name. No one knows whether C. J. Moore is a woman or a man.

The chief negotiator for a major trading company claims that the kinds of problems she encounters on the job have nothing to do with being a woman. Rather, the problems are all about cultural differences: When negotiating contracts, one should be very conscious of the fact that the environments in which she is doing business are culturally and politically different. A partner of a firm in the male-oriented field of providing management services for overseas engineering and construction says that women just have to use a little extra common sense. For instance, the Saudis aren't ready to accept women engineers and contractors, but they are in the Philippines and Indonesia.

Women have a strong role in Africa, both in the home and in business. Yet visitors should remember that in Muslim and Buddhist nations the religious stricture against mixing the sexes socially is still very strong. One woman traveling as chief emissary for her company was surprised after meeting with men all day to be placed at a table with their wives that evening at dinner. On the other hand, some women executives find this an advantage. Sometimes they find out more about the country and company from the wives than from the men.

One woman gives this advice. At presentations, conversations, and sales meetings avoid using "I did" or "I know." She says it is better to use "We do this," or "Our company does this."

■ Hot tips for women

1 Send your biography ahead of time.
2 Have your title on your card.
3 Sit in a power position.
4 Position your staff on both sides of you.
5 Keep the tone of your voice low.
6 Don't be aggressive, but be assertive.
7 Never give a man a gift, no matter how close the business relationship. A small gift for his family might do.
8 Give gifts from the company, never from you.
9 If you are married, use Mrs. when overseas, even if you don't at home.
10 Avoid eating or drinking alone in public. Use room service, or invite a woman from the office where you are doing business to join you at a restaurant.
11 If the question of dinner arises and is useful to cement the deal, avoid any doubts by inviting your counterpart's family.
12 Make a point of mentioning your husband and ask about your male counterpart's family. Some businesswomen who are not married invent a fiancée or steady back home.
13 Try not to be coy about flirtations. Turn them off immediately with a straightforward, "No."
14 Be aware of the culture, and dress to fit as closely as your wardrobe will permit. Conservatism works.
15 Use your intuition.

Former citizens

By former citizens I'm referring to those persons who now reside in a land not of their origin, a German living in South Africa or a Chinese living in the United States who faced the difficulties of entry into a new culture but now is right at home in the adopted country. Such people often have a natural expertise and understanding of their original culture which helps them do business overseas.

In most of Africa it is an advantage to have colored skin. Most newcomers to Europe or the United States have a disadvantage because their skin has color, but their advantage is they speak another language and understand another culture. Getting off the ground in business in their original nation is often easier because contacts are already in place.

■ Hot tips for former citizens

1 Don't get caught in the "racial discrimination trap." Every country has discrimination of one kind or another, so avoid discussions of this sort.
2 Be proud of your heritage and use it to your best business advantage, but do your homework and know your adopted country's history as well as that of your ancestors.
3 Dress conservatively—business dress is similar all over the world.
4 Use your multilingual capabilities.

About jokes

The people of every country enjoy humor and they all have their funny stories, but explaining complicated jokes to business people who don't share your culture can be very tricky. Here are a few dos and don'ts:

■ Hot tips

1 Remember that each culture reacts differently to jokes.
2 Don't tell foreigners a joke that depends on word play or punning.
3 Be careful of the subject of your joke. It could be taken seriously in a culture different from your own.
4 Be informed about the sensitive issues in the country you are visiting.
5 Ask to hear a few local jokes. They will give you a sense of what is considered funny.
6 Tell jokes; everyone enjoys a good laugh.

> ### ■ Hot tip
>
> *Learning the Hard Way*: Once, while training a group of Russian business people, the author learned the hard way about the importance of selecting the right joke. He told a complicated joke through a translator and used the word "stupid" in the punch line. Later he learned that even though they laughed none of the Russians understood the joke and the only thing they remembered was the word stupid, which they thought referred to them.

Culture shock

Most people accommodate changing situations, environmental conditions, and cultures, but some have problems, particularly when facing a long-term situation. This phenomenon has been identified as "culture shock." The phrase "culture shock" was first used by the anthropologist Kalervo Oberg to describe problems of acculturation among Americans who were working on a health project in Brazil. Oberg found it to be a "malady, an occupational disease of people who have been suddenly transported abroad" (Oberg 1955). The symptoms of culture shock can be apparent in people who don't even leave their own culture. It is possible for you to put on your blinders in your own home office. Women can experience "culture shock" in almost every place.

Let's not overstate culture shock. Only about 25–30 percent of those going abroad for the first time are unable to adjust to a new culture. And it should be recognized that culture shock is primarily a matter of adjusting to frustration–the psychological dynamics that everyone finds when encountering new and confusing situations. Most of us have experienced the bewildering ambiguity caused by the inability to predict the behavior of others in a new social situation, maybe joining a new church or going to a new school. Anxiety in these situations ranges from mild discomfort to panic, rage, or flight.

Each person reacts differently. Some people jump right into the new situation and adjust easily. Some become aggressive and angry, which scholars have labeled "fight." Others try to escape or withdraw. This is called "flight." Yet others "filter," distort, or deny the reality of culture shock. Those that cope best take up what is called "flex" or behavior adjustment.

Fight

This reaction often manifests itself in scoffing at foreign nationals and, in the extreme, becomes aggressive to the extent that there may be overt destruction of life and property.

Flight

In an effort to overcome frustration some people reject those who cause discomfort; that is, they completely avoid foreign nationals and seek the exclusive security of expatriates from their home country. On the other hand, the complete opposite might happen. By literally joining the host culture you could relinquish your own cultural identity, thus never resolving the conflict between the two cultures.

Filter

People engaging in filter reaction tend to glorify things in their country of origin. As if they were wearing special glasses, they forget the harsh reality that places like Germany, Japan, and the United States have homelessness, racism, and crime.

Flex

This is the reaction you should be encouraged to adopt. By suspending judgment of the foreign cultures, you can learn and use new cues as guidelines for behavior. Dr. Sunny Chung, Ed.D., a counselor for international students, suggests that there are five distinct stages of culture shock, and she experienced all five when she came from South Korea to live in America.

1 *Honeymoon*: this is often a happy time when the new arrival falls in love with the new culture.
2 *Disintegration*: this is the period of immersion into new problems with language, transportation, shopping, food, and everyday life. During this period common feelings experienced are mental fatigue, bewilderment, alienation, depression, and withdrawal.
3 *Reintegration*: acceptance of the new culture takes place and some negative feelings about the foreign culture are healthy.
4 *Crisis*: you may experience deep frustration, a loss of identity, confusion, and anger—or, in some extreme cases, even feel suicidal.
5 *Autonomy and independence*: this is a period of acceptance and adjustment, with small bouts of residual culture shock. At this final stage people become fully capable of accepting and drawing nourishment from cultural differences. These people become expressive, creative, and relaxed enough to enjoy humor.

Knowing something of another culture helps smooth the way to adjustment and prevents unrealistic expectations. On the other hand, when you understand and are conscious of your own cultural conditioning you begin to see that the customs and ways of your country of origin are not "natural" for all people. Overcoming culture shock requires a willingness to try as well as learn about foreign cultures.

The next chapter offers some helpful tips about world travel.

CHAPTER FIVE

Travel tips

Remember that wherever our life touches yours, we help or hinder . . .
wherever your life touches ours, you make us stronger or weaker. . . .
There is no escape—man drags man down, or man lifts man up.
Booker T. Washington

Nothing improves a business connection, or for that matter any relationship more than a face-to-face meeting. Don't let technology over-
whelm your sale. Facsimiles, World Wide Webs, and satellite televised
meetings are not a substitute for the personal touch. This chapter is
intended to provide suggestions that can facilitate that trip which you
know will locate and cultivate new customers and improve relationships
with foreign representatives.

Planning

Your trip begins long before you actually travel. It begins two or three
months in advance, when you visualize why you are undertaking this
voyage to other countries and what you expect to accomplish. Give some
thought to your goals and their relative priorities. Begin by obtaining the
names of possible contacts, confirming appointments, and checking
transportation schedules. The more planning you do, the more time,
opportunity, and money you will save in the long run. Double-check holidays and make sure you are not wasting your time sitting in a hotel on
a foreign non-work day. Make sure you know the normal work day of the
destination nations. For instance, in many Middle Eastern regions the
work week typically runs from Saturday to Thursday. Another thing to
take into account is potentially dangerous in-country situations such as
civil unrest or a disease infestation. The State department of most
nations has a travel alert system that can be tapped for current situations.

Itinerary

Travel is expensive; therefore care should be taken to have a full but
not overloaded schedule. Two or three definite appointments, spaced

comfortably throughout the day, are more productive and enjoyable than a crowded agenda that requires you to rush from one meeting to the next without allowances for concluding business. Keep your schedule flexible enough to allow for both unexpected problems and opportunities. You are reminded that time is reckoned from Greenwich, England, in time zones that span the globe. Make sure you think ahead about the local time and arrange schedules accordingly.

Preparations

Travel agents can help arrange your transportation and hotel reservations, and they can be helpful in planning the itinerary, obtaining the best rates, and explaining such things such as visa requirements.

Passports

A valid passport is normally required for all travel outside your home country. Make certain it is still valid and will remain so for your entire trip.

Visas

Visas are provided, for a small fee, by the foreign country's embassy or consulate in your country. To obtain a visa you must have a current passport. Allow several weeks to obtain visas, especially if traveling to Eastern Europe or developing nations. Some countries do not require visas for tourist travel but do require them for business travel.

Vaccinations

Health requirements vary from country to country. A travel agent or airline can advise you of the different requirements. In some cases vaccinations against typhus, typhoid, and other diseases are advisable even though they are not required.

Travel checklist

- Seasonal weather conditions
- Healthcare requirements
- What and what not to eat
- Electrical current (do you need a transformer or plug adapter)
- Money (currency requirements, credit cards, and traveler's checks)
- In-country transportation
- Tipping (how much and whom?)
- Customs regulations

Assistance

Every country is attempting to help businesses sell their goods abroad, so your first stop before leaving your country and on entering the foreign country should be your economic and/or foreign commercial offices. These services are free or at least very low cost, so why not take advantage of them. Both often provide in-depth briefings and can arrange introductions to appropriate firms, potential clients, and government officials. Discuss your needs with the staff of the local embassy or consulate.

Carnets

Foreign customs regulations vary widely from place to place, and the traveler is wise to learn in advance the regulations that apply to each country to be visited.

If you plan to carry product samples be alert to the fact that you may be required to pay import duties. In some countries duties and extensive customs procedures may be avoided by obtaining an ATA (*admission temporaire*/Temporary Admission) carnet. The ATA carnet is a standard international customs document used to obtain duty-free temporary admission of certain goods into the countries that are signatories to the ATA Convention. Under the ATA Convention, commercial and professional travelers may take commercial samples, tools of the trade, advertising material, and cinematographic, audiovisual, medical, scientific, or other professional equipment into member countries temporarily without paying customs duties and taxes by posting a bond at the border of each country to be visited.

Applications for ATA carnets are made to the Council for International Business in your own country. Since countries are continuously added to the ATA carnet system, the traveler should contact the Council for International Business to learn if the country to be visited is included on the list. The fee charged for the carnet depends on the value of the goods to be covered. A bond, letter of credit, or bank guarantee of 40 percent of the value of the goods is also required to cover duties and taxes that would be due if duties on goods imported into a foreign country were not paid by the carnet holder.

The next chapter offers tips on negotiations.

CHAPTER SIX

Negotiating tips

Let the other person save face.
Dale Carnegie, How to Win Friends and Influence People

When the global stakes increased and the competition forced your hand, instinct told you it was time to learn how to negotiate across borders. Negotiating is a complex process even when the parties are from the same country. It becomes even more complex in international transactions because of the added chance of misunderstandings stemming from cultural differences. As was discussed in Chapter 2, it is essential to know who the negotiators are, their names, and to understand the importance of rank. Beyond that the nature of their business methods and agreements in the context of their negotiating style becomes of major importance.

People from some nations are born cultural negotiators. Even so, all too many people wander into international bargaining with no plan and no idea how to proceed. For them, its an ad-lib and ad hoc operation all the way. For some, a sense of corporate superiority explains their lack of preparation, but for most it is pure ignorance of the competence of the ferocious competitors out there scouring the world for scraps of business. Different styles of doing business stem from cultural and protocol differences. A better understanding of these differences will strengthen the ability of a businessperson to negotiate a better deal.

This chapter is divided into two parts. The first discusses ethics, then goes on to describe the five steps of the negotiating process. It includes many tips for successful execution. The second offers anecdotal information about what to expect when negotiating with business people from seven selected countries: Middle East (including Turkey) Asia (general), Taiwan, Japan, Switzerland, Indonesia, Mexico, India.

Ethics

There is ongoing debate about the meaning and interpretation of ethics as they relate to business. Some argue that ethics vary by country and are linked to differences in national ideology and culture. Others argue that ethics vary by industry. Discussions shift about the use of information for insider trading, personnel issues like theft or inaccuracy of books and records, and improper relations with foreign governments. Highest among these is employee and managerial conduct such as gift giving, and national customs related to bribery.

Outright graft and bribery are still common in much of the world, especially in fast-developing countries. Access to markets by some hyper-aggressive Asian and European companies is levered by lucrative under-the-table offers. To win contracts, some American companies—who face stiff penalties under the 1977 Foreign Corrupt Practices Act, which bars U.S. firms from paying bribes to win business—substitute corrupting junkets to Disney World or Super Bowl games. Almost all multinationals make small "facilitation" payments (an accepted practice, like a tip) for such things as speeding up building inspections, expediting customs clearances, and installing telephones.

The question is how pervasive this behavior is and whether there is a global merger of moral reasoning. Today we find many companies with greater power than some nations. Presidents and CEOs of global businesses are among the most respected leaders of the world. Thus global business expansion brings with it greater ethical responsibilities and a need to eliminate questionable business practices. It is beyond the scope of this book to offer solutions; however, because of the destructive and harmful consequences of unethical behavior it is hoped that competition will be based on the commercial qualities of products and services, and that high moral reasoning will remain significant in the minds of all negotiators.

The negotiation process

Negotiation is a process in which one individual tries to persuade another to change his or her ideas of behavior. It is the process in which at least two partners with different needs and viewpoints try to reach an agreement on matters of mutual interest. They want to do business or they would not be talking in the first place.

Success in international business results from the ability to bring people together but all too often the obstacle is our perception of people from other countries. Frequently one party enters into a negotiation with expectations of the other party that are completely unrealistic. Representatives of companies from industrialized nations expecting to take advantage of an abundant supply of cheap labor from a less developed country can be surprised by a higher set of values from those across the table. While Americans, for instance, might be worried about profit, people from other countries might worry more about whether or not you can be trusted. As an example, they may hold a vision that all American businessmen are predatory.

Three things are common among successful international negotiators: (1) they understand cultural differences; (2) they know that preparation for a meeting is essential; and (3) they want to do business or they wouldn't show up in the first place. The more they know of the other culture and the better prepared they are for the meeting, the better their chances of negotiating the best possible outcome.

The fact that international trade is growing steadily makes international negotiations a necessity. Cross-cultural differences in values, personality, and nature, as well as social, economic, and political systems within a specific cultural environment, stress the need to recognize differences. For the international negotiator the importance of intercultural understanding is the key not only to interpersonal relationships but also to business relationships.

Whenever we negotiate we try to find out what our opponents think, how far they will go, and their limits. One of the keys to success is to see oneself in the eyes of another person and their culture. This is called role reversal and consists in putting ourselves in their position and looking at ourselves from their point of view. It is difficult, but it is the negotiation imperative.

Once I was faced with the task of describing how Americans negotiate. I experienced great difficulty in describing my own culture. Try it!

The key to having empathy is to fight parochialism and ethnocentrism and to recognize cultural diversity.

■ Hot tip

Intercultural understanding is a prerequisite to becoming a successful negotiator in cross-cultural management.

We know that negotiators can influence the success or failure of a negotiation most directly by managing the process. An effective process includes the negotiation's overall strategy, and the stages and the tactics (approaches) used. In international trade there is no perfect recipe that describes how to negotiate with people from a particular country, but there are general guidelines we surely must take into consideration.

Step one: preparations

All too often, when we go abroad on business the only two things we want to know are how profitable a project will be and how quickly it will happen. So we prepare for the international negotiation by picking up a book for a quick read about the country. We really don't want to learn about the culture; all we want to know is whether we should bow or shake hands.

The truth is that we must prepare for international negotiations. You can't just pick up a briefcase, jump on a plane, and go. We must know the country, the people, and understand the culture with which we are dealing. We need to know the specific tips and traps, because it is important not to offend business people in the host country. For every ten minutes of international negotiations we may need ten, twenty, or thirty hours of preparation. Preparation is the most important priority in international negotiations.

The first step will always be collecting data about the country. Demographics give us insight into helpful information for our needs. Gross national product (GNP) and per capita income tell us about the standard of living, the literacy rate, and about the skilled and unskilled labor force. Life expectancy tells us about the health system; distribution of GNP per capita (wealth) tells us about population growth and about the present availability of labor; knowledge of the government explains stability and continuity; general information about the economy explains the structure of industry, agriculture, and service; the currency tells us about the power of purchase. We need to know the geography, the climate, and about the resources. We can get a lot of information from demographics.

The second step is more difficult. We need to understand the character of the people. The best way to do this is to visit the country and meet them, but this is not always possible. Another way is to ask somebody who has been to that particular country. We know every culture has certain characteristics regarding values, attitudes, and behavior, and the more we find out about the targeted culture, the better we will recognize culture differences and be prepared to deal with them.

Step two: culture and protocol

Next, analyze your target—the company (in the country) where you intend to sell your product. Get to know as much about the firm and the people you will be meeting. Find out what their experiences have been. Sometimes all that's required is to pull out the old reports and review the facts and the names of the people.

■ Hot tip

The calling card is very important in international business.

Typically we only exchange cards once, but there is nothing more embarrassing than forgetting the name of someone you have already been introduced to. It is a good practice to attach a copy of a key person's card to the agenda and all meeting reports; then you have the names and positions of all the people who were involved. There is nothing that a foreign businessman likes better than that when you walk into a room you remember his name. It is important before a meeting to sit down and memorize the names of the players.

Keep in mind that the human and behavioral aspects of your negotiations are vital:

- Understand the place in the world where you will be traveling.
- Know the culture, history, and political processes.
- Pay particular attention to the importance of face-saving to the people of the country where you will be negotiating.
- What is the host government's role in country negotiations?
- How important are personal relations?
- How much time should you allow for negotiations?

■ Hot tip

In Ethiopia the time required to make a decision is directly proportional to its importance. This is so much the case that low-level bureaucrats attempt to raise the prestige of their work by taking a long time to make decisions. If you, a foreigner, attempt to speed up the process, you could innocently downgrade the importance of their work.

Step three: prepare for business

The third step is to know your competitors and be prepared for business. What is their financial position, what are their strengths and weaknesses, and what are their capabilities in terms of negotiating gambits. Know your own product and your boundaries. Prior to the meeting you should make a complete list of your product's strengths and weaknesses, particularly in terms of managerial skills, product delivery, technical abilities, and global resources. Develop a complete assessment of your firm's capabilities. Be prepared to show that your strengths outweigh your weaknesses and how your product is superior to those of your competitors. It is very important that you anticipate as many of these points as possible prior to the meeting. You should also determine your ideal price and your minimum price prior to entering into negotiations.

Step four: training

Preparing and training the negotiating team are necessities. In today's increasingly competitive business world there is no substitute for extensive advanced preparation and thought. Many companies have taken to role-playing their negotiations long before the initial quote is submitted or the actual marketing of a product begins. Teams are formed and each team is given a set of negotiating alternatives. Each team pretends to represent a product, company, or country which is a competitor. With a chalkboard nearby on which a team presents its position, the negotiators go through a sufficient number of rounds to get a sense of the process. Sometimes price is reduced by 10 percent, or service warranties are offered. Even specific advertising concepts are discussed. Little is left to chance.

Competence in formulating strategy and negotiating skills are subjects ruled by so many variables that there is no substitute for experience and knowledge. Nevertheless, preparation and role-playing act as excellent training devices and serve to sharpen the skills of even the most experienced.

Step five: execution

Preparation and planning are pointless unless you are prepared to put the thinking part into practice. This step explains some of the key activities that lead to a successful negotiation.

Participants

Use team assistance wisely. Take along financial and technical experts. The extra expense will prove to be an excellent investment. It shows the other party you are serious about the importance of the negotiation. It also serves to train younger members of your organization by having them take notes and listen, thereby learning the negotiation process. Too many people enter into a negotiation as a team yet use the "John Wayne approach," trying to run the whole show themselves. They tend to put their goal before the group's. It is not uncommon, for example, to see the members of a foreign team arguing with each other in the presence of the other negotiating group. This causes loss of bargaining power with other cultures.

Formality

Dress for business. Show by your appearance that the event is of major importance. Wear proper, conservative clothing and have a neat appearance. Learn how to address people. To make foreign clients more comfortable, follow their traditions and customs.

Language

Although English is the most popular negotiating language, it is always advantageous to have somebody in your team who speaks the other side's language. Knowledge of key foreign terms or numbers eases the process.

Authority

An important part of any negotiation is the question of authority limits. To maintain good interpersonal relationships, a useful strategy is the ploy of having to check with a higher authority for a decision. However, having to check with the home office may be a disadvantage in some countries. In Indonesia and Switzerland you could lose the respect of the other party.

Silence, breaks, and getting to the point

Put your watch in your pocket. Let the other side bring up business. Recognize that silence can be a much more powerful negotiating tool than good argument. Look at your notes, fiddle with your pen—anything— but let them break the silence. Ask questions and, when you think you understand, ask more questions. Feel (carefully) for pressure points. If any impasse occurs, do not pressurize your counterparts; suggest holding another meeting. Minds can be changed later, behind the scenes. It's important to know how to ask questions, how to get information, how to listen, or how to use questioning as a powerful persuasive tactic. All these skills are most critical at the international table. The person who asks questions controls the process of negotiation and wins more in bargaining situations. Anticipate having to ask the same question in several ways to get so-called straight answers.

Concession and agreements

Avoid concessions on any issue until all issues have been discussed. Do not necessarily measure progress by the numbers of issues that have been settled. Recognize that agreement means different things across cultures. Be careful about involving legal institutions. In most countries personal relationships are more important than legal systems.

Playing in the major leagues

When confronted with making your terms or price known, use the ploy of recalling a similar deal. It gets your point across without moving the other party into a defensive position, and might get the other side thinking at higher levels. Adjust your initial offer accordingly.

Round numbers

Round numbers like $100,000 beg to be negotiated, usually by counter-offering round numbers. Odd numbers sound harder, less negotiable (e.g. $95,500 or $104,500).

Emotions

Any emotional outburst in a business dispute is perceived as the beginning of the end of negotiation. You should focus shifts on getting something off your chest rather than getting what you want. When you feel emotional, step back and relax. You must be calculating, not emotional.

Communications

Once the negotiation begins, the biggest problem is failure to understand the language. Ninety-nine percent of all international negotiations are conducted in English, making them extremely slow and difficult for foreigners who speak English as a second or third language. Learn to speak slowly, and use textbook English, not slang.

Often it is necessary to repeat something a number of times. One tip is to repeat important points in a number of different ways throughout the conversation. Quite often two people don't fully understand each other, and the other party will be too polite to interrupt, but will nod. A nod in the Orient does not mean that people understand you, only that they heard you. If the person said "No" to the original question, then he or she should say "No" to the back-up question. This approach can be quite difficult because you have to think of more and more ways of saying or asking the same thing. This method also tends to be very time-consuming. It is helpful to maintain eye contact during conversation. If their eyes cloud as they listen, then people probably don't fully understand what you are saying.

When it is possible to use them, visual aids help a great deal, whether they are paper sketches or drawings on a blackboard. If you do not understand what a person is saying, have them write it down. It is often easier to communicate concepts and ideas on paper than through conversation. If a communication problem still exists, then at least you have the ideas on paper for another person to evaluate later.

In general, technical terms are easier to understand than vague business and finance terms. Words like "guarantee" are legal jargon and are hard to communicate, whereas technical words usually break down nicely. Every word should be understood; don't use adjectives, adverbs, or vague terms, i.e. "several" or "a lot." It is important that everything be precise. In the international field don't confuse your issues with language barriers.

What to put in writing

Depending on the detail involved in the negotiation, use different approaches as to what should be put in writing and what should be left as a verbal commitment. For highly technical discussions it is best to draft a position paper stating what was said and what was agreed upon. At the end of the meeting both parties agree to the points on the paper and then sign or initial the agreement.

When the details are not so specific and both parties are discussing concepts, then seldom is anything put into writing. When points go on paper most negotiators don't want to close off negotiations prematurely, simply because one point has gone too far and it is on paper and perceived as unchangeable. With Americans, there is the problem that everything needs to be on paper. Attorneys tend to reinforce this practice. The best negotiators in these situations don't put a thing in writing until all of the details have been ironed out.

Politics in negotiations

In social discussions you are best to steer around political obstacles. Most businessmen operate on a professional level and want only to do business, but the world is changing rapidly and you must always have your ear open to politics.

Debriefing and evaluating an international negotiation

Directly after the final negotiating meeting, team members should review their notes and make sure they agree on all the points stated. If there is a misunderstanding there is still time to make a phone call or to go back to the other party to clarify the issue. Debriefing works best as a team effort.

It is good practice, time permitting, not to schedule meetings for the last day of a business trip, so that in the event that the last meeting goes over schedule there is still the next morning to iron out loose ends. The worst way to end a negotiation is to rush through important details, then forgo debriefing or conduct it while rushing to the airport. A free final day allows you the time to meet with agents or to review meeting notes to clarify confusing points.

■ Hot tip

When evaluating the progress of a specific negotiation, use the following scale:

1 Do I have a check in my hand?
2 Have they signed the contract?
3 Is there a memorandum of understanding?
4 Do I have a verbal commitment?
5 Do I feel good about the results?

Negotiating with selected countries

This part of the chapter offers anecdotes from selected countries in Europe, the Middle East, and Asia. The information can be incorporated into negotiations with people from almost any country.

The Middle East

Middle Easterners are among the toughest negotiators in the world. They set-up their negotiation to separate the technical people from the finance people. The finance people begin by negotiating a contract for a specific dollar amount, without prior resolution of any technical details. Then the engineers come in and build the project beyond the limits of the contract. You must constantly monitor the Middle Eastern activity, because their technical people try to go beyond the terms of the contract.

Middle Easterners use all the negotiating tricks in the book. During one negotiation in Israel, they set up the meeting in a room without air conditioning, when it was 42°C outside (over 100°F). The room was hot, smoke-filled and sweaty, and all they gave the visitors to drink was a cup of warm, thick tea. The smoke was so thick you could cut it.

Middle Easterners turn on their negotiating face when they get into the negotiating room. They argue a technical point for ever. Meetings go on for hours without a break. You ask them if they would like to stop for a break, and they say "No," and continue to work. It becomes a question of who can go the longest without going to the bathroom. Of course, after the meeting the Middle Easterners turn off their negotiating face, and relate with you on a very personal level.

Turkey

The secret of success in Turkey, as well as any other place, is solid preparation, a first-hand exploration of business conditions, a market survey, and a good local contact. Traditionally, Turks tend to be warm-hearted and often go slow, showing a preference to talk about a common sport such as soccer before business matters.

Turkey varies on such key aspects as the amount and type of preparation for a negotiation, the number of people present, and the extent of their influence; the relative emphasis is on task versus interpersonal relationships, the use of general principles versus specific details. There is no one best way to negotiate, no guaranteed formula for success; however, research into aspects of business when negotiating is considerably helpful. The following guidelines are important:

■ Negotiations are conducted in a formal but familial manner. Candor and businesslike behavior are most respected. Quite often family relations and school ties enter into the process. Lawyers and other third parties enter into the negotiating process once the principals have agreed in principle.

■ Do business in hard-currency terms (preferably dollars). Letters of credit should be confirmed by banks or secured by goods. Financing needs to be nailed down early.

■ Written materials, proposals, and specifications should be provided in English and, if possible, in advance of meetings. Bring interpreters to take notes at meetings.

■ Retain reliable local contacts, consultants, or brokers. The cost is repaid by avoiding the unexpected and obtaining up-to-date information on government and private-sector initiatives.

■ Most importantly, do not underestimate the sophistication of the modern Turkish businessman. Many have been educated in the U.S. or Europe. The younger they are, the more certain it is that they will have been to university.

■ Respect for age and status requires common courtesies. Family-owned holding companies have been passed down to younger family and/or gone public.

■ Dress in suit and tie.

■ Honesty and mutual respect play an important role.

Asia (general)

In the Orient things move much more slowly. Above all, insist on an agenda or the meeting will wander. When you walk into a meeting the first thing they give you is a page full of questions. You may be allowed ten minutes to review the questions before they start going through them one by one. Asians prefer to have your data in advance. If this is not a problem, it will pay off in meetings, which will progress much faster.

Taiwan (China)

Asian culture has a large impact on the negotiation process. One time a foreign firm was negotiating with a company in Taiwan to supply a telecommunications system. The president of the foreign company was present, so the Chinese company counterbalanced his presence by having the Chinese president sit in. However, in the Orient the Chinese president does not make decisions in public. He prefers to be in the background where he can be consulted. If a Chinese president makes a decision in public it is very difficult for it to be changed. The only way to overcome this dilemma was to have the American president leave the meeting and take a vacation. Once the American president dropped out of the meeting, the Chinese president also dropped out. The engineers could then continue with the technical details. This was the only way the meeting could proceed.

Japan

The Japanese are similar to the Chinese, in that they tend to be very careful about what they say in the presence of their chief. In Japan all the people in the meeting are important and you must treat them accordingly. It is important not to push for an answer, but to make sure that they are all in agreement. The Japanese use a consensus decision-making approach, and will keep talking about a topic until everybody nods. This process, known as *nemawashi*, is a political process by which an unofficial understanding is reached before a final decision is made. The process is rooted in the Japanese family system, where the head of household makes all significant decisions for the entire family. Today, more interested in maintaining harmony than upholding his authority, the CEO consults with other company (household) members. The group will make a decision, only when its members are in a separate meeting with their boss. The Japanese do not like to make their decisions in public.

It is important to understand the background and culture of the people you are working with. For instance, one negotiator read up on Japan's history and when the Japanese realized he was interested in their culture they offered to take him to museums and show him their cultural sights. Another negotiator took an English translation of a famous Japanese book, *The Book of the Five Rhinos* by Miyamota Musashi. The book deals with the skills and art of the samurai. He had the book wrapped and gave it to them, which did two things: demonstrated his respect for a book by a famous samurai and showed them that he thought they could read English well, which delighted them.

Here is another example of how cultural differences affect the relationship. On one project with the Japanese a foreign firm proposed a design and asked the Japanese engineering group to review it. Instead of saying they did not like it, or the design would not work, the Japanese said, "We will study it." That was their polite way of saying "No." The foreign firm really thought that they would study it and, as you can imagine, it was upsetting when they received no response.

The Japanese use silence as an effective negotiating tool. It is not uncommon for them to schedule a 7.30 p.m. meeting knowing you will be arriving late in the evening on a trans-Pacific flight. When you show up at the meeting they will usher you into a conference room where the Japanese negotiators are sitting. They will then give you a cup of tea. The Japanese simply sit and wait, and say nothing. Most foreigners feel uncomfortable with the silence, and after a couple of minutes begin to talk business. Before you know it the foreigner has all his cards on the table, and the Japanese haven't said a word.

In general the Japanese are much more thorough than Americans or Europeans. After a meeting the Japanese break off for a separate meeting and spend an additional two hours reviewing what you said. The Japanese review every sentence to determine exactly what is meant.

Below is a general outline of the differences between Japanese business habits and those of the West. When a company is under a contract to ship a product by a certain time and falls behind schedule due to problems:

- the European firm will say, "Don't worry about it, we need the product, just ship it;"
- the American firm will say, "We need the product, so ship it and we will fix it;"
- the Japanese firm will say. "We need the product, but don't ship it until it meets the specification. We have a contract and you must honor your commitment."

Switzerland

Switzerland is a multicultural nation with a highly developed economy. Whenever you do business with its people, keep attributes such as quality, reliability, and punctuality in mind. The Swiss take business very seriously, and that's what they expect from their partners. Due to the country's cultural diversity, negotiations in Switzerland might differ from state to state. But there are common characteristics that multinational firms will encounter when sitting at the negotiation table.

Typically a representative or a delegation will welcome you at the airport and take you to your hotel. Depending on your time of arrival and how much time you are spending in Switzerland, lunch or dinner might be organized so that you can be shown around and get better acquainted. They will then briefly discuss the time and place of the negotiation meeting. It is well understood that you would like to take a shower, relax, and go through your documents with your associates before entering into negotiations. Business language in Switzerland can be English, German, French, or Italian. If you don't speak any of these languages it is likely that they will provide a translator. Swiss negotiators ask a lot of questions and they expect answers. It might be very useful to bring some experts and your own translator.

The typical physical setting is a conference room with a round table, either in the company's building or at a neutral location. The negotiators will be introduced, followed by presentation of the negotiating subject and opening of discussions. The negotiation is always formal and starts punctually. Normally, negotiations take one or two days. A very important factor for the Swiss is time. For them, time is money. The typical Swiss way of dealing with negotiations is business first, then pleasure. Age, title, and seniority are highly valued. Negotiators are addressed by their last name and title. Formal suits and proper appearance are required. The Swiss love recognition and compliments.

The contract under negotiation, and the problems will always be treated in sections (broken down into discussion categories). Where an agreement can't be reached after a certain time period, it will be discussed later. Concessions are very rarely made unless they are of minor importance to the whole subject. Agreements are notarily authorized and signed by both parties, with a legal contract.

In international negotiations with the Swiss you will always face experts such as engineers, lawyers, finance managers, technicians, and multilingual advisors. The head of the Swiss delegation generally has full authority, and is the only one who knows the deadline and the bargaining limits. Swiss negotiators are always involved in other business issues and are therefore very busy. Only competent and qualified personnel are selected for negotiations.

Indonesia

The Indonesian government offers many incentives to attract foreign investors. When foreign partners arrive the Indonesians usually send a representative who has an important position in the company. Usually, the welcoming representative will take care of everything you need.

The preferred business language in Indonesia is English, but if you are not fluent in English it is likely that you will be provided with a translator who speaks your language. You will usually have a free day after your arrival before the meeting begins. During your free day the Indonesian partners will visit you. This is your chance to get acquainted. After you have rested you will be presented with any working papers you need to review.

Typically the meeting will be held in the conference room in the company's building. It is very rare for the meeting to be held in a hotel or restaurant. The delegations will introduce to each other, but it is preferred that only the head of the delegation speak. It is considered rude or impolite to use your hands when you talk. The length of the negotiation depends on the size of the deal that is being negotiated. Expect a break if the negotiation goes on for more than two hours. During the break you'll be served a formal lunch. Indonesian negotiators expect that you have the authority to reach agreements without delay.

Mexico

Mexican business people tend to pick a neutral arena, like a well-known restaurant. They do this in order to create trust and to get to know the other person as an individual or friend. When negotiating, they always look for mutual goals, needs, interests, and benefits. A hierarchical relationship exists throughout Mexico and the owner of the company is the one who always makes the final decision. Lawyers and subordinates do the paperwork. Businessmen are usually related to people with political influence or economic power and they let the opponent know about their status. A negotiating opponent should be strong, decisive, and know everything about the business deal. To secure success, be prepared to bargain beneficial options. Mexican business people are always well informed about their opponents. Cultural differences are used to benefit the negotiation. Cultural misunderstandings occur when foreigners use stereotyped images and ideas they have about Mexican society and corruption. Be open and respectful.

India

Indians are known to have a less hurried attitude toward time than most North Americans and Europeans. The concept that "time is money" is alien to most; therefore small talk leading to highly personal relationships takes up much of the time. Indians are very competitive technology-wise, so one should be prepared to offer competitive technology packages with close technical follow-up.

■ PART TWO ■

Tips and traps

Country-by-country practical applications

Fear and suspicion are obstacles to clear thinking, especially on matters where foreigners are concerned.

Jan Pen, former Professor of Economics and Director of Economic Policy, The Netherlands

The remainder of this book lists, country by country, a short discussion of business and economic conditions, and various protocol suggestions that will contribute to successful business and help you enjoy a foreign land. Neither the snapshots of business and economic conditions nor the lists of protocols are exhaustive, but they do, in most cases, provide the salient points about each country.

CHAPTER SEVEN

North America

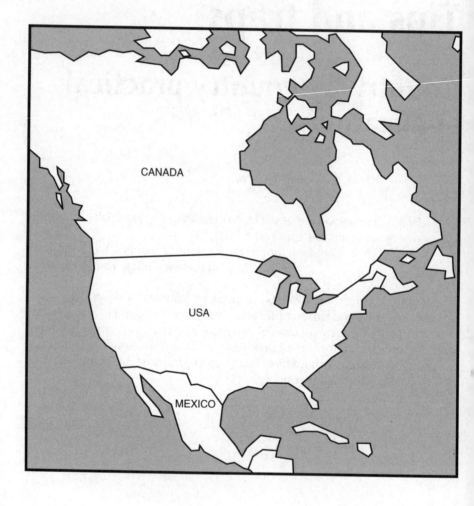

Canada

The second-largest country in the world (after Russia), Canada is a land of richness in resources and people. It is a blend of closeness to Europe as well as the United States, with two-thirds of its more than 28 million residents living within 190 miles (300 km) of twelve adjacent American states. Before going there take time to learn the geography of Canada and its fertile history with its linkages to Great Britain and France. With a per capita income equal to the highest of the industrial nations, Canada is a market that cannot be overlooked. When deciding to sell in this important market, consideration must be given to the implications of the North American Free-Trade Agreement (NAFTA), of which Canada is a vital member. As an affluent, high-tech industrial society, since World War II Canada has had impressive growth in the manufacturing, mining, and service sectors, which have transformed the nation from a largely rural economy into a primarily industrial and urban one. With its great natural resources, skilled labor force, and modern capital plant, Canada has excellent economic prospects. Among its generous resources is an international transportation system extending, by way of the St. Lawrence Seaway and the Great Lakes, from the Atlantic Ocean to the western end of Lake Superior. With excellent nationwide highway and rail systems, cargo can move by land as well as water to and from the main ports of Halifax, Montreal, St. John's, Toronto, and Vancouver.

Tips

✔ Greetings are English expressions similar to those in Great Britain and the U.S.A., i.e. good morning, good afternoon, good evening, goodnight, hi, hello, nice to meet you, how are you?, etc.
✔ Be careful of name pronunciation, especially with French.
✔ Business cards are exchanged, but not on initial greeting.
✔ Possibly because of their heritage of strong links with Great Britain, Canadians tend to be more conservative and a bit more rank- and title-conscious than U.S. citizens.

✔ Business hours are typically 9 a.m. to 5 p.m.
✔ Make appointments and be punctual.
✔ Shake hands on greeting and departing.
✔ Part of the Canadian population speaks French (Quebec, and parts of New Brunswick and Nova Scotia). The remainder speaks English.
✔ Expect Anglophiles to be monolingual, while Francophiles are bilingual.
✔ Safe subjects in conversation are sport, commerce, and geography.
✔ Expect to be entertained in restaurants and clubs.
✔ Business lunches are usually short (1–1½ hours), with light foods and no alcohol.
✔ If invited to a home for a meal, present an inexpensive gift to the host.
✔ Expect Canadians to partake of strong drink.

Traps

✗ Be aware that Canadians are sensitive to comparisons with the United States.
✗ Know where you are, and avoid becoming involved in any disparaging discussions about the two different cultural parts of the country and the continuing impasse between English- and French-speaking areas threatening to split the nation.

Mexico

Mexico is a country of four distinct regions. The northern region, dominated by Monterrey, extends from Tijuana in the west, to Hermosillo and Chihuahua in the center, to Ciudad Victoria on the east and Zacatecas in the south. Monterrey is a modern city of nearly 3 million; Tijuana and Monterrey each have grown to populations of more than 2 million, and because of their proximity tend to emulate the drive and work ethic of the United States. The central region extends north to San Luis Potosí and Guadalajara, and south to Puebla and Veracruz. Guadalajara is the largest and most important center of industry in this region. The south-east is primarily an agrarian region with little industry except for tourism. Mexico City is the largest region because it has rapidly grown to become the largest city in the world, with a population of over 20 million. Consequently, infrastructure lags behind the growth, and, on the one hand, the atmosphere is alive and exciting and, on the other, even simple tasks sometimes often take days and weeks. People here are professional, sophisticated, and well educated.

This nation's economy is a mixture of state-owned industrial facilities (notably oil), private manufacturing and services, and both large-scale and traditional agriculture. Petroleum, border assembly plants, and tourism are the largest earners of foreign exchange. Mexico is a full member, with the U.S. and Canada, in the North American Free-Trade Agreement (NAFTA), and the United States is Mexico's major trading partner, accounting for almost three-quarters of its exports and imports. Mexico faces substantial problems, for example rapid population growth, unemployment, and serious pollution, particularly in Mexico City; however, the government, in consultation with international economic agencies, has been implementing programs to stabilize the economy and foster growth. For example, it has privatized more than two-thirds of its state-owned companies (parastatals), including banks.

This is a country of family-owned businesses, and 95 percent of them are small or medium-sized. It is also a place where family members are trained to take over when the "*patrón*" steps down. Control and business decision-making power therefore rest in the paternalistic hands of the owner. Care must be taken not to send the wrong person to negotiate. To send only a middle manager might be a slap in the face to a Mexican business owner. If a negotiator does not have an impressive title conversations may take place with only Mexican middle managers who lack the authority to make key decisions.

Tips

✔ Be careful about names. Men and women adopt their mother's family name as an extension of the father's family name. For instance, for the name Israel Moreno Lares, Israel is the given name, Moreno is the father's family name and Lares is the mother's family name. What to use? Señor (or other title) Moreno would be correct until the relationship becomes more familiar.

✔ The morning greeting is ¡*Buenas días*!; afternoon: ¡*Buenas tardes*!; night: ¡Buenas noches! You can use ¡Hola! or ¿Cómo esta? anytime.

✔ Professional titles should be used when addressing a Mexican, i.e. doctor, architect, lawyer, engineer, certified public accountant (CPA).

✔ The form, presentation, and appearance of everything, including attire and written reports, is very important.

✔ Appointments are scheduled; however, it is not unusual for them to be made from 30 minutes to 1 hour in advance of the time the meeting will actually take place.

✔ Working hours in this country are 8 a.m.–2 p.m.; 3 p.m.–5 p.m..

✔ Mexicans rarely work on Sundays, a day reserved for church and family.

✔ Mexican's are gracious and formal, and treat everyone with great respect.

✔ Greetings among men who know each other usually include a bear hug called the *abrazo*, which is a sign of friendship. The *abrazo* is accompanied by vigorous slapping on the back with the free hand, followed by a handshake. Foreigners should learn this form of greeting. It is welcomed as a sign of goodwill, and is an important asset when dealing with the Mexican associate or customer.

✔ The psychological space of Mexicans is relatively close; that is, it is not unusual for men to stand near to each other and women, and to touch frequently.

✔ In Mexico it is common for workers to exchange personal greetings each morning; these include a handshake and a kiss on the cheek for the women.

✔ Expect the Mexican viewpoint to be cosmopolitan and European, yet be aware of the strong national pride Mexicans take in their rich heritage.

✔ Learn some Mexican history.

✔ Honor is important and plays a vital role in business.

✔ You should attempt to learn the language. Mexicans appreciate the effort.

✔ Mexicans tend to use ornate phrases in this very formal language and they expect you to do likewise.

✔ Influence is critical. The power of influence is favoritism, which is an important factor in doing business.

✔ You should have a cosmopolitan frame of mind when doing business in this country.

✔ Expect mealtimes to be similar to those of Southern Europe, i.e. breakfast: 7–8 a.m.; lunch: 2–3 p.m.; Supper: 8–10 p.m..

✔ Be careful with presents. Inquiring in advance can be offensive; if you are not familiar with your business counterpart bring a small gift such as a book or a piece of handicraft..

✔ Expect Mexicans to be creative in business deals.

✔ Unless he or she is a close friend, do not call a person at home.

✔ Sharing the intimacy of family with an invitation to a Mexican's home symbolizes a change in the relationship from acquaintance to friendship. Friendship means trust, and is the key to closing a business deal.

✔ Nothing is more important to the Mexican than his family, which includes not just the immediate members, but also aunts, uncles, and cousins several times removed, as well as all the members of his in-laws' families. Family members often account for much of the management of Mexican companies.

✔ Mexicans have a tradition of making the other party feel comfortable which takes precedence over other circumstances.

✔ The honor of the woman is sacred. Use great care when meeting and dealing with women in Mexico.

✔ Beware of the macho stereotype, which is on the wane in the modern age. Mexicans have become aware of the implications of population growth on their lifestyle and economy.

Traps

✗ Don't be too direct or frank. It may be seen as rude and pushy. It is better to establish the relationship over drinks, a meal, or recreation then, when the time is right, get down to business.

✗ Don't draw comparisons with the United States or discuss illegal immigration.

✗ At a business meeting, don't throw documents on the table. This is highly offensive to Mexicans and may well be the end of your business deal.

The United States of America

America, a country of more than 270 million people, with a per capita income equal to the highest among the industrial nations, is the world's largest and richest target market. Expect great diversity across this large country, particularly in and around the major port cities, where immigrants from around the world first settle. The business culture of this land is fairly consistent—suits and ties, and reasonable formality. The exception is in many of the high-technology businesses, where people tend to dress informally, but take their work very seriously. It is a nation of high productivity where the work ethic rivals that of any nation.

The United States has the most powerful, diverse, and technologically advanced economy in the world. The economy is market-oriented, with most decisions made by private individuals and business firms, and with government purchases of goods and services made predominantly in the marketplace. America's transportation and maritime port systems rival the finest in the world. Most major cities have international airports and free-trade zones. Manufacturing plants are connected to air and marine ports by the finest intermodal processes, consisting of a superb national highway and rail system.

Tips

✔ Americans are future-oriented people who value their freedom and equality.

✔ They are also very competitive at work and at play.

✔ Don't expect great formality.

✔ Expect women to be a major part of life in this continually changing nation. Women compete in all aspects of life.

✔ A handshake is the customary greeting for both men and women, although you should wait to see if the woman offers her hand.

✔ Business hours are typically from 9 a.m. to 5 p.m., Monday through Friday.

✔ Americans typically do not work on weekends.

✔ Be prepared to speak English. Unlike Europeans, most Americans know only one language.

✔ Americans do not speak British English. They speak American English and they use a lot of jargon in their speech. They say things like "Keep a low profile," "It's raining cats and dogs," "It's as flat as a pancake," and they ask "What's the bottom line?"

✔ Expect to be entertained in the home, with the spouse (or significant other) a full partner in discussions.

✔ Be on time for a visit or business.

✔ Expect to get right down to business.

✔ Pleasure has high value. Americans like to get away from the workplace.

✔ Expect diversity in dress. In some parts of the country (particularly the east) everyone wears business suits. In others (west coast), sport shirts are the norm for everyday work. Most executives dress more formally than work-center people. Check with your counterpart, but on first meeting you cannot go wrong if you dress conservatively.

✔ Americans like sports and their pastime is baseball, which is played from early spring until late fall. Americans play football (not soccer) in the fall and basketball in the winter. Soccer (known as football everywhere else in the world) has a foothold in only a few sectors of the country.

✔ Golf is a growing sport, and a pastime during which business is often discussed and where deals are made.

✔ It is OK to talk politics; however, fewer than 40 percent of Americans care about it enough to vote.

✔ Drink the water and eat the food, but be careful of your diet when visiting the United States because the fat content is higher—you are in danger of gaining weight.

✔ Practice driving before getting on the freeways, particularly during work hours. Driving is an intense exercise and almost all Americans drive their own car.

✔ It's OK to tell jokes. Americans like to laugh, but be careful of ethnic and religious humor. Know your audience. They like self-deprecating humor.

✔ It is nice, but not expected, to present a gift.

✔ Because the United States is dominantly Christian, Sunday is the typical religious day.

✔ The psychological space of Americans is about 18–20 inches. They are generally not huggers. American men (except for athletes) don't hug and are suspicious of touching.

✔ Americans like children, animals, and cars. The American dream is to have several of each in their own home.

Traps

✗ Don't be fooled by Americans' informality away from the workplace. Most ordinary Americans on the street, while respecting titles and rank, prefer just to use first names. Nevertheless, they do understand rank and titles, and a visitor should take great pains to know who ranks who in an organization and give due respect.

CHAPTER EIGHT

Central America

In general, you should expect the people of the modern nations of Central America, the narrow bridge of land that connects the continents of North and South America, to reflect a blend of cultures. However, you should also remember that great early civilizations once existed in this area of the world, providing a rich heritage.

Belize

This is the tiniest nation in Central America, with a population of only about 210,000; however, it is rich in unspoiled beaches, lush forests, and abundant wildlife, and there are few restrictions on foreign investment. It is becoming an economic target for tourism developers. There are no railroads in Belize, but there are over 900 miles of all-weather main and feeder roads, as well as a deep-water port at Belize city. The international airport only 9 miles from Belize City can accommodate medium-sized, jet-engined aircraft.

Tips

✔ A valid passport is required for all visitors.
✔ Recall the British colonial history of this nation and expect a residue of those ways.
✔ Expect to be greeted with a handshake.
✔ The verbal greeting is often, "You all right?" It's their way of asking "How are you?"
✔ Make appointments and be on time.
✔ The languages are English (official), Creole, Spanish, Garifuna, and Mayan.
✔ Most Belizeans speak Spanish in addition to English.
✔ The work week is Monday–Friday, 8.00 a.m.–12 noon; 1 p.m.–5 p.m
✔ Dress comfortably for this tropical, hot, and humid country. Take informal, comfortable clothes.
✔ Taxi drivers are generally not tipped.
✔ Many hotels and restaurants automatically add a service charge to the bill. Nevertheless, add a small tip on top.

Traps

✗ Be prepared for frequent devastating hurricanes during the period from September to December.

Costa Rica

The name means "rich coast" in Spanish, and its people are mostly of European (Spanish) descent. Costa Rica has a stable government—political risk is quite low. This country, whose main exports are bananas, cattle, seafood, flowers, foliage, and sugar, has an international airport at El Coco, about 10 miles from San José, and an excellent port on its west coast, with truck and rail service to both. There are free-trade zones in most industrial areas.

Tips

✔ Confirm airline reservations for flights in and out of the country.
✔ Because tickets are heavily taxed, buy your airline tickets outside of the country.
✔ People here are very literate.
✔ Expect to be greeted with a handshake.
✔ Spanish is the official language.
✔ Expect women to kiss each other's cheeks on greeting.
✔ Dress comfortably for this tropical, hot and humid, wet country. Take informal, comfortable clothes and be prepared to change often.
✔ Taxi drivers are generally not tipped.
✔ Many hotels and restaurants automatically add a service charge to the bill. Nevertheless, add a small tip on top.

Trap

✗ The rainy season is very long—from May to November.

Cuba

Times change, and doing business in Cuba is not such a far-fetched idea now as it once was. Since the end of the Cold War Cuba has gradually warmed to trade and investment with Western countries. Following the loss of massive amounts of economic aid from the former Soviet bloc, Cuban banking officials opened foreign-exchange houses, which now offer hard-currency transactions and credit card services. Nevertheless, most arrangements are still restricted to barter deals and buy-back arrangements. Foreign firms may tap into strategic industries through joint ventures and economic associations with Cuban state-run companies. Cuba has several international airports, as well as a container service with northern Europe, the Mediterranean, and the Black Sea. The country does have a paved central highway system, but is disadvantaged by having one of the world's least-developed telephone systems.

Tips

✔ Expect to be greeted with a handshake.
✔ Only friends are hugged, and with regularity.
✔ Dress comfortably—Cuba lies within the tropics, and because of the north-east trade winds has a pleasantly warm climate.
✔ Be prepared for a rainy season from May to October.
✔ Remember that this country still operates on the Spanish clock with siesta time from about 1.30 p.m. to about 4 p.m.
✔ For conversation—politics no, sports yes.
✔ Leave your English at home and be prepared to do business in Spanish.

Traps

✗ Don't expect Cuba to be inexpensive. Food, hotels, and transportation are expensive—about the same as other Caribbean countries that cater to business people and tourists.
✗ Don't change money into pesos—the currency is worthless outside the country.

El Salvador

This very picturesque nation—with mountains in the north, valleys and plateau in the center, and plains along the Pacific Ocean—is the most industrialized of all Central American countries. It is also the region's most densely populated country. Spurring the high growth of this nation (about 5 percent) are the government's five-year programs, which include modernization of telecommunications and infrastructure. Public and private investment have increased as a result of post-civil-war rebuilding and expansion in manufacturing and services. The nation has extensive highways linked to air and sea ports, all of which are being upgraded to support increasing international trade. There is a free-trade zone in San Bartalo, 6 miles from San Salvador.

Tips

✔ Expect to be greeted with a handshake, but friends are hugged with regularity.
✔ Don't address Salvadorans by their first name unless you know them well.
✔ Spanish is the official language, but Nahua is a common Indian language.
✔ Talk sports, especially football (soccer).
✔ Don't point your fingers or feet at anyone.
✔ Expect the clock to run on Hispanic time—lunch in the late afternoon, about 2 p.m. and late supper, about 9 p.m. or 10 p.m., or even later.
✔ Don't be surprised by a two-hour lunchtime siesta.
✔ If invited as a guest in someone's home, do try all the food. It is a compliment to the host .
✔ Shake hands with children when you're introduced.
✔ Don't tip taxi drivers unless they have been hired for the day.
✔ Tip hotel and restaurant employees the usual 10–15 percent.

Traps

✗ Salvadorans think of themselves as Americans; therefore U.S. citizens should introduce themselves as such.
✗ A mostly mountainous country, El Salvador is subject to frequent and sometimes destructive earthquakes.
✗ Exercise great care traveling in this country—ask about conditions.

Guatemala

This is a country of 10 million people, and is dominated by agriculture, which accounts for roughly 25 percent of its total output, two-thirds of its exports, and half of its employment. On the other hand, a growing portion of its 3 million labor force is actively participating in non-traditional exports, mainly textile assembly. Guatemala has an international airport, a national railway, and the inter-American highway, linking ports on the Caribbean as well as the Pacific.

Tips

✔ Carry your passport at all times; it is the law.
✔ Expect a handshake on first arrival.
✔ Leave your English at home and be prepared to do business in Spanish.
✔ The work week is 9 a.m.–5 p.m., Monday through Friday.
✔ Dress comfortably.
✔ Make appointments.
✔ Expect to be entertained in public restaurants.

Traps

✗ Don't argue or offer resistance if stopped at a roadblock.
✗ Don't drive after sunset—many cars don't have headlights.

Honduras

This is a nation growing in importance in Central American trade. It has a market for most high-technology products and its export-led economy is growing as it modernizes its industrial sector. The country is aggressively marketing high-value products such as seafood, especially shrimp, as well as cut flowers and tropical fruits. It is also trying to market itself as a foreign processing zone for textiles and other manufactured goods under the Caribbean Basin Initiative.

Tips

✔ Be certain to have confirmed reservations during the high season, space quickly becomes limited.
✔ Hugs are the usual greeting for friends and acquaintances, but expect a handshake on first arrival.
✔ Topics of conversation might include the ancient civilization and fascinating history of the country.
✔ Dress comfortably.
✔ Make appointments.
✔ Expect to be entertained in public restaurants.
✔ Tip waiters the normal 10–15 percent.
✔ Tip taxi drivers according to the number of bags/suitcases.

Traps

✗ Don't go to Honduras during the high season without a confirmed hotel reservation—they sometimes overbook.
✗ Don't expect to cash a personal check.
✗ Don't carry bills of large denominations.

Nicaragua

The largest country in Central America has an ambitious economic improvements program aimed at shedding its war-torn image. Having made the transition from a centralized to a market-oriented economy by privatizing more than 300 non-financial public-sector companies, Nicaragua is making progress toward a stabilized economy and positive economic growth. With an international airport, free-trade zones in multiple cities, and the pan-American highway that links its port cities and its neighbors north and south, Nicaragua is well positioned to achieve its long-run export-driven economic goals.

Tips

✔ Expect the way of life in this country to be similar to that of other Central American countries—primarily agrarian.
✔ Spanish is the primary language; don't expect English to be widely spoken.
✔ The people, in general, follow the ways of the Roman Catholic Church.
✔ Make appointments. Respect appointments, but don't be surprised if precise time is not kept.
✔ Expect a handshake on first arrival.
✔ Don't be taken aback when Nicaraguans refer to you as *mi amor* (my love). The expression is a common greeting when addressing someone of the opposite sex.
✔ Business hours are Monday through Friday, 8 a.m.–5 p.m.
✔ Dress comfortably.
✔ Expect to be entertained in public restaurants.
✔ Keep your arms but not your elbows on the table during meals.
✔ Tip waiters the normal 10–15 percent.
✔ Tip taxi drivers according to the number of bags/suitcases.

Traps

✗ Don't be offended if someone refers to you by the color of your skin or body type. It means no insult—they think of it as an endearment.
✗ Don't expect to use your credit card or traveler's checks.
✗ Don't criticize someone's personal traits—honor is important, as is machismo.

Panama

The people of this nation refer to their country as "the crossroads of the world," for it lies on the traditional trade routes between North and South America. It has the fastest-growing, lowest-inflation-rate economy in Central America. Panama's free-trade zone in Colón, the oldest and most widely used in the Western Hemisphere, has long been a vital part of Panama's trade by spurring a growing manufacturing and export sector. In addition there are four export-processing zones. Panama has an international airport and excellent deep-water ports, all linked by excellent roads and an inland waterway.

Tips

✔ Expect many Panamanians to speak English.

✔ This is a tropical country, with a rainy winter from May to December and a dry summer from January to April.

✔ Although a handshake is the norm on first arrival, don't be surprised to receive an *abrazo* (hug), some kisses, and a *gritando* (howl) from people whom you have not actually met before. The shriek of delight is because you are finally meeting for the first time.

✔ Don't be upset if someone refers to you as a *chueleta* (pork chop). This is a term of endearment similar to the word "buddy" in American English.

✔ Normal business hours are Monday through Friday, 8 a.m.–5 p.m.

✔ Expect your Panamanian partner to work with you late into the evening if business requires it. Panamanians don't walk away at quitting time.

✔ Dress comfortably, but sharply.

✔ Wear suits and dresses.

✔ Panamanians wear a tie; you should also.

✔ Expect to be entertained in public restaurants.

✔ It is a great compliment to be invited home for dinner.

✔ It is impolite to take a gift to the home, although you may be given one.

✔ If you wish to return the favor, invite the host to a meal with you at a local restaurant.

✔ Stick to bottled water.

Traps

✗ Don't talk politics, and be sensitive to Panama's nationalism and independence.

✗ On departing, never say "*adios*" to a Panamanian. If you do, they will assume they will never see you again. Instead, say "*ciao*".

CHAPTER NINE

South America

The continent of South America is an expanse of land rich in resources, with a literate population, an export-oriented industrial sector, and a history that extends to the earliest man. It stretches some 17.8 million square kilometers from the Atlantic Ocean in the east to the Pacific Ocean in the west. Central America and the Caribbean Sea are found to the north. The Andes mountains form the longest mountain chain in the world and the Amazon river surpasses all others in volume of flow. The Amazon basin holds the world's largest area of tropical rainforest.

The cultural characteristics of the modern people are derived from immigrant settlers who brought the Spanish and Portuguese languages, the Roman Catholic religion, a two-class social system, and a belief that large landholdings impart great prestige to the owner. Only recently have the latter two characteristics begun to disappear.

The first European explorer of South America was Christopher Columbus, but the land is named after Amerigo Vespucci, the first to recognize the Western Hemisphere as separated from Asia. Recent years have brought a struggle to find the right social and economic mechanisms to bring lasting welfare to the people.

In 1994 an accord similar to other international economic integrations developing in the world, such as the North American Free-Trade Agreement (NAFTA) and the European Union (EU), was reached between Argentina, Brazil, Paraguay, and Uruguay. It is called the Southern Cone Common Market or MERCOSUR, and it adopted a common external tariff (CET) on about 85 percent of the Harmonize Tariff Schedule categories, with the phase-in of the remainder by 2006.

Doing business in Latin America is about developing relationships before tasks with people who are expressive and personal yet proud of their way of life.

Generalizing is dangerous; however, in an attempt to conserve the limited space of this book several observations about cultural commonalties of this region of the world are offered.

Common cultural characteristics

■ In general men and women shake hands on greeting and departure. Close friends often hug and pat each other on the back.

■ Women friends often greet each other with a kiss on the cheek.

■ The clock generally runs on southern European time, that is lunch and supper are usually taken at 9 p.m. Expect business luncheons to be held in restaurants. Let them pay the check, but make an effort otherwise.

■ "American" is not an exclusive term for those who live in the United States. It includes those who reside in Central and South America as well as the north. After all, the name comes from Amerigo Vespucci, the Italian who discovered the continent of America in 1492.

■ Family ties, the church, and business loyalties are extremely strong and highly valued by South Americans. Nothing is more important.

■ Class, rank, and social status are very important.

■ Beware of title inflation.

■ People of these nations go to great lengths to avoid offending.

■ How something is said is more important than what is said.

■ A business person will avoid being brisk or "businesslike." Instead he or she will try to make each conversation friendly and warm even though the deal is being made at the same time.

■ Expect verbal prowess, even what may seem flowery language to some foreigners. South Americans are in general cultured and well educated.

■ Aristocratic top executives and government ministers will seldom negotiate with you at the outset. Instead expect middle-class middle managers to lay the groundwork.

■ Whom you know is what generally matters, rather than what you know.

■ Be patient in business matters. Don't expect immediate results.

■ Show your humanity—Latins expect and want to see a person's inner qualities.

■ Latin women tend to be classically feminine, not manly—it would be unlikely that they would wear a tie.

■ Machismo is the concept that men are superior to women. This is an extremely strong feeling among the people of the nations of the South American continent. Being manly is constantly on the minds of men, and it is important to them that they appear brave and have great self-confidence.

Argentina

This nation of about 35 million mostly Catholic people is going through a period of modernization. Argentina is the second-largest country in Latin America (after Brazil) and occupies the southern portion of the continent. Following years of mismanagement and statist policies, this country, rich in natural resources and with a highly literate population, is fast returning to its former status as one of the most-developed countries in the Western Hemisphere. Prior to World War II it was the sixth richest nation in the world. Electric power and telecommunications have improved dramatically following the recent privatization of the state electric power company and national telephone company. In recent years its economy has made the courageous shift from a traditional large-scale livestock and agricultural base to an export-oriented, diversified industrial base. Argentina is one of the founding members of the Southern Cone Common Market, or MERCOSUR, and has a transportation system which includes ten international airports and excellent ocean cargo ports. Several free-trade zones are under construction. The zone in La Plata province, only 45 miles from Buenos Aires, has been in operation for several years.

Tips

✔ See the Common cultural characteristics on p. 80.

✔ Expect to be greeted with a handshake.

✔ Expect Argentina to be a mix of immigrants from around the world. It has been described as a nation of Italians who speak Spanish and think they are British.

✔ Expect to make appointments and be on time.

✔ Take or arrange for delivery of a gift for the hostess if invited home for dinner.

✔ This country is 95 percent Roman Catholic and 85 percent ethnic white. The 15 percent non-white population is dominated by *mestizo* Indians.

✔ Expect Argentinians to speak Castilian (with an Italian accent) rather than Spanish.

✔ Sports and art are acceptable conversation topics. Avoid politics and religion.

✔ Don't tip taxi drivers but do tip ushers in the cinemas.

Traps

✗ See the Common cultural characteristics on p. 80.

✗ Don't go to Argentina during the high season without a confirmed hotel reservation—they sometimes overbook.

✗ Don't expect all banks to cash traveler's checks.

✗ Don't expect to be understood if you have studied the Mexican dialect of Spanish—Argentinians speak Castilian Spanish.

Bolivia

Named for Simón Bolívar, the liberator of South America, this land-locked country straddles the Andes mountains in the west central portion of the continent. With a population of only about 7 million, it has achieved an annual gross domestic product (GDP) growth rate of 3–4 percent. Bolivia has experienced more than 190 coups; however, it has remained stable since 1982, when the last military regime was replaced by a democratically elected president. In 1994 a Bill passed the legislature which will privatize the electrical sector and strengthen free trade.

Tips

✔ See the Common cultural characteristics on p. 80.
✔ Expect a handshake in personal greetings, going or coming.
✔ Carry your passport with you at all times. If you don't have it and the police stop you, expect to be fined and to spend several hours in jail.
✔ Learn and use some Spanish.
✔ Make appointments.
✔ Be on time for meetings even if others are late.
✔ Dress in moderate, conservative taste.
✔ Direct eye contact influences positive communications in this country.
✔ Eating on the street is not good manners; often the food found there is not of good quality.
✔ Watch your manners—this is considered very important.
✔ Expect a closer body-language distance. Expect patting on the shoulder as a sign of friendship.

Traps

✗ See the Common cultural characteristics on p. 80.
✗ Don't bring up the "war on drugs". There is resentment over U.S. military activity in Bolivia.

Brazil

This is the largest market economy in Latin America, occupying almost half of the continent and stretching about 4,350 kilometers from the foothills of the Andes mountains eastward to the Atlantic Ocean. Brazil's name is derived from the Portuguese word for the reddish color of brazil-wood, an important export during the sixteenth century. Throughout the 1980s and 1990s Brazil has suffered incredible debt, high inflation, a shaky democracy, and even the threat of secession by the three southernmost states. It has had at least six different currencies, the latest being the real, which replaced the cruzeiro in July 1994. Today this nation of about 162 million people is undergoing a trade liberalization drive to develop its vast resources and industrialize the country. Inflation is at a low point and the country has one of the most stable democracies on the continent. There are about 20 airports, excellent highways, and several export-processing zones throughout the country. Brazil is a member of the Southern Cone Common Market (MERCOSUR).

Tips

✔ See the Common cultural characteristics on p. 80.
✔ The language of this country is Portuguese. Try to learn some and don't worry about making mistakes. Brazilians appreciate your efforts even if your vocabulary is small. English is spoken by many of the well educated and is widely used in the business community.
✔ Say "*oi*" (sounds like "boy" without the "b") for "hello" and "*tchau*" ("*ciao*") for goodbye.
✔ Brazilians generally greet each other with long handshakes and noticeable eye contact; good friends often embrace.
✔ Women tend to exchange kisses, touching cheek to cheek and kissing the air.
✔ Expect Brazilians to be casual about time and work. But don't mistake this attitude for laziness or indifference. They just consider time in the context of events, not hours and minutes. Work is a necessary evil rather than an essential part of life.
✔ Avoid creating an agenda that immediately launches into business discussions.
✔ Dress conservatively for work and even dress modestly (no shorts or tank tops) when at leisure.
✔ Business hours are Monday through Friday, 8 a.m.–6 p.m.
✔ The midday meal is generally the main meal of the day.
✔ Carry your passport (or a photocopy) with you at all times.
✔ Expect men to value their manliness. It is all important to be brave and to display great self-confidence in every situation.
✔ Body language will be different. It is a simple friendliness for a Brazilian to stand close to you when he or she speaks, to pat your shoulder or back, or even to rearrange your tie or scarf. Don't misinterpret this familiarity as sexual; their psychological space is quite close.
✔ Expect family ties to be extremely strong and very important.
✔ Dress discreetly and in good taste. The upper class is very fashion-conscious. The lower class (about 80 percent of the people) are more casual.
✔ Be soft-spoken and gentle-mannered.
✔ Knock on office doors but, after knocking once, stand back and wait. Many offices are becoming more informal.

✔ If invited home, don't knock on the door of a Brazilian. Stand back and clap.
✔ Take a tasteful gift for the hostess. If your gift is flowers, don't bring purple, a sign of death.
✔ Speak about the things you admire about Brazil, such as its culture and arts, and the nation's progress in developing its resources.
✔ Holding your earlobe between your thumb and index finger signifies appreciation.
✔ Brazilians consider themselves to be among the best football (soccer) players in the world, so don't hesitate to talk sports.
✔ Use the "thumbs-up" sign when things go well.
✔ Most people do not eat on the street or on public transportation.
✔ Be careful when crossing streets—traffic is chaotic and fast.
✔ Don't yawn or stretch in public.
✔ Most restaurants will add 10 percent to the bill. Leave another 5 percent for a tip and you'll be fine.
✔ Don't tip taxi drivers.
✔ Don't overpay for domestic help or other services.
✔ Although Brazil is definitely a male-dominated society, machismo in this country takes a milder, more subtle form than is generally found in neighboring Hispanic America.
✔ Expect Brazilians to be very fashion-conscious, but actually casual dressers. A suit and tie for men, and suits and skirts or dresses for women are the office standard.

Traps

✗ See the Common cultural characteristics on p. 80.
✗ Don't make a circle with your fingers to show that everything is OK. This is considered an extremely vulgar gesture in Brazil.
✗ Don't snap your fingers. This is also considered vulgar.
✗ Avoid controversial topics such as Argentina, personal issues and ethnic jokes.

Chile

Chile, from the Indian *tchili*, meaning "the deepest point of the earth," is considered by many to be South America's most dynamic economy. Although it stretches like a ribbon more than 4,000 kilometers along the west coast of the continent, Chile is deceptively large. It is slightly bigger than the American state of Texas, with a population of about 14 million. Manufacturing and mining make Chile one of the most important industrial nations. It has a prosperous, essentially free-market economy, with government intervention varying according to the philosophy of the differing political regimes. It achieved its independence in 1818, but it wasn't until about 1988 that its economy began to sustain the economic growth of its potential. The new government returned many factories, banks, and expropriated land to private owners. Business investment, exports, and consumer spending are currently growing substantially. International airports, maritime ports, and excellent rail and road systems link many free-trade zones, north and south in this energetic nation.

Tips

✔ See the Common cultural characteristics on p. 80.
✔ Expect Chileans to greet one another with an *abrazos*, or hug, but you will, at least at first, receive only a handshake.
✔ Instead of shaking hands, women often greet each other with a pat on the forearm or shoulder. They may hug and kiss each other on the cheek if they are close friends.
✔ Spanish is the official language, but English and German are also spoken.
✔ Business cards should be printed with your own language on one side and Spanish on the other, and should be presented to everyone except the secretaries at a meeting.
✔ Dress for temperate desert in the north and cool, damp weather in the south.
✔ Dress conservatively. Men wear dark blue or gray suits; women should wear a suit and heels.
✔ Don't be surprised if no one makes a move to eat supper before about 8.30 p.m.—like many Latins, Chileans eat late.
✔ You will be entertained at public restaurants and hotels.
✔ Don't be late to appointments.
✔ Expect Chilean negotiations to be serious and straightforward.
✔ Arrive late for social functions—15 minutes for dinner, 30 minutes for a party.
✔ It is not customary to send a thank-you note following an invitation to a Chilean home, but sending flowers or candy to the hostess in advance is appreciated—avoid sending yellow roses (they signify contempt).
✔ Chileans converse at a closer distance than some other cultures, often with a hand on the other person's lapel or shoulder. Don't back away; they will just follow you, closing the distance again.
✔ Tip 10 percent in restaurants and hotels, but do not tip taxi drivers.

Traps

✗ See the Common cultural characteristics on p. 80.
✗ Slapping your right fist into your left open palm is an obscene gesture.
✗ An open palm with the fingers separated means "stupid."

Colombia

Columbia, under the leadership of the Great Liberator, Simón Bolívar, became the first South American country to fight and win its independence from Spain. Today the Colombian economy is growing at a favorable rate of about 3 percent. This has been brought about by a stable government, which has put in place an economic liberalization program, and the rapid development of oil, coal, and other non-traditional industries. Colombia is still a leading producer of both coffee and emeralds. Located in the northern part of South America, this nation of about 35 million people is modernizing its transportation system, including privatizing maritime ports, railroads, and highways. Because it is the only South American nation with coastlines on both the Pacific Ocean and the Caribbean Sea, it has eight or more free-trade zones linked to more than 100 domestic and about ten international airports.

Tips

✔ See the Common cultural characteristics on p. 80.
✔ Expect to be greeted with a handshake.
✔ Expect to be entertained in restaurants.
✔ Expect time to be less important than establishing a good relationship. Negotiations can wait until you know your business partner.
✔ This is a nation that loves to talk about sport, particularly soccer and bull-fights.
✔ Because of Colombia's high altitude, expect your body to need time to adjust.
✔ Prepare for rain. The Pacific coast of Colombia has some of the highest rainfall in the world.

Traps

✔ See the Common cultural characteristics on p. 80.
✔ Don't dress too flashy, wear expensive jewelry, or change money on the street.
✔ Don't travel by intercity bus, wear valuables, or accept food, drink, or cigarettes from strangers.
✔ Use only official taxis from legitimate taxi stands.
✔ Be aware that narcotics traffickers have turned violent. Exercise extreme caution when traveling in Colombia.
✔ Don't bring up the "war on drugs." There is resentment over U.S. military activity in the country.

Ecuador

Ecuador was once a Spanish colony, and today this republic on the northern Pacific coast of South America is the nation where traditional society remains most nearly intact. The population is ethnically and racially mixed. About 40 percent is *mestizo* (of mixed Indian and European ancestry) and another 40 percent is Indian. The remainder is equally divided between Europeans and negros or mulattos. The country, which derives nearly half of its export earnings from oil and is therefore subject to the swings of world market prices, is attempting to reduce its dependence on traditional exports by developing a better mix of industry. There are two international airports at Mariscal Sucre, near Quito, and Simón Bolívar, near Guayaquil, the principal seaport, which handles most trade.

Tips

✔ See the Common cultural characteristics on p. 80.
✔ Expect strong nationalist feelings.
✔ The work week is six days, eight hours a day.
✔ Don't expect dignitaries to eat in public.
✔ Expect to be greeted by handshake.
✔ Although punctuality is not essential, it is impressive.
✔ Expect doing business to be somewhat difficult, and getting paid to be a drawn out process.
✔ Avoid political topics and any issues or subjects that imply the superiority of the United States.
✔ Control your body language. Don't fidget with the hands, or answer with the head, or move your feet unnecessarily while seated.
✔ Dress well. All people of this nation, rich or poor, attempt to be well-dressed in public.
✔ Avoid sunglasses except when they are actually needed.
✔ Expect a cool climate. Equador is at about 13,000 feet or 4,000 meters altitude.
✔ Change your money at the airport on arrival.

Traps

✗ See the Common cultural characteristics on p. 80.

Paraguay

Paraguay means " a place with a great river" in the Guarani Indian language, and most of this landlocked nation in the northern part of the continent is bounded by rivers. Paraguay, which gained its independence from Spain in 1811, is primarily an agricultural country, yet, beginning in 1989, it has undergone dramatic political and economic change. Gearing up to compete in the global economy, Paraguay's democratic political and market opening has progressed even with occasional setbacks. Paraguay is a strategic member of the Southern Cone Common Market (MERCOSUR), because of its status as the region's lowest-cost provider of electricity and labor.

Tips

✔ See the Common cultural characteristics on p. 80.
✔ Keep your passport with you at all times. There are frequent checks by the military police.
✔ Expect to be greeted with "*mucho gusto*" on first meeting (pleased to meet you). Thereafter the greeting will be "good morning" or "good evening."
✔ Be on time for appointments, even though strict punctuality on the part of Paraguayans is not demanded.
✔ Discuss family, sports, current events, and the weather, but avoid politics.
✔ The national pastime of this country is conversation. Do not expect as great a division between work and play as in the United States.
✔ Expect business hours to extend from early morning until late afternoon, with a midday siesta.
✔ Don't be surprised by the three- or four-hour lunchtime siesta.
✔ Expect compliments to be given freely and expressively, but they should be about personality traits rather than about objects or appearance.
✔ Sit erect, with both feet on the floor. Crossing of legs is acceptable but only with one knee over the other.

Traps

✗ See the Common cultural characteristics on p. 80.
✗ Never use the U.S. OK sign or make a sign with crossed fingers—these gestures are considered offensive.
✗ Don't snap pictures of anything associated with the military.

Peru

The Republic of Peru, which declared its independence from Spain in 1821, extends about 2,400 kilometers along the western coast of South America. The Peruvian economy has become increasingly market-oriented, with major privatization in the mining and telecommunications industries. Its economy is continuing a strong growth rate of about 6 percent and is eagerly seeking foreign investment. The strongest growth has taken place in the fisheries sector, especially in the production of fishmeal for animal feed. The largest share of international air commerce is handled at the Jorge Chavez airport near Lima. There are industrial and commercial free-trade zones located throughout the country, all linked by extensive transportation systems between cities.

Tips

✔ See the Common cultural characteristics on p. 80.
✔ Expect to be greeted with a handshake, but Peruvian men will exchange hugs.
✔ Make appointments and be on time for business—being late a casual half-hour is expected.
✔ Don't miss your departure flight because of confusion about time. National time (tiempo nacional) is generally held to throughout the country, but there are some localities rebeling where they still set their clocks by the old time.
✔ Take or arrange for delivery of a gift for the hostess if invited home for dinner.
✔ Sports and art are acceptable conversation topics. Avoid politics.
✔ A 19 percent service charge is normally included in the bill, but an additional 5 percent is normal.
✔ Don't tip taxi drivers.

Trap

✗ See the Common cultural characteristics on p. 80.

Uruguay

Uruguay is the smallest country in South America, with a population of only about 3 million. It is an open economy, allowing 100 percent foreign ownership in many sectors. There are few remnants of its pre-colonial and colonial past. By the turn of the twentieth century Uruguay had developed a model social-welfare state, which lasted until the late 1960s. Today its goals are to privatize many of its industries, including airlines, telecommunications, and seaports. Uruguay is committed to the Southern Cone Common Market (MERCOSUR) customs union. The nation has free-trade zones, several deep-water ports and an excellent international airport.

Tips

✔ See the Common cultural characteristics on p. 80.
✔ Expect the urban educated elite to know some English, but you should count on doing business in Spanish.
✔ Men wear a coat and tie, women conservative dresses. After 6 p.m. many restaurants require them.
✔ Expect to dine about 9 p.m.
✔ Business hours are Monday through Friday, 8 a.m.–4 p.m.
✔ Government hours are Monday through Friday, 12 noon–7 p.m.
✔ Banks hours are Monday through Friday, 12 noon–5 p.m.
✔ Uruguayans work hard on projects that interest them but do not consider being efficient, keeping busy, and learning to conquer the material environment virtues in themselves.
✔ Personal relationships are valued highly and in most cases preferred to impersonal, functional connections.
✔ Expect men to be well dressed, but in a conservative manner.
✔ Women here have extensive political and legal rights—they are generally accepted as equals in social and cultural life, and often in the political, business, and financial world.
✔ Expect to find career women, and those that you meet to be exceptionally talented people.
✔ Pay about 10 percent for a tip for taxi drivers and in restaurants.

Traps

✗ See the Common cultural characteristics on p. 80.
✗ Don't go without a coat and tie—most restaurants require them.
✗ Don't be surprised by how late they eat supper—about 9 p.m. or later.

Venezuela

European explorers named the region "Little Venice" when, in 1499, they saw Indian villages built on pilings over Lake Maracaibo. The most northerly South American nation, Venezuela has a long Caribbean and Atlantic coast, and is a lightly populated but mineral-rich nation. It is a founding member of the Organization of Oil-Producing Countries (OPEC), and as a result of its lucrative petroleum business is one of the continent's wealthiest nations. The main international airport is Simón Bolívar, located in Caracas. There are nine major maritime ports, three major highways, and new rail tracks linking petrochemical and mining operations. The total population is about 20 million and the labor force is about 5.8 million, about half whom are employed in the service sector.

The beauty industry has to be taken very seriously. Venezuelans have won three Miss Universe and four Miss World titles.

Tips

✔ See the Common cultural characteristics on p. 80.

✔ Travelers must have a passport and a round-trip airline ticket.

✔ Carry your passport with you at all times.

✔ This is a country that considers titles and position to be very important. Instead of saying "Mr. Johnson," the Venezuelans would say "Engineer Johnson."

✔ Make appointments.

✔ Be prepared for fast chaotic traffic, especially motorcyclists.

✔ Be careful crossing streets.

✔ Smaller firms are less formal.

✔ Because of the hot weather, dress casually.

✔ Conversation among men, when not talking business, is usually about women.

✔ Expect to be invited out to discuss business. Luncheons at nice restaurants are common.

✔ Tip 10 percent in restaurants, but do not tip taxi drivers.

✔ Expect black to be considered the most fashionable color among women; subdued colors are usually selected for men's suits.

✔ Expect, as a result of the far-reaching mixture of races, that this nation has greater opportunity, is less tradition-bound, and has less class prejudice than most other Latin American cultures.

✔ Expect to learn that business training in this country puts a high value on spiritual and social aptitudes.

Traps

✗ See the Common cultural characteristics on p. 80.

✗ Don't speak badly about Simón Bolívar.

CHAPTER TEN

Asian Pacific Rim

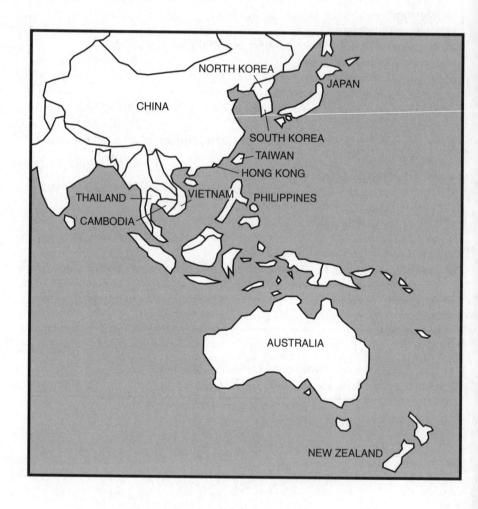

Historically, trade has been dominated by European cultures, but recently international business has become global and growth has migrated toward the Asian Pacific Rim.

Excepting the southernmost countries, i.e. Australia and New Zealand, which have closer cultural ties to England and the United States, the Asians are extremely sensitive about "losing face"—the behavioral characteristic of maintaining self-esteem. Go slow and learn as much as you can about Asian cultures before you embark on an enterprise there.

Australia

Nicknamed the "the Land Down Under," Australia is the smallest of the earth's continents but is the world's sixth largest independent sovereign nation. It was discovered by the Dutch in 1606 but claimed by Captain James Cook in 1770, and much of Australia's culture is derived from Great Britain and the European continent. It has about the same area as the United States, but with only a fraction of the American population. Its people (estimated in 1996 at about 19 million) are concentrated along the eastern and southeastern coasts. It is a mostly dry desert land situated south of Indonesia, between the Pacific and Indian Oceans, and it has large differences in climate, from extremely warm climates in the north to cold, windy climes in the south. Australia is rich in natural resources and has a prosperous Western-style capitalist economy, with a per capita GDP comparable to that of industrialized Western European countries. Its GDP averages 2.5–3 percent a year. Australia is a major exporter of agricultural products, minerals, metals, and fossil fuels. The government is pushing for increased exports of manufactured goods. There are abundant transportation systems, including world-class international airports, domestic air service, modern highways, and transcontinental rails connecting all major cities and ports. Telecommunications are extensive and modern. There is only one free-trade zone, located near the Darwin Airport.

Tips

✔ Australians generally respond to their full name and use first names only after getting to know you.

✔ Expect to be greeted with a handshake.

✔ Greetings are casual and often accompanied with "Good day," pronounced "gidday," and "mate," meaning friend or pal.

✔ Although Australians are characterized as a warm and friendly people, this is not a hugging place.

✔ Outward signs of emotion, such as hugging, are not considered manly and are avoided.

✔ Class structure and rank are recognized, but signs of self-importance are not looked on kindly.

✔ Promptness is important.

✔ Business hours are Monday through Friday, 9 a.m.–5 p.m., Saturday, 9 a.m.–Noon.

✔ Banks are open Monday through Thursday, 9 a.m.–3 p.m.; Friday, 10 a.m.–5 p.m.

✔ Expect less formal dress in the warmer cities. Safari suits are often worn.

✔ Speaking frankly and directly, with head-on resolution of disagreements is not unusual.

✔ Australians generally like Americans and Europeans, but keep in mind their historical connections with Britain.

✔ It is not unusual to be invited to the home of your Australian business associate.

✔ Although gifts are seldom exchanged, when visiting a household a modest bunch of flowers for the hostess or a bottle of wine is an acceptable gift.

✔ Gifts should be small and inexpensive, and are best if they reflect where you are from.

✔ Australians like their sport so it is a safe topic of conversation.

✔ You should expect to hear Americans referred to as "Yanks," and the British by the not so nice term "Pommies," which some say comes from "Prisoners of Mother England."

✔ When yawning, always cover the mouth, and excuse yourself.

✔ Men keep their emotions to themselves.

✔ Sportsmanship is very important and is often cheered, even in a losing team.

✔ Expect this nation to come to a stop on the first Tuesday of November for Melbourne Cup Day. Everyone watches this famous horse race, first run in 1861.

✔ Australian's beer has a higher alcohol content, so be careful!

✔ At parties or get togethers, it is not uncommon for the men to congregate together and the women separately.

✔ Australians drive on the left side of the road.
✔ Tipping is not always necessary, but it is often expected at better restaurants.

Traps

✗ A clenched fist with a raised thumb, as in the American hitchhiking sign, is a vulgar gesture.
✗ If an Australian is asked to do something, he or she will endeavor to please, if told what to do, the same person may reject the command.
✗ Avoid winking, especially at women. Winking at women, even to express friendship, is improper.
✗ Eating anything but ice cream on the streets is not proper.

Cambodia

This is a country whose economy is held hostage by continued political unrest and factional hostilities. However, it is making slow progress from the cut-off of aid from former Soviet-bloc countries and its shift to free-market mechanisms. Cambodia is essentially rural, with severely degraded infrastructure because of the war. A number of companies from industrialized nations are testing the waters and taking advantage of new foreign investment laws which encourage foreign capital and expertise. There is an international airport at Pochentong near Phnom Penh and a deep-water port at Sihanoukville on the Gulf of Thailand, with an adjacent industrial free zone. Telecommunications is barely adequate but is being upgraded.

Tips

✔ The customary greeting is to place of the hands together in the praying position before the face and to bow slightly or nod the head. This is the equivalent of a handshake.
✔ Always respect the royal family.
✔ Remove your shoes before entering a Cambodian home, shrine or temple. Place your shoes soles down when removing them.
✔ It is all right to take pictures of temples, but be respectful and avoid loud talk.
✔ Be patient.
✔ Make appointments and be on time.
✔ Expect business decisions to take a long time.
✔ When invited to dine, don't decline and say you dislike their food. It is better to taste it, but if you decide not, then make up another excuse not

to eat it at all.
✔ Gifts are proper, but wrap them.
✔ Do not immediately open a gift you may be given.
✔ Tip 10 percent for good service from taxi drivers, waiters, and hotel staff.

Traps

✗ It is considered rude, in poor taste, and contrary to their religious attitudes to take photographs of people in informal dress, such as swimming suits, using a temple as a backdrop. Certainly you would expect the taking of nude pictures in front of a temple to incense the Thai people, and it did when one foreign magazine attempted to do this.
✗ Do not use profanity.

China (People's Republic of China, PRC)

Mainland China—or the PRC, as it is often called—is the third largest country on earth, with the largest population in the world. With its more than 1.2 billion people you may expect great extremes of wealth and living conditions. The Chinese name for this country is *Zhong Guo*, which means "The Middle Kingdom." China's history extends more than 4,000 years and it is the oldest of the great nations. Since about 1978 the Chinese leadership, while still operating within the framework of a monolithic Communist-controlled government, has been trying to move the economy from a sluggish Soviet-style, centrally planned economy to a more productive and flexible one with elements of market economy. To this end more authority has been given to local officials and plant managers in industry. Small-scale enterprise, including light manufacturing, is thriving. Industry has posted major gains, especially in the coastal areas, and output has doubled since 1978. On July 1, 1997, Hong Kong became part of China again (it had been leased to Great Britain). The large population of this country, its rich resources, and low labor costs make China a highly attractive market for foreign investors and exporters. The country has excellent international airports in Beijing, Xiamen, Shanghai, and Chengdu, which connect China with major cities around the world. A national rail network runs through all provinces except Tibet (where construction is in progress) and links economic free zones and sea ports in most coastal cities. Domestic and international telephone services are increasingly available.

Tips

✔ The Chinese are a formal people.

✔ This is a country with one class but many ranks.

✔ Respect titles and show respect for the elderly.

✔ Refer to the country as the "People's Republic of China" or simply as "China".

✔ Don't go without doing some reading about the country and culture and reviewing Chinese geography—it's a big and varied country, with many provinces.

✔ Mandarin, also known as Putonghua or common speech, is the dominant language spoken in China. Other dialects include Cantonese, Shanghainese, Fukienese, and Hakka.

✔ Learn some Chinese, if only a few words—it pays off.

✔ Expect the Chinese to have a very strong work ethic—they would be considered workaholics by most standards.

✔ Most businesses keep 8 a.m.–5 p.m. hours, with a break from noon to 1.30 p.m. six days a week.

✔ Even though China is vast, the entire country keeps the same time as Beijing.

✔ "Saving face" is an important principle to understand. In China a person's reputation and social standing are often based on this complex concept. Causing someone to lose face, even unintentionally, is a certain way to halt business negotiations.

✔ Personal relationships play a big role in business.

✔ Foreign business delegations are usually welcomed at the airport by a person of equivalent stature. Similarly, they attach great importance to seeing their guests off.

✔ Take a large supply of business cards–they are exchanged frequently in China. They should be printed in your language as well as Chinese (preferably in the local dialect). Exchanging business cards is a common way to start a conversation with the people you wish to do business with.

✔ Present your business card with two hands, with the Chinese translation side of your card facing the recipient. Then expect to receive the other person's card in the same way.

✔ The Chinese shake hands and make a small bow.

✔ When receiving a business card, examine its contents carefully before putting it in your card case or pocket for future reference.

✔ In Chinese practice the surname precedes the personal name, and married women do not use their husband's name.

✔ Generally, when Chinese enter a room for a meeting it is in protocol order; therefore they assume that the first foreigner to enter the room is the delegation head.

✔ The leader of the guests is seated to the right of the main Chinese host.

✔ Meetings generally begin with small talk. Safe subjects are the weather, how many visits you have made, and what Chinese cities you might have visited.

✔ The Chinese approach to business is subtle, and often indirect compared to the American approach of "laying all your cards on the table."

✔ When it is your turn to state your business, pause frequently and speak slowly to allow the interpreter a fair chance to keep up.

✔ Negative replies are considered impolite in most Oriental cultures. When in doubt say "maybe" and clarify later.

✔ The Chinese prefer to know in advance exactly what will be discussed— they don't like surprises.

✔ The typical Chinese executive leads a frugal life, but don't be surprised if you are invited to frequent banquets over lunch or dinner—it is a polite Chinese gesture, and an opportunity for a good meal at state expense.

✔ The visitor need not reciprocate this hospitality while in China, but you should be prepared to entertain your Chinese hosts if and when they come to the visit you.

✔ At these banquets, Chinese hosts are expected to arrive before the guests and seating is rigidly by rank.

✔ Learn to use chopsticks before you go, or take a fork with you.

✔ It is the responsibility of the hosts to serve their counterparts from the platters. Of course, the guest of honor is served first by the principal Chinese host. It is perfectly polite to serve yourself once the dish has been first served. Help yourself and enjoy it.

✔ The cardinal rule when you are finished eating a particular course is to leave some food on your plate, else your host will continue to serve you and you will be expected to eat.

✔ The Chinese understand if you elect to pass on duck blood soup, sea slugs, duck brains, or fish stomach.

✔ As you grow in the art of Chinese banqueting you will soon learn that drinking plays no small part. People who do not drink should not feel compelled to imbibe. But do return toasts with soda or some other drink.

✔ Although more and more Chinese women are getting involved, you should expect few women in business or social settings.

✔ At the end of a toast all are expected to rise and say "ganbei," the equivalent of "bottoms up," then turn the glass upside down to demonstrate that all has been consumed.

✔ Stay on safe subjects at banquets. Food, sport, geography, climate, or art are generally non-controversial.

✔ Although there are exceptions, like the bigger hotels, generally the Chinese consider tipping anyone an insult. Many younger people working in hotels are used to the tip for their service.

✔ In China it is wise to be a patient listener.
✔ In China friendship probably means good working relationships rather than personal relationships, which are very hard to establish.
✔ Leave your tuxedo at home. The Chinese don't care what their foreign guests wear during the business day—but no shorts for men.
✔ Generally Western-style suits are required for formal occasions.
✔ Women should stay away from revealing, see-through blouses.

Traps

✗ Be careful of gifts—follow their lead.
✗ Gifts from foreigners are generally politely declined—the Chinese have rigorous rules about bribery and corruption, and the offering of lavish gifts may embarrass the intended recipient.
✗ If, in friendship, you wish to give a gift, do it in private—gifts are never accepted in public.
✗ A presentation to the business organization as a whole is a better idea.
✗ Public embarrassment is considered a major breach of etiquette, so be careful not to pose questions to a ranking Chinese that puts him on the spot.
✗ Do not use expressions such as "Red China," "Mainland China," or "Communist China."
✗ Avoid mentioning Taiwan, but if it comes up do not refer to that country as the "Republic of China" or as "Nationalist China." "Taiwan Province" or simply "Taiwan" will do.

Hong Kong (China)

This place of historical international trade is a island ceded to the British as a result of an unequal treaty by the last Emperor of the Ming Dynasty. It then became populated by many capitalist Chinese, who fled Canton and Fusian during the Communist civil war. Hong Kong, which was returned to the People's Republic of China (PRC) in 1997, is one of the best examples of a bustling free-market economy with few tariffs or even non-tariff barriers. It is the growth model for nations without natural resources. Virtually everything must be imported, and 90 percent of its output is exported. Hong Kong, centered around Victoria Harbor, a naturally sheltered deep-water port, is one of the world's leading shipping centers, and more than fifty international airlines offer regular flights to and from Kai Tak and its new airport Chek Kok. With its excellent bus, train, water taxi, and Hong Kong–Kowloon ferry systems, it enjoys excellent domestic transportation and telecommunications with China.

Tips

✔ Business appointments generally start on time.

✔ Reserve and tact are highly stressed.

✔ When invited to dinner the guest usually takes a gift of fruit, candy, or cookies to the hostess and presents it with both hands.

✔ Expect most businesses to have family relationships.

✔ Expect the Chinese to want to acquire Western technology—although the government would want the technology without importing Western culture, nevertheless the country is fast becoming Westernized.

✔ After entering a home, visitors are usually offered tea, a soft drink, or warm water. Younger generations are now offering Coca-Cola.

✔ Before starting a meal, guests should recognize the older members of the family.

✔ Don't be surprised if the Chinese burp and slurp loudly; they are just showing they are enjoying their meal.

✔ Sincere compliments are given and appreciated, but denying them is the Chinese way of accepting them.

✔ If one receives a gift, he or she tries to give a gift in return.

✔ It is very impolite to open a gift in front of the person who gave it. If, for good reason, you wish to open it, make sure you ask the giver's permission.

✔ When social appointments are made, a half-hour courtesy time is allowed for most people.

✔ When sitting, visitors should place their hands in their lap and be sure not to wiggle their legs.

✔ The open hand, rather than the index finger, should be used for pointing.

✔ Call for a waiter with your palm down, never up.

✔ Most police officers wearing red shoulder tabs speak English.

✔ Tipping is not expected, but more and more people, especially the young, want tips for their service in hotels and restaurants.

Traps

✗ Take your time, slow down, don't try hard-driving, get-to-the-point tactics. Business discussions are best left until a certain amount of familiarity has been established with your counterpart.

✗ Blinking at someone is impolite.

Japan

This is a nation of very industrious people, who live on a number of islands stretching from climates of ice and snow in the north to somewhat sultry temperatures in the south. Japan made the most economic progress of any nation in the last half of the twentieth century. This improvement from a war-torn agrarian economy has come about by combining excellent government-industry cooperation with a strong work ethic. Japan, like Hong Kong, Taiwan, and Singapore, has demonstrated that nations with limited natural resources can make extraordinary, if not spectacular, economic progress by adopting an export-oriented world business strategy. Japan's is the second most powerful economy in the world. Industry, the most important sector of the economy, is heavily dependent on imported raw materials and fuels. There are international airports at each of the larger cities and they are in the process of building five new airports. Throughout the islands, highways and the rail service link most urban areas. There are large free-trade zones in Naha and in Okinawa Prefecture. Japan's marine port facilities are considered among the most modern and extensive in the world.

Tips

✔ Expect the Japanese to place importance on rank and titles.
✔ Be punctual for business meetings. The Japanese consider it rude to be late.
✔ The Japanese don't expect Americans to act exactly like they do, but awareness of manners and customs is important in the conduct of business.
✔ The written language has three forms: *kanji* (Chinese characters), to express proper nouns and verbs; *hiragana*, to express verb endings and other inflections; and *katakana*.
✔ Although the Japanese will often use English, the business traveler should not assume this.
✔ Learning Japanese and trying even a few words will generate great respect for you and your company.
✔ Try using some Japanese language phrases even if you only know a few greetings like *"konnichiwa"* (hello) or *"konbanwa"* (good evening). The result will be that the Japanese will feel closer to you.
✔ Speak slowly and wait for the translator.
✔ Expect the Japanese to be hierarchical and place high value on protocol.
✔ Third-party introductions should be made in advance at the highest level of the firm.
✔ You should exchange the *"meishi"* or business card. It is very important, and indispensable for both social and business use. Use a card holder.
✔ Place your rank on both sides of your business cards in both languages.
✔ The proper exchange of business cards is a formal ritual. Present your card with both hands (the Japanese language side facing your partner) and a formal bow.
✔ It is improper to pass out cards or leave them fanned on a table.
✔ When offered a card you should bow and accept it with both hands, then study it. Treat business cards with respect. Pause to read the card and

make uplifting remarks about the person's status. To do otherwise is an insult.

✔ Expect the Japanese to look closely at your card to see what company you are with.

✔ They will want to know the size of your company relative to theirs and your position in the company.

✔ Be polite and considerate.

✔ Observe how the Japanese act.

✔ If you have a previous relationship with them (correspondence etc.), bring a small gift for the people you will be doing business with, especially if the business is small or in a rural area—the Japanese are gift givers. If this is the first contact, don't

✔ If you are presented with a gift, you should respond by giving a gift.

✔ To approach a business, you may do well to go throught the International Chamber of Commerce.

✔ Take a group with you at negotiations. You'll be making a deal with five or six Japanese.

✔ The Japanese deal through trading companies (*sogo shosha*) and they earn their profits as a percentage of sales. They are motivated by sales.

✔ In Japan you rarely negotiate directly with the decision-maker; therefore, the lesser employees take copious notes verbatim. They'll spend hours on what seems to be a very minor subject. For that reason negotiations take a lot of time.

✔ Expect Japanese negotiators to require consensus among several groups before making a decision.

✔ Don't expect a lot of feedback from your business counterpart. It's not that they are secretive, it's just not in their culture to be direct. The Japanese are much more subtle than Europeans or Americans.

✔ If a Japanese answers "maybe" or "probably" to your question, the likelihood of positive action will be great, even higher than when Americans respond in the same manner. If the same Japanese were to answer "I'm thinking about it," your expectation should be that the result will probably be yes.

✔ You should be prepared to ask a key question several times to gage the response and to confirm a commitment.

✔ Don't wear your shoes (*kutsu*) in Japanese houses.

✔ Normally you should not smoke on Japanese trains; however, night trains and express trains often have special smoking sections.

✔ Don't soap up in a Japanese bath. Washing is done outside of the tub. The Japanese-style bath is for soaking.

✔ Don't tip waiters. A 15 percent gratuity is included in the bill. However, in night clubs and bars customers sometimes will leave a tip.

✔ The Japanese bow (*ojigi*) is famous the world over and is very convenient since it can be used for greeting, thanking, leave-taking, or apologizing.

It can be used when saying "good morning" (*ohiyo*), "hello" (*kon-nichiwa*), "good evening" (*konbanwa*), "thank you" (*arigato*), "goodbye" (*sayonara*), or "sorry" (*sumimasen* or *gomennasai*).

✔ Bows are used for expressing appreciation, making apologies, requests, greetings, and farewells.

✔ The seriousness of the bow cannot be overstressed. It is a symbol of both respect and humility.

✔ The Japanese have differing greetings for different situations. They wave their hand to say hello to a friend, and give a quick bow of their head in passing.

✔ The direct business bow is deep, and considered an extremely polite bow. It is simultaneous with an extended handshake.

✔ The depth of the business bow depends on your status and rank compared to the other person's. The Japanese are familiar with the handshake and often shake at the same time that they bow.

✔ When passing in front of people, do excuse yourself by stooping slightly and holding out your hand with the edge downwards as if you were cutting your way through.

✔ In a business environment the Japanese like to entertain guests from abroad, sometimes in the evening.

✔ You should try Japanese food.

✔ You should slurp your noodles (*ramen, udon, soba*) and Japanese tea.

✔ Scratching the head is a way of hiding confusion or embarrassment.

✔ Folding the arms implies that a person is thinking hard; this gesture can be misunderstood as aggression.

✔ Holding a clenched fist beside the head and suddenly opening the fingers expresses the opinion that a person is "*paa*" (stupid or crazy).

✔ Holding a clenched fist in front of the face in imitation of a long nose implies that the person under discussion is, like the long-nosed goblin *tengue,* a conceited braggart.

✔ Touching the index fingers together like swords clashing indicates that people are quarreling.

✔ The gesture of applying saliva to the eyebrow shows that you are not taken in by the tall story your friend is telling you.

Traps

✗ Never call a Japanese by his or her first name unless you are invited to do so. Use Mr. or Mrs., or *san* after the name. *San* is appropriate for both men and women, married or single.

✗ Don't misinterpret silence during negotiations. It does not imply that the Japanese counterpart is upset or not pleased. It just means he or she is contemplating the deal. Sit back and wait for them to speak first.

New Zealand

The 3 million people of this nation live on two large islands, logically called North Island and South Island. North Island, where most of the people live, has a warmer, more temperate climate. South Island is colder but gorgeous, with glorious, dramatic glaciers, fjords, and hundreds of streams and lakes. Since about 1984 the government of New Zealand has been reorienting an agrarian economy previously dependent on guaranteed British sales to an industrialized, open, free economy that can compete in the global market. The results of the new approach have been excellent, as growth in the 1990s has picked up to levels of 3 percent or better and industrial production now accounts for about 20 percent of GDP. This country has a modern infrastructure of excellent railways, highways, water ports, international airports, and an excellent communications system.

Tips

✔ In informal situations the people are very casual and easygoing, but again, as with the Australians, remember their British connection. In situations requiring formality they are very formal and expect others to conduct themselves properly.

✔ The greeting "how do you do?" is used in formal meetings.

✔ Always use people's titles when addressing them in informal situations.

✔ Shaking hands is acceptable at all meetings.

✔ Gifts such as flowers are not expected of guests, but it is not improper to give them.

✔ The European style of eating is used in New Zealand. The check, at a restaurant, is often paid to the waiter at the table.

✔ Children are required by bus company regulation to stand and allow adults to be seated if there are insufficient seats.

✔ Cover your mouth when a yawn cannot be suppressed.

✔ Friday night is the major social night.

✔ Tea is a ritual in New Zealand–morning and afternoon. If you are invited for tea it probably means supper.

✔ Good topics of conversation include sports—sailing, sport-fishing, and "tramping" (which is what they call hiking).

✔ Ask about the Maoris (pronounced "MAU-rees") and their long tradition of oral history, which includes the story of how the islands were first inhabited.

✔ Drug stores are called chemist's shops.

✔ Expect lots of rain.

✔ Taxi drivers never expect a tip.

✔ Tipping is not necessary unless one receives special service beyond normal duties. To offer a waiter or porter money for preferential treatment could offend them.

Traps

✗ New Zealanders are very proud of their country. Comparison with the U.S. or other countries is not appreciated.

✗ Visitors should not excessively compliment their host on items of decor and clothing, as the host might customarily feel obligated to give the item as a gift. This is especially true among the Polynesians.

North Korea

More than 90 percent of this command economy is socialized; agriculture is collectivized; and state-owned industry produces 95 percent of manufactured goods. However, as a result of disruptions in economic relations with the former Soviet bloc and China, the possibility of doing business with North Korean firms becomes more of a reality each year. Despite the history of animosity between the North and South Korean governments, both sides profess a desire for unification since about 5 million Koreans families were divided by the conflict. The customs of North and South Korea are similar; therefore, most of the tips and traps are the same. North Korea remains far behind South Korea in economic development and living standards.

Tips

✔ See also South Korean tips, pp.107–8.

✔ Rank and titles are highly valued.

✔ Bow slightly and shake hands.

✔ Remember that this is a centrally controlled economy and many of the business practices differ in that regard from those of South Korea.

✔ Make appointments far in advance and be on time.

✔ In this country you will need a translator. Foreign languages are seldom spoken. Speak slowly, emphasize important points, and avoid colloquialisms.

✔ Friendships are highly valued, as is modesty.

✔ Emotional considerations and face are often more important than Western logic.

✔ Pass food with the right hand, with the left supporting the right forearm.

✔ Both hands are used when giving objects to or receiving from another person.

✔ You should try to use the Korean greetings and language. This is much appreciated.

Traps

✗ See also South Korean traps, p. 109.
✗ When visiting a Korean home one should wait to be urged two or three times before entering.
✗ Shoes are always removed.
✗ Talking or laughing loudly is often offensive.
✗ Do not open a gift at the time it is received.

The Philippines

This is a multicultural country, with Moslems a strong minority in the south (Mindanao) and Christians (mostly Catholics) in the north. Much of the Philippines is still marginally subsistence living, but the nation has undertaken a series of open, market measures that have brought strong economic growth in recent years. It realized a 4.3 percent growth in 1994 and a GDP of $173 billion (PPP) by taking advantage of great familiarity with United States' business methods, the widespread use of English, and a 90 percent literacy rate. There has been a marked increase in capital goods imports, particularly power-generating equipment, telecommunications and electronic data processors. There are international airports at Manila and Cebu, and a network of 84 airports that connect the nation's more than 7,000 islands. The airport at the former U.S. Air Force base in Clark is due to open to international flights soon. Bus is the most widely used form of inland transportation; however, a light-rail network has recently been built in Manila. There are free-trade zones in Baguio City, Subic Bay, Mactan Island, Bataan Peninsula, and the province of Cavite.

Tips

✔ A smile always works wonders
✔ The initial greeting should be friendly and informal.
✔ The everyday greeting is a handshake for both men and women.
✔ You should be polite.
✔ Older people should be shown great respect and allowed to take the lead.
✔ There are 111 dialects and 87 languages in the Philippines. Filipino is based mainly on the Tagalog (pronounced "tah-GAH-lahg") languages; however, English and Spanish are dominant in government and business.
✔ Try some words. You will gain respect. "*Mabuhay*" (pronounced "ma-BOO-high") means welcome, hello, good luck.
✔ When in another person's home, guests should direct questions to the father.

✔ When greeting a young child, allow the child to show respect rather than lower yourself to the child's level.
✔ The word "hostess" should not be used.
✔ Add a small tip of about 5 percent for good restaurant service even if a service charge has already been added to the bill.
✔ Tip taxi drivers and bellboys.

Traps

✗ You should be security-conscious—there is a high incidence of petty thievery.
✗ Do not use the curled finger gesture to call or motion a Filipino towards you. It is extremely offensive. Use the entire hand, palm down.

South Korea

This country is the envy of a great majority of the world's people because it has a dynamic economy driven by export-oriented, planned development and a highly entrepreneurial society. The result has been, except for occasional downturns, a real gross national product (GNP) that has increased between 5 and 10 percent annually since the mid-1980s. International air and marine ports are modern, and are served by excellent domestic highways and high-speed railroads. There are free-trade zones at all major ports which allow for the bonded processing of imported materials into finished goods for export. Despite the history of animosity between the North and South Korean governments, both sides profess a desire for unification since about 5 million Korean families were divided by the conflict.

Tips

✔ Meeting the right person in Korea depends on having the right introduction; therefore avoid popping in or trying to make direct contact.
✔ A man greets his male friends by bowing slightly and shaking hands. Women usually do not shake hands.
✔ Use the Korean greetings and language. This is much appreciated.
✔ You may say, "*Annhonghasimnika*" (phonetic), a greeting that translates in English as "how are you?" "Thank you very much" is "*dae-danhi gamsa hamnida.*"
✔ You should pay complete attention to the person you are greeting.
✔ Don't be late for prearranged meetings and events. Koreans are punctual and expect you to be.

✔ Koreans like to know your company and your position in that company.

✔ Take plenty of business cards.

✔ After the exchange of business cards, place them on the table in front of you, then proceed with the meeting.

✔ Korean family names generally precede the given name.

✔ The real level of understanding of English may be less than courtesy implies. Speak slowly and emphasize important points.

✔ Koreans are considered to be good negotiators, but be patient and don't push your position too hard. Sensitive issues and details should be deferred, to be worked out by your staff or middlemen.

✔ In Korea legal documents are not as important as human rapport, relationships, mutual trust, and benefit.

✔ For the Korean businessman the important thing about a contract is not so much what it stipulates, but who signs it and the fact that it exists.

✔ Try to personalize your business relationship. Learn as much about your counterpart as possible–family status, hobbies, philosophy, birthdays, etc.

✔ Friendships are highly valued, as is modesty.

✔ As in Japan, entertainment plays an important role in any Korean business relationship. When offered, it should always be accepted, and in some way reciprocated.

✔ Expect to be entertained in restaurants—wives might sometimes be included.

✔ Be prepared to use chopsticks.

✔ Good topics of conversation are sport—especially baseball, table tennis, golf—and cultural events such as classical music.

✔ The giving of small gifts is an accepted practice.

✔ Emotional considerations and "face" are often more important than Western logic.

✔ When visiting a Korean home one should wait to be urged once before entering.

✔ Shoes are always removed.

✔ Pass food with the right hand, with the left supporting the right forearm.

✔ Don't be surprised if you are offered dog meat, deer antlers, snake soup, blood worm soup, and other exotic dishes. You need not eat your fill, but at least take a taste–who knows, you might like it!

✔ Tipping is usually expected in modern tourist hotels.

✔ In meetings and on formal occasions you should cross your legs one knee over the other, soles and toes pointed downward. On very formal situations do not cross the legs at all. Hands should remain in sight at all times.

✔ Korean women often hold hands in public.

✔ Putting one's arm around another's shoulders or slapping a person on the back is reserved for close friends.

✔ Both hands are used when giving objects to or receiving them from another person.

✔ Reluctance to accept high honours is the mark of a true Korean gentleman.

Traps

✗ Talking or laughing loudly is often offensive.
✗ Do not open a gift from a person who is older than you at the time it is received.
✗ You may see plenty of barbed-wire runs on the border between North and South Korea. The two Koreas are still on a war footing.

Taiwan (China)

This country, which has three names—Taiwan, Formosa, and the Republic of China—is an island nation off the east coast of mainland China. Named *"Ilha Formosa"* (Beautiful Flower) by early Portuguese seafarers, it is a place of two primary ethnic groups: native Taiwanese and the ancestors of the Kuomintang, who were the nobility who fled from the mainland to set up a government in exile in 1949. Earlier settlers include Dutch and Spanish explorers, and migrations from mainland China during the eighteenth and nineteenth centuries. The island was ceded to the Japanese after the Sino-Japanese war. As it was one of their colonial showplaces during World War II, the Japanese improved the infrastructure and brought modernized agricultural methods. Today, Taiwan, one of the so-called Asian Tigers, is a vigorous high-tech land of business enterprise with a dynamic capitalistic economy which has considerable government guidance in terms of investment, foreign trade, and industrial planning. Traditional labor-intensive industries have been steadily replaced with more capital- and technology-intensive industries. Taiwan has two international airports, Chiang kai-shek near Taipei and Haiaokang in Kaohsiung. There are four maritime ports, an excellent freeway, and four export-processing zones, including Kaohsiung, one of the world's largest.

Tips

✔ Taiwanese business people are generally formal.
✔ They have great respect for family, elders, and nature.
✔ They respect titles. Even retired civil servants use their titles and are treated with great respect.
✔ The handshake is the normal form of greeting, along with the words *"ni hao ma"* (phonetic).
✔ *"Xiexie ne,"* which sounds like "shay-shay-knee," means "Thank you." Use it often and you'll be well received.
✔ After the initial handshake a slight bow is appropriate.
✔ Avoid effusive greetings, gestures, and body contact.

✔ Make appointments and arrive on time even though the Taiwanese are not always punctual.

✔ Expect them to work six days a week from about 9 a.m. until 7 p.m.

✔ If doing business with the government you should observe channels—they have perfected bureaucracy to an art form.

✔ Be prepared to exchange business cards with everyone you meet.

✔ Have your cards printed in both Chinese and your language.

✔ Expect Confucianism, which is both a religion and a philosophy—the theme is "civilized behavior."

✔ Although Mandarin Chinese is the official language, expect English to be spoken by many business people.

✔ Try a few simple Chinese words. Its means a lot.

✔ Remember that Chinese surnames precede the given or personal name. For instance, Shang Han-Wu would compare to Washington George.

✔ In general, do not expect Taiwanese women to be liberated. Most dress beautifully and accept the traditional role.

✔ However, a new class of Taiwanese woman is emerging—like American-style women.

✔ You should expect to find more female managers than in many Western countries.

✔ By Western standards the Taiwanese take longer making business decisions.

✔ Expect the Taiwanese to be shrewed, clever negotiators.

✔ The hot season is from May through October.

✔ Taiwan has a tropical climate with frequent rains, so dress in light-weight clothes and take an umbrella.

✔ For a good impression, dress in business suits. Men should wear a tie.

✔ Like many other Asians, the Taiwanese entertain in restaurants or executive clubs. These meals are commonly heavy-drinking affairs with many courses.

✔ Expect to be served tea.

✔ Learn to use chopsticks before you visit.

✔ The toast is "*kampai*," which means "bottoms up."

✔ Gifts are presented with both hands and are not opened in the presence of the giver.

✔ Corporate gifts should be unique but not overly expensive. They like hard liquor, perfume, anything high-tech.

✔ Thank-you notes are appreciated.

✔ The Taiwanese like American baseball.

✔ Don't tip taxi drivers, but do expect 10 percent to be added to restaurant and hotel bills.

Traps

✗ Don't leave your chopsticks sticking straight up and down in your rice bowl. it is a sign of death to the Chinese.

✗ Avoid discussing the People's Republic of China.

✗ Don't give a clock or watch as a gift—it's considered a wish of death.

Thailand

Thailand, known as Siam until 1939, has enjoyed more than 700 years of independence—more than any other country in Southeast Asia. For the Thai people, the king stands as a sacred being and the head of the family. He is more than a symbol, he is the godhead of Thai pride, nationalism, and majesty. Westernization and modernization have been adopted voluntarily and have resulted in Thailand being one of the more advanced developing countries in Asia. The country depends on exports of agricultural manufactures and the development of the service sector to drive the nation's rapid growth. With an expanding middle class and a growing industrial sector, Thailand, despite its roller-coaster economy, is increasingly becoming an economic magnet for foreign investment. To continue its rapid economic development for the long term, Bangkok is producing more and more college graduates with technical training and is upgrading worker skills. Thailand has six international airports, including a new one only 19 miles from Bangkok. There are also six major deep-water sea ports connected by a network of rail and roads.

Tips

✔ Thais are always smiling and are very friendly. This is the "Land of the Smile."

✔ Travelers must carry a passport and visa.

✔ Make appointments and be on time.

✔ Expect business decisions to take a long time.

✔ Be patient.

✔ The proper and customary greeting in this country is the *wai*, which is similar to the Indian *namaste*. You may say *"sa wa di"* (phonetic), accompanied by placing the hands together at chest level in the praying position before the face, and slightly bowing or nodding the head. This is both a mark of respect and a greeting equivalent to a handshake.

✔ Always respect the royal family.

✔ The national anthem is customarily played daily at 8 a.m. and 6 p.m., and the king's anthem is played after plays and other events–it is bad manners not to stand to erect attention.

✔ The Thai flag has three colours, red, white, and blue, which represent the nation, the religion, and the king respectively.

✔ Remove your shoes before entering Thai homes, shrines, or temples. Place your shoes soles down when removing them.

✔ It is all right to take pictures of temples in proper dress. It is contrary to their religious attitudes to take photographs of people in informal dress such as swimming suits using a temple as a backdrop. Certainly you would expect the taking of nude pictures in front of a temple to incense the Thai people, and it did when one foreign magazine attempted to do this.

✔ When invited to dine, don't decline and say you dislike their food. It is better to taste it, but be prepared for the spicy taste. If you decide not to try it, then make up another excuse not to eat it at all.

✔ Gifts are proper, but wrap them.

✔ Tip waiters 10 percent if there is no service charge added to the bill.

✔ Don't tip taxi drivers.

Traps

✗ Avoid loud talk.

✗ Avoid pointing with the finger–Thais take offense at this.

✗ Do not use profanity.

✗ The feet are a most unworthy part of the body. To point a toe, sit cross-legged, or show the bottoms of the feet is offensive.

✗ Never touch a Thai on the head or shoulders. To a Thai, the head is a sacred part of the body and is considered off-limits for touching—the soul resides there. Don't even pat a child's head.

✗ Never step on Thai currency, as the king's image is embossed on it.

Vietnam

The legacy of war and Communism left Vietnam's 75 million people out of the Asian growth of the 1970s and 1980s. Once two sovereign nations, this controlled economy is now doing more business with the West. The trade embargo with the West was lifted in 1994. With a per capita GDP of only $1,200, the Vietnamese know they have a lot of catching up to do. But the fundamentals are in place for accelerated economic development as well as major trade opportunities because it is a nation with an 85 percent literacy rate, strong work ethic, and government commitment to boosting foreign investment. Vietnam's economy is expanding rapidly, led by a movement away from the planned economic model and toward a market-based economy that invites foreign investment and encourages exports. International airports are at Ho Chi Minh City and Hanoi. Its major marine ports are at Haiphong, Da Nang and Ho Chi Minh City. Plans are underway to upgrade the air, road, and port systems. There is an export-processing Zone at Ho Chi Minh City, and others are under construction.

Tips

✔ When greeting say *"xin chao"* (pronounced "seen chow"), followed by their given name or *"ong"* (man), *"ba"* (older woman), or *"co"* (girl).

✔ Expect the Vietnamese people to be very industrious. They work a six-day week.

✔ Business hours are 7.30 a.m. to 4.30 p.m.; closed for one hour from noon.

✔ Punctuality is important.

✔ You should exchange business cards.

✔ Initial business meetings often begin with informal conversation over tea or coffee, fruit, and sweets.

✔ Expect the Vietnamese to be a formal people.

✔ Wear conservative business clothes.

✔ Respect titles and the elderly.

✔ Refer to the country as "Vietnam."

✔ Foreign business delegations are usually welcomed at the airport by a person of equivalent stature. Similarly, the Vietnamese attach great importance to seeing their guests off.

✔ Expect to be greeted with a bow and a handshake.

✔ When shaking they use both hands, and you should also.

✔ Women usually bow instead of shaking hands.

✔ On special occasions women wear the *ao dai* (pronounced "owl yai"), a tailored, form-fitted ankle-length dress.

✔ When the Vietnamese enter a room for a meeting they do so in protocol order. Therefore they assume that the first foreigner to enter the room is the delegation head.

✔ The leader of the guests is seated to the right of the main Vietnamese host.

✔ Meetings generally begin with small talk. Safe subjects are the weather, travel, sports, and cities you might have visited.

✔ When it is your turn to state your business, pause frequently and speak slowly to allow the interpreter a fair chance to keep up.

✔ Negative replies are considered impolite in most Oriental cultures. When in doubt say "maybe" and clarify later.

✔ The Vietnamese prefer to know in advance exactly what will be discussed—like us, they don't like surprises.

✔ You should expect to be entertained at a restaurant.

✔ To be entertained at home is a special honor.

✔ Tipping is not expected in most restaurants.

✔ At banquets, Vietnamese hosts are expected to arrive before the guests. Seating is rigidly by rank.

✔ It is the responsibility of the hosts to serve their counterparts from the platters. Of course, the guest of honor is served first by the principal Vietnamese host. It is perfectly polite to serve yourself once the dish has been first served. In fact the host may invite you to do so.

✔ Expect food to be served in large bowls in the center of the table.

✔ Learn to use chopsticks. It is not difficult.

✔ It is perfectly correct to hold your rice bowl in your hand while eating your rice.

✔ The cardinal rule when you are finished eating a particular course is to leave some food on your plate, else your host will continue to serve you and you will be expected to eat.

✔ The Vietnamese understand if you elect to pass on duck blood soup, sea slug, duck brains, or fish stomach.

✔ Stay on safe subjects at banquets. Food, geography, climate, sports, and art are generally non-controversial.

✔ Gifts from foreigners are generally politely declined–a presentation to the business organization as a whole is a better idea.

✔ Gifts of flowers, incense, tea, or small gifts for children or elderly parents are appreciated.

Traps

✗ Do not touch the head of young children. The head is considered a sensitive spiritual point.

✗ Avoid mentioning their many wars.

CHAPTER ELEVEN

Indian Ocean

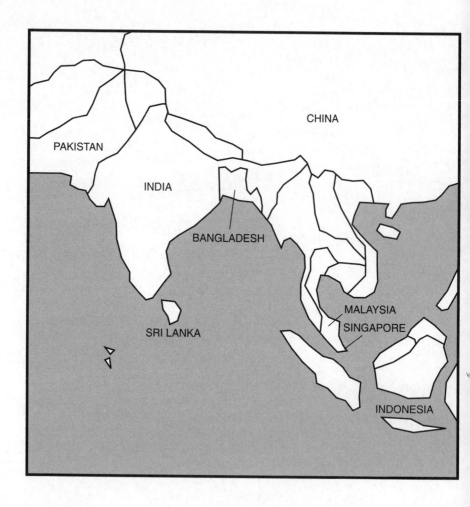

These countries, which extend west from Singapore and rim the north Indian Ocean, comprising Bangladesh, India, Indonesia, Malaysia, Pakistan, Singapore, and Sri Lanka, have been influenced by a mixture of British and Chinese cultures.

Bangladesh

This nation is in its infancy compared with most countries. Formerly known as East Pakistan, Bangladesh became an independent state in 1971 but remains one of the world's poorest, most densely populated, and least developed nations. Nevertheless, after a rocky start it is a place of growing business energy. Major impediments to growth include frequent cyclones and floods, and historical government interference with the economy. Bangladesh has recently instituted reforms intended to reduce government regulation of private industry and promote public-sector efficiency. To offset a rapidly growing population that cannot be absorbed by its overwhelming and traditional agriculture base, an export garment industry has begun to make a contribution to national growth.

Tips

✔ Shake hands with men, but only nod to women–if the hand is extended, of course you may shake it.
✔ British influence still exists, particularly about being on time.
✔ Bangladesh's laws are based on Islamic law (sharia), but the court system is closer to English law.
✔ Don't wear shorts, no matter how hot it is.
✔ Women should wear shirts with sleeves, and dresses or long pants.
✔ Ask before you take photographs.
✔ It will be unusual to be entertained at home.
✔ Wives usually are not invited to accompany their husbands.
✔ Knowing this country's history will make an impression.
✔ Avoid political talk.
✔ Tip about 10 percent in restaurants and taxis.

Traps

✗ Don't use the thumbs-up sign to show approval—its a vulgar insult in Bangladesh.
✗ Don't wear shoes into a mosque.

India

This country, whose population will be over 1 billion by the year 2000, is the world's largest democracy. India is driven by its religious beliefs, and is dominated by Hindus (83 percent), followed by Muslim (only 11 percent, but the world's third largest Muslim population, about 115 million), Sikh (2 percent), and Christian (2 percent). Hindi is the language spoken by 30 percent of the population, but its people speak twenty-four other languages, including English as one of the fourteen official languages. Its economy has been a mixture of traditional village farming, modern agriculture, and handicrafts, but an economic revolution has brought a myriad modern industries and support services. Recent government reforms have thrown open the economy and begun a liberalization to reduce controls on production, trade, and investment. The country's welcome is extended to foreign investment, particularly in infrastructure sectors. India has seven international airports, but the number is expected to grow to twenty-two by 2000. The railway system is the largest in Asia and fourth largest in the world. It also has an excellent national highway system connecting all major cities, maritime ports, and there are export processing zones at Kandia, Bombay, Calcutta, Falta, Cochin, New Okha and Visakhapatnam.

Tips

✔ Understanding the religions of this nation is a must before doing business.
✔ India is a land of castes and it is well to study them before traveling there.
✔ The British left their conservative influence.
✔ Titles and age are important factors of life in India.
✔ Make appointments and be punctual.
✔ The handshake is an acceptable greeting but you should expect and may use the *namaste* greeting as well. This is formed by placing the palms together, fingers pointed up near the chin, and nodding the head.
✔ When greeting a woman avoid touching—not even a handshake, unless she offers her hand. Use the *namaste*.
✔ Expect to speak English when doing business.
✔ Dress conservatively.
✔ Most business people wear business suits.
✔ A woman can wear regular-length suits or even pant-suits.

✔ Indian women often wear a sari to special affairs; Western women can too.

✔ Expect Indians to be a flexible, tolerant and conversant people so be careful you are not drawn into conversations about religion and politics.

✔ Expect Indian negotiators to be sharp at the bargain table.

✔ Don't over-tip—10 percent in better restaurants that haven't added a service charge to the bill.

✔ Tip taxi drivers by rounding off the fare.

✔ Food customs are very important.

✔ Hindus are vegetarians who believe the cow is sacred.

✔ Cow manure is used for fuel.

✔ Muslims eat no pork and do not drink alcohol.

✔ Sikhs eat no meat and can be identified by their turbans.

✔ Jains do not eat meat or honey, or most vegetables. These people practice non-violence.

✔ Muslims, as well as Hindus, generally keep their women hidden away in the kitchen, although this practice is less pronounced among Hindus.

✔ Use your right hand to accept or pass food.

✔ You may talk about sport, travel, art, literature, and Indian culture.

✔ Expect a swirl of bicycles, motorcycles, and cars—be careful crossing streets.

Traps

✗ Don't talk about poverty, homelessness, etc.

✗ Never talk to a woman walking alone.

✗ Avoid talking politics.

Indonesia

This, the fourth most populated nation in the world, with almost 200 million people, consists of 17,508 islands (only 6,000 of which are inhabited) and extends approximately 3,000 miles east to west. Only six islands are considered major: Bali, Java, Sulawesi, Sumatra, Irian Jaya (on new Guinea), and Kalimantan (part of the island of Borneo). As diverse as it is exotic, Indonesia has gradually undergone a transition from a protected, import-substitution, oil-dependent market to a comprehensive, diversified manufacturing and services economy. The result is GDP of $588 billion in 1994, an increasingly open economic system, and a government that is playing a leading role in fostering the Asia-Pacific Economic Cooperation (APEC) process. Indonesia is a mixed economy with many socialist institutions and central planning, but with a recent emphasis on deregulation and private enterprise. It is a land of opportunity for outsiders because prior to 1995 foreign companies had to have an Indonesian partner; however, now they can own 100 percent of their businesses. The Sukarna-Hatta airport in Cengkareng, near Jakarta, is the largest of Indonesia's international airports. There are adequate road networks on Java, Sumatra, Bali, and Madura, but on most other islands traffic moves by jungle track or row boat. Telecommunications networks are being overhauled, with expectations of 5 million new lines by 2000. Export-processing zones exist near each primary sea port.

Tips

✔ Although handshaking is common, physical contact is usually avoided. Smiling, bowing, or nodding is considered more gracious.

✔ You should say "*selamat pagi*" (phonetic for "good morning") or "*selamat sore*" (phonetic for "good afternoon").

✔ Exchange business cards at first greeting.

✔ Business hours are Monday through Friday 8.30 a.m.–5 p.m.; and Saturday 8.30 a.m.–12.30 p.m.

✔ Make appointments and be on time.

✔ You should expect business to take time; sometimes it will be long and frustrating. No business transaction or decision is completed immediately.

✔ Plan on more than a week to accomplish even the smallest venture.

✔ English is commonly spoken in business circles; however, the official language is Bahasa-Indonesia, which is a modified form of Malay. There are some twenty-five local languages, mainly Javanese and more than 250 different dialects.

✔ You should hire a translator.

✔ Exchanging small gifts is common. However, avoid offering with the left hand; it is better with both hands.

✔ Don't expect wrapped gifts to be opened in front of you—it's considered impolite.

✔ Keep your feet and legs in a downward position.

✔ Expect Indonesians to use an indirect approach, going around an issue before getting to the point.

✔ Patience is the key. Never lose your temper or show emotion.

✔ Remove your shoes when entering any holy place.

✔ Expect to eat in restaurants, not in the home.

✔ You should tip about 10 percent.

Traps

✗ Do not use the word "no." Indonesians will not say no when they mean no.
✗ Avoid turning your back when departing.
✗ Do not talk about local politics, socialism, or foreign aid.
✗ Never drink the tap water.

Malaysia

This nation, with a population of about 17 million, is a mixture of many ethnic groups, of which the Malays constitute about 50 percent. The economy of this country has grown at a remarkable rate of about 9 percent since the mid-1980s. This growth has been the result of strong foreign investment and substantial demand for Maylasian goods. In recent years integrated circuits manufacturing has made this country the hub for global electronics. The Malaysian economy is a mixture of private enterprise and a soundly managed public sector. The Subang airport in Kuala Lumpur is the largest of Malaysia's six international airports. The already excellent intercity telecommunications service on the main peninsula is being digitized, and an excellent rail and highway system links Malaysian cities, ports, and its neighbor Singapore. A second bridge linking Malaysia to Singapore is underway.

Tips

✔ Be on time and make appointments.
✔ The handshake is common among men.
✔ Out of deference, a slight bow should be shown to the elderly.
✔ It is advisable not to touch a woman on greeting–a slight bow or nod will do.
✔ Exchange business cards on first meeting.
✔ You should say "selamat page" (phonetic for "good morning") or "selamat petant" (phonetic for "good afternoon").
✔ Business hours are 8.30 a.m.–5.00 p.m. with one hour for lunch. Many Malaysians work a half-day on Saturday.
✔ Most Malaysians wear Western-style clothes to work.
✔ This is a land of mixed religions. Expect to be among Buddhists, Hindus, and Muslims.
✔ Remove your shoes when entering a home or holy place.
✔ Respect the elderly—they do.
✔ Expect to be entertained at a restaurant.
✔ Expect some hot and spicy foods.

✔ Chopsticks are used in some restaurants.
✔ The left hand is never used to touch food, particularly among Muslims.
✔ Safe topics of conversation are sports, business, or art.
✔ Do not tip—it is considered impolite.

Traps

✗ Never gesture to a person with a curled index finger.
✗ Don't compare Malaysian lifestyles with Western.
✗ Don't bring up the topic of ethnic relations.
✗ Touching in public is uncommon.
✗ Drug trafficking brings a mandatory death penalty.

Pakistan

Pakistan has a long history. Before 1947 it was a part of India and the history of the two countries was inseparable. Pakistan is a poor third-world country faced with a rapidly increasing population, sizable government deficits, and heavy dependence on foreign aid. However, in 1990 Pakistan embarked on a sweeping liberalization program to boost foreign and domestic investment and reduce dependence on foreign aid. As a result a real growth rate of above 5 percent has helped the country to deal with its problems. Karachi has a new airport to complement four others located in the cities of Islamabad, Lahore, Peshawar, and Quetta. An extended rail and road network connects all major cities, maritime ports, and the export-processing zone at Karachi.

Tips

✔ The traditional greeting is the handshake, but close friends may embrace.
✔ Appointments are necessary.
✔ Be punctual.
✔ Dress modestly.
✔ Working hours are 9 a.m. to 5 p.m.
✔ Lunch is the business meeting meal.
✔ Do not shake hands or otherwise touch a woman in public.
✔ Avoid name familiarity.
✔ Stick to titles and last names until you have established yourself, although this is a very friendly nation and first names are used early on.
✔ Learn to interpret local gestures. A motion of the head from side to side indicates yes; a slight backward flick of the head, often accompanied by a quick "tsk" or "tut" means no.
✔ Using the left hand to touch food is a no-no.

✔ Do not expect pork, it is forbidden, but do expect some highly seasoned beef, lamb, or poultry.

✔ Alcohol is not encouraged, although it might be offered in very private situations.

✔ For elders use *"Aap"* and for casual friendships and young adults use *"Tum."*

✔ Gifts are welcome, particularly if the gift is something for their children.

✔ The northern part of Pakistan is known as Kipling country, especially around Peshawara and Lahore, where Rudyard Kipling lived and worked.

✔ Tip about 10 percent.

Traps

✗ Avoid talking politics, especially domestic politics.

✗ Do not talk about nuclear weapons development.

Singapore

Singapore (singa Pura, meaning Lion City), is the home of the world's second largest container port, tied to an aggressive business orientation. It is an open entrepreneurial economy with strong service and manufacturing sectors, and excellent trading links derived from its entrepôt history. Because of its rate of growth, and technological and labor discipline, Singapore is now considered a developed country.

Tips

✔ Because of the great diversity of cultures in Singapore, greetings usually depend on the age and nationality of the person. The handshake is the most common gesture of greeting with the addition of a slight bow for Orientals.

✔ Great respect is paid to the elderly. The door is held open for them. On buses, a man gives his seat to an elderly person before he gives it to a woman.

✔ Westerners are expected to be punctual.

✔ Shoes are removed before one enters a mosque and sometimes a home.

✔ Compliments are appreciated, but usually denied for modesty's sake.

✔ As in most other Asian countries, gifts are not opened at the time they are received.

✔ Singapore is considered the most corruption-free state in Asia.

✔ Touching another's head is impolite.

✔ When beckoning someone the whole hand, palm down, is waved.

✔ A slight bow when entering, leaving, or passing a group of people shows courtesy.

✔ Wear neat, clean clothing.
✔ Expect Singapore to be clean and orderly.
✔ Don't tip taxi drivers or waiters.

Traps

✗ Risqué magazines such as *Playboy* and *Penthouse* are taboo. A court could fine you upwards of S$500.
✗ Don't litter! One cigarette discarded on the street can cost you S$50 or a night in jail.
✗ Never become drunk in public.
✗ Legs are crossed one knee over the other. The foot or sole is never pointed at anyone.
✗ Hitting the fist into a cupped hand shows very poor taste.

Sri Lanka

Previously known as Ceylon, the island was renamed Sri Lanka ("Resplendent land") by the national government in 1972. This country is torn by internal strife between the Singalese Buddhist government and the Tamil Hindu minority in the north and east. Historically, agriculture, forestry, and fishing have dominated this island economy; however, recently Sri Lanka has plowed ahead with a massive privatization program which has encouraged foreign investment. The main container ports and international airports are at Colombo and Trincomalee, which are connected by a domestic rail and road system to the remainder of the island. A massive fiber-optic cable network improvement program is underway.

Tips

✔ Greetings vary from ethnic group to ethnic group and from caste to caste. Again remember the British influence—common English greetings are acceptable.
✔ English is considered the language of business; however, Sinhala is the official language. In the north and northeast Tamil is the common language of a minority but often aggressive and business-wise population.
✔ Titles are very important. It is proper to address acquaintances by their titles unless otherwise invited.
✔ Exchange business cards on first meeting.
✔ Sri Lankans shake their heads up and down to say "no" and bob their heads from side to side to indicate "yes."
✔ Dress conservatively but comfortably—don't bother with a tie. They are not necessary at business meetings.

✔ Sri Lankans are extremely polite and friendly.
✔ The pace of life is very slow.
✔ Observe before you speak.
✔ Take off your shoes before entering a temple or mosque.
✔ Expect a tropical monsoon climate.
✔ Sri Lankans are careful of the types of food they eat. Before inviting a Sri Lankan to a meal, check with your embassy or consul which types are acceptable.
✔ Tipping is rare.
✔ Do not tip taxi drivers.

Traps

✗ Avoid discussion about relationships between Sinhalas and Tamils.
✗ Ask permission before taking pictures of people.

CHAPTER TWELVE

Western Europe

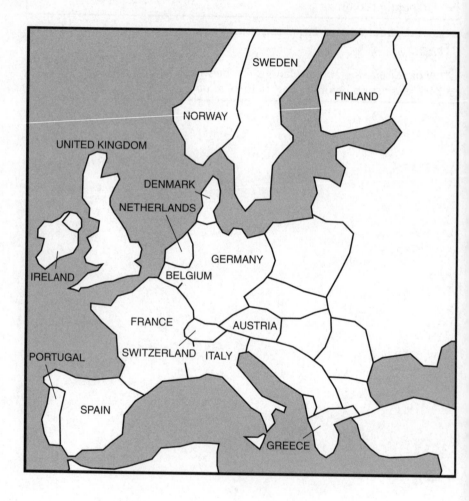

Before we begin, I'd like to make a few general statements about the tips and traps of Western Europe.

These are the nations (except for Switzerland and Norway) of the European Union (EU), which is undergoing a transformation and harmonization of laws and procedures to become eventually an integrated market with a common economic policy and free movement of people, goods, capital, and services. It is of major business importance in this region to understand the EU integration process and its laws. Take time to become up to date about membership, its latest issues and implications for your firm. Of course, you should also understand that the terms "Great Britain" or "British" are geographical terms and not political. They should only be used when referring to the island comprising England, Scotland, and Wales. They cannot be used interchangeably with the terms England or United Kingdom, which more properly is the United Kingdom of Great Britain and Northern Ireland. For purposes of clarity I have grouped the protocols for these nations together at the end of this section.

Although punctuality differs somewhat from country to country, in general it is at the top of the list of not only good business practice but good manners, so be on time. Most Europeans are not as familiar as Americans at first meeting. First names are used only after developing a relationship. If a person has a title, don't forget to use it just as a matter of course, to show respect. July and August are the months when Europeans vacation—don't expect to do heavy business during the summer months.

Austria

This is a land with excellent raw materials, a technically skilled labor force, and strong business ties to German industrial firms. However, it is also a country with great pride in its own accomplishments. Austria's prosperous and stable socialistic market economy has a sizeable portion of nationalized industry and extensive welfare benefits that provide a living standard comparable to that in any of the large industrial countries.

Austria is a member of the European Free Trade Association (EFTA), the European Economic Area Treaty and the European Union (EU).

Tips

✔ Arrange business appointments in advance.
✔ Rank and titles are routinely used.
✔ Think conservative.
✔ Use a few words, such as *"grüß Gott"* or *"guten Tag"* (hello) and *"auf Wiedersehen"* (goodbye).
✔ Wear dark suits and smart dresses.
✔ Be punctual.
✔ Flowers or a small gift are appropriate if invited to a home for dinner.
✔ Expect a 10–15 percent gratuity to be added to most hotel and restaurant bills.
✔ Tip taxi drivers—about 10 percent.

Trap

✗ Never refer to Austrians as Germans—they have distinctly different customs and values, although they speak the same language.

Belgium

The kingdom of Belgium is known as the diplomatic capital of Europe because of its central location, and because it is home to the headquarters of many of the world's most distinguished organizations (such as the World Trade Organization (WTO), European Union (EU), and North Atlantic Treaty Organization(NATO)) and several multinational corporations. A land of limited natural resources, Belgium depends heavily on imports of raw materials. Therefore this small private-enterprise economy has capitalized on its geographical location to provide a highly developed transportation network and a diversified industrial and commercial base to enhance its trade in world markets. The people of Belgium have comfortable living standards and benefit from extensive welfare measures. Brussels, its capital, has a large international airport which serves as a hub for European and African carriers. Its rail service reaches most of the country and has a high-speed link to other European nations. Telecommunications are considered excellent. Belgium is a member of the European Economic Area Treaty and the EU. Belgium conforms with the European Union's Common Customs Tariff.

Tips

✔ Belgium is culturally divided into two groups: the more populous Flemish in the north (known as Flanders), who speak Dutch, and the Walloons in the south, who speak French. The people think of themselves as Belgians first and Flemish or Walloons second.

✔ Unless you are sure of your audience, have your material translated into both languages.

✔ Address French-speaking contacts as *"Monsieur"* or *Mademoiselle"* followed by their last name.

✔ Make appointments.

✔ Greetings are often accompanied by kisses on the cheek—three times, alternating cheeks.

✔ In a business meeting it is customary to greet and say goodbye with only a handshake.

✔ Belgians like to get down to business right away.

✔ Have your facts and figures ready.

✔ Belgians are known as tough negotiators.

✔ Business hours are Monday through Friday, 9 a.m.–noon and 2 p.m.–5.30 p.m.

✔ A luncheon is the typical form of business entertainment.

✔ Business gifts are rarely exchanged.

✔ If invited to a Belgian home it is nice to send flowers in advance. Don't send chrysanthemums; they are mainly used for funerals.

✔ Do not be surprised to see men embracing.

✔ Tipping is not necessary in restaurants, as most places include a service charge.

✔ Tip hotel doormen and washroom attendants.

✔ Do not tip taxi drivers.

Trap

✗ First names are never used in business or social situations.

Denmark

Denmark has the oldest monarchy (founded in AD 985) and flag (AD 1219) in the Western world. This is a modern nation, with high-tech agriculture, up-to-date small and large industries, and a high dependence on international trade. This is a place of high foreign investment because of excellent market access, high product quality, strong export orientation, and a talented and dependable workforce, with excellent labor-management stability. Denmark is a member of the European Free Trade

Association (EFTA), the European Economic Area Treaty and the European Union (EU).

Tips

✔ Punctuality is expected.

✔ Call ahead if you will be late.

✔ The Danes are very formal people.

✔ Shake hands on greeting, but don't use a firm grip and pumping style. A single shake is considered more appropriate.

✔ Expect English to be the language of business.

✔ Danes work only five days. Saturday and Sunday are for the family.

✔ Wear a coat and tie and conservative dress.

✔ Take a raincoat.

✔ A business lunch is typical. Often it will be a "*koldt bord,*" like a Swedish smorgasbord.

✔ Danes like their drink *aquavit.* Be careful; it is potent.

✔ Danish sandwiches are always open face and eaten with a fork, not picked up and eaten by hand.

✔ Expect Danes to like their beer.

✔ Toast by saying the word "*skoal.*"

✔ Wait until your host has made the toast before you begin your meal.

✔ July and August are the months when the Danes vacation–don't expect to do heavy business during the summer months.

✔ A 15 percent tip is usually included in hotel and restaurant bills.

✔ Don't tip taxi drivers.

Trap

✗ Stay with family names until they tell you. First names are seldom used in business or social situations.

Finland

Finland is a highly industrialized and largely free-market economy that attributes about 30 percent of it's gross national product (GNP) to exports. It shares a 600-mile border with Russia, before the break-up of the Soviet Union a major barter partner. Except for timber and several minerals, this nation must import most of its raw materials, energy, and many of its components for manufactured goods. Finland is a member of the European Free Trade Association (EFTA), the European Economic Area Treaty and the European Union (EU). International and domestic transportation is very modern and there are free-trade zones located at Helsinki, Oulu, Turku, and Kotka.

Tips

✔ The Finns are generally not very formal people.

✔ Make appointments in advance and be on time. They are punctual for all appointments; you should be also.

✔ Business hours are Monday through Friday, 8 a.m.–4.15 p.m.

✔ Shake hands when meeting, including with children.

✔ If invited to your host's home, take flowers.

✔ If you are the honored guest don't touch the wine until after a toast is made at the beginning of the meal. You will be expected to make a reciprocal toast of thanks.

✔ Topics of conversation include ice hockey and fishing sports, architecture, and literature.

✔ The Finns enjoy saunas, so be prepared for a relaxing evening.

✔ A tip is usually included in hotel and restaurant bills.

✔ Don't tip taxi drivers.

✔ Tip bellhops and sauna attendants.

Trap

✔ It is quite rude to be more than five minutes late.

France

France is one of the world's most developed countries, with a highly diversified industrial sector and excellent agricultural resources. Its international air and marine ports also rank among the world's best. This is a nation producing world-class products and competing strongly in the global arena. France is a member of the European Economic Area Treaty and the European Union (EU). There are international airports at Orly, Roissy, and Le Boourget (all in Paris), Bordeaux, Lyon, Marseilles, Nice, Strasbourg, and Toulouse. Le Havre is the largest sea port to ocean cargo. Telecommunications and land transportation services are modern. There are free-trade zones associated with most significant business districts.

Tips

✔ The French call their country "*l'hexagon*," for its roughly six-sided shape. Unlike its complicated contour, France enjoys the simplicities of living and is noted for being remarkably comfortable and intimate. Make the most of your visit to enjoy this rare country, with excellent fashion designers, wonderful chefs, art, and a sense of style.

✔ Be on time for your appointments.

✔ Gifts are not usually exchanged at first meeting, but you will not be wrong if you do give a gift.

✔ The handshake serves as the standard greeting, but don't be surprised to see kissing on the cheeks.

✔ Unlike the U.S.A. and elsewhere, few French women participate in business.

✔ Learn and speak some French, no matter how little; it is very much appreciated.

✔ Expect business to be conducted in a formal way.

✔ Expect the French managerial elite to have family or school connections, so access to the right network or decision-makers requires skill.

✔ Most business is done after being introduced by a banker, an attorney, or a friend.

✔ Appearance is very important for first impressions. Expect business dress to be fashionable. Famous designer suits, shirts and ties, and dresses are often worn in business circles.

✔ The French tend to take negotiations cautiously and do not make decisions quickly.

✔ Expect the hard sell not to be appreciated. Go slow.

✔ Expect business to be conducted over meals—a lunch could last more than two hours and be a gastronomical delight.

✔ Business dinners often last all evening and are seldom in the home.

✔ Business will often wait until coffee is served.

✔ Don't expect to be invited home, but if you are take flowers or candy.

✔ In some cultures, particularly Asian, socializing comes first, but the French tend to get right to business. They may take their time making the decision, but they are forthright and direct in their intentions.

✔ The French are known for their fine food, but don't be surprised if you are offered snails and horse meat.

✔ Expect a 10–15 percent gratuity to be added to hotel and restaurant bills.

✔ Taxi drivers are generally not tipped.

Traps

✗ Even though many French speak English they will seldom admit it, so bring a translator.

✗ Don't put your hands in your pockets in public; its considered rude.

Germany

After World War II the "economic miracle" of the Marshall Plan brought prosperity to West Germany. Even though East Germany enjoyed the highest standard of living among the Warsaw Pact countries, that prosperity was significantly less than in the rest of Western Europe.

Following the collapse of Communism in Eastern Europe and the incorporation of East Germany into the Federal Republic, Germany sank into a significant recession. However, in less than five years eastern Germany privatized almost all of its 12,000 government-controlled firms and, with the aid of subsidization from the German government, resurrected itself as a manufacturing base of meaningful importance. Today, even with all its problems, the united Germany is the clear economic powerhouse of Europe. Western Germany continues to be an advanced economy and a world leader in exports, with a highly skilled population that enjoys excellent living standards, abundant leisure time, and comprehensive social-welfare benefits. Germany has many world-class companies that manufacture technologically advanced products.

The Federal Republic of Germany is a member of the European Economic Area Treaty and the European Union (EU). Germany's highway and inland waterway transportation systems are among the best in the world, and Germany has a long history of excellent international air and marine ports supporting many free-trade zones.

Tips

✔ Until invited, never take the liberty of using a first name.

✔ Do not expect Germans to greet strangers or say hello to people on the street.

✔ Germans say *"guten Tag,"* which means the same as "hello" in English. *"Hallo"* is reserved for acquaintances.

✔ Learn a few basic words of German. *"Danke"* means "thank-you," and *"bitte"* means "please," as well as "you are welcome."

✔ Be sure to use titles.

✔ This is a country of conservative thought, attitudes, and bureaucratic approaches.

✔ Make appointments and be punctual—it is essential.

✔ Almost every German speaks English, the language of business—they learn it early in school. However, on some occasions if you are not fluent in German and you don't understand English you may need help. Don't hesitate to take a translator.

✔ Introduce women first, then always start with the highest-ranked man.

✔ Use the handshake. It is important in both business and personal relationships.

✔ The body language (psychological) distance of most Germans is 18 inches or more.

✔ Do not expect to establish a close relationship during a short duration. Germans maintain relationship distance until they are sure business will be long term.

✔ Use your last name when answering the telephone.

✔ Expect Germans to respect authority and older people.

✔ Respect the "line of command" in a German company.

✔ In meetings, as they are on the production line, Germans are big planners, so don't expect much to be done impromptu.

✔ Germans dress conservatively and you should also.

✔ Expect to find more and more German women have joined the workforce, are becoming managers, and are not staying home.

✔ If invited to an intimate dinner with a family or couple, take a gift such as flowers or candy.

✔ Breakfast typically consists of breads, no meats.

✔ Lunch is the big meal of the day and also the big business meal.

✔ Germans eat continental style, that is, fork in the left hand, knife in the right—they leave their wrists and arms on the table, but not the elbows.

✔ Germans generally use their knife to cut, never their fork, and cut only what they are eating next.

✔ Expect Germans to drink in the evening.

✔ Topics of conversation are politics, sports, arts, and business.

✔ Although it is not recommended as a high-priority topic of conversation, talking about World War II, especially among later generations, is no longer taboo.

✔ Expect presents and gift exchanging with business associates, particularly during the Christmas season.

✔ Expect working hours during the work week for government to be 9 a.m.–12.30 p.m. and 2 p.m.–4.30 p.m.; lunch 12.30 p.m.–2 p.m.

✔ Banking hours are usually 8.30 a.m.–12.30 p.m. and 2 p.m.–4 p.m.

✔ Commercial hours vary with location and the market but generally are Monday through Friday, 8.30 a.m.–5 p.m. Shops are closed everywhere from 1 p.m. to 3 p.m.

✔ Germans stores are usually open Saturdays from 9 a.m.–4 p.m., and are closed Sundays.

✔ Tips are OK in restaurants.

✔ Do not tip taxis.

Trap

✔ Beer and wine consumption is among the greatest in the world and the beer is strong, so take it easy.

Greece

Greece has a mixed socio-capitalistic economy with an entrepreneurial system overlaid on a large public sector. It has the lowest labor costs in Europe. This Mediterranean country favors business with other European Union (EU) and European Economic Area Treaty members, but has growing trade relations with the former Eastern-bloc nations of Russia,

Bulgaria, and the Ukraine. Greek telecommunications services are highly developed and there are several free-trade zones.

Tips

✔ Be prepared for a handshake, a hug, or even a kiss at each meeting.

✔ Expect the "psychological" distance of Greeks to be less than that of most other Europeans.

✔ This is a country of generosity and sincerity. Expect to be invited home for dinner.

✔ Age is revered in Greece. The elderly are served first, addressed with respect, and have authority.

✔ Make appointments and call if you are going to be late.

✔ Punctuality is less important here than in most European countries, but you should not be the offender.

✔ Expect Greek business people to be astute bargainers.

✔ Be patient at the bargaining table.

✔ The Greek business day begins early, about 7.30 a.m., and continues until mid-afternoon, about 3 p.m., when they close for the day.

✔ Most business entertaining is done in the evening at a local taverna, with spouses often included.

✔ Business relationships usually begin over a dinner—getting to know each other in a relaxed setting is important.

✔ Standard tipping rules apply (10–15 percent), but in restaurants do check to see if the service has already been included. If so, you should leave a small additional amount, usually change in the plate.

✔ Don't tip taxis but do round up the fare to an even amount.

Traps

✗ Avoid conversations about Turkey or Albania.

✗ Don't refuse offers of food or drink from business associates—it's considered an insult.

Ireland

Ireland, as a member of the European Economic Area Treaty and the European Union (EU), is a small, trade-dependent economy. It's labor force of about 1.5 million people has a 98 percent literacy rate. The manufacturing sector now accounts for about 40 percent of the GDP of this once agriculturally dominated nation. Dublin aggressively courts foreign investment for industry and provides substantial aid to small indigenous firms.

Tips

✔ Expect to be greeted with a handshake.
✔ You should say *"dia dhuit,"* which, translated from the Gaelic, means "God be with you" (formal), or "how's the craíc?" (informal).
✔ Exchange business cards.
✔ Dress and act formal until the relationship warms.
✔ Don't ask for a scotch in an Irish pub.
✔ The Gaelic language is taught in schools along with English.
✔ Take a small gift if invited to an Irish home.
✔ Show your keen appreciation of this nation's contribution to world literature. It is the land of Becket, Joyce, Shaw, Swift, and Yeats.
✔ Tip 10–15 percent in restaurants and taxis.

Traps

✗ Avoid debate about the political or religious struggles.
✗ Don't expect anyone to accept currency issued by Northern Ireland or England.

Italy

This member of the European Economic Area Treaty and the European Union (EU) may have made the greatest economic change of any European nation since World War II. Once an agriculturally dominant country, it now ranks among the strongest industrialized countries and has about the same total and per capita output as France and the United Kingdom. The country remains divided into an industrial north, dominated by private companies, and an undeveloped agricultural south, with large public enterprises. However, Italy is actively luring foreign investors with a sweeping privatization program. There are large international airports in Rome and Milan and seventeen other cities. Extensive public transportation systems connect its several world-class ports and free-trade zones.

Tips

✔ Address Italians by their last or family name.
✔ Learn the professional titles of the people you are doing business with and use them.
✔ Most college graduates have a title. University graduates are given the honorary title of *"Dottore."*
✔ This is a less formal country than many of the northern European nations, but expect business to be reserved.

✔ Dress in business clothes.

✔ Expect personal dress and style to be important to Italians. Hand-made suits rather than off the rack are considered part of business attire to make a good impression.

✔ These are a very warm and friendly people. Shaking hands is part of the culture here. Expect it often and vigorously.

✔ Some Italians do speak other European languages, such as German and French, but most do not speak English—bring a translator for English.

✔ Many businesses are family owned. You should expect the head of the family to be the decision-maker. In those that are not family owned, expect the head of the organization to make the decisions.

✔ Expect Italian business circles to be small but powerful.

✔ In Rome and other cities expect a long midday break—about two hours from 1.30–3.30 p.m.—but they work until 7 p.m.

✔ Government hours are Monday through Friday, 8.30 a.m.–1.45 p.m.

✔ Bank hours are: 8.30 a.m.–1.30 p.m.

✔ Commercial business hours are: 8.30 a.m.–12.45 p.m. and 5 p.m.–8 p.m.

✔ Expect to spend a lot of time at lunch, and expect to get some business done during this meal which sometimes takes two or three hours.

✔ Expect to be entertained in restaurants, not at home.

✔ Although punctuality is not an Italian virtue, don't pick up the habit.

✔ The Italians do take business very seriously, so be on time and make appointments.

✔ Gift giving varies. Follow their lead.

✔ Nominal gifts such as a bottle of Cognac are OK.

✔ Don't be surprised by the excessive hotel taxes.

✔ Expect a 10–15 percent gratuity to be added to your restaurant bill, but do give a bit more.

✔ Tip taxi drivers.

Traps

✗ Do be careful of your gestures. The Italians find the upward hand or fingers offensive. Call for waiters with your fingers pointed down.

✗ Remember Italians are not Sicilians and vice versa.

✗ Do be careful of thievery—pickpockets are at work in all major metropolitan areas.

The Netherlands

This is a country with a highly developed sense of private enterprise. Over 70 percent of the population speak at least one foreign language. Favorable telecommunications laws have attracted major foreign corporations to centralize their telephone marketing efforts in this country.

The Netherlands is a member of the European Economic Area Treaty and the European Union (EU). Rotterdam is the principal maritime port and Schiphol, near Amsterdam, is the major international airport. Because of its extensive network of customs bonded warehouses, Rotterdam is a widely used transshipment point for trade between Europe and the rest of the world.

Tips

✔ The Dutch are formal in their business dealings.
✔ Be on time and make appointments.
✔ Expect 100 percent of the people of this country to speak English. It is bad form to ask if somebody speaks English—it is assumed and they don't even like to be questioned about it.
✔ Expect a 10–15 percent gratuity to be added to your restaurant, hotel and taxi bills, but give a bit more for exceptional service.

Traps

✗ Don't call the Netherlands "Holland" since that term specifically refers to only two of the twelve provinces that make up the country.

Norway

Norway is first and foremost a maritime nation—most of its population lives along the coast or on one of the hundreds of coastal islands. It is a mixed economy, combining free-market activity with government intervention in key areas such as petroleum and welfare, as well as extensive subsidies for agriculture and fishing. This small entrepreneurial country is rich in natural resources—petroleum, hydropower, fish, forests, and minerals. As a result, the Norwegian standard of living is among the highest in the world. It maintains a high dependence on international trade, exporting raw materials and semi-processed goods. Norway is a member of the European Free Trade Association (EFTA) and the European Economic Area Treaty but is not a member of the European Union (EU).

Tips

✔ Norwegians are private people (much more so than the Danes or Swedes).
✔ You may be invited to a Norwegian home, if so take a small gift.
✔ Be on time.
✔ Dress conservatively.

✔ You should expect, among the achievements of this modern society, an appreciation of the equality of women, both in theory and practice.

✔ These are outdoors people. Talk about sports, including skiing, boating, rustic cabin life, and travel, but don't talk about social status or other personal topics.

Traps

✗ It takes time to get acquainted and build trust.

Portugal

Portugal is known as the "Land of Discoveries," because of a history of many voyagers that ventured into uncharted waters. Since Portugal became a member of the European Economic Area Treaty and the European Union (EU) it has experienced strong growth—at least 4 percent each year. To prepare for its entry into the EU Lisbon, the capital, fully liberalized its capital markets and most trade markets. International airports are at Lisbon and Oporto, and are connected by an excellent interstate transportation system.

Tips

✔ These are a warm, if somewhat reserved, people.

✔ Using a few words of Portuguese will make you even more welcome.

✔ Be punctual for appointments.

✔ Most business meetings begin reasonably on time.

✔ Exchange business cards.

✔ The Portuguese respect age, titles, and rank.

✔ Women have played important roles in business and government for many decades.

✔ Third-party introductions are important in business circles.

✔ The correct title for men is "*senhor.*"

✔ Women are addressed "*minha senhora,*" which simply means "my lady."

✔ Use professional titles such as professor in lieu of general titles.

✔ Expect to shake hands.

✔ The main meal is in the middle of the day and there is a "siesta" from about 1.30 p.m. until about 4.30 p.m. Most people join their families, and even take a short nap. Others spend the time in restaurants with their friends.

✔ Close friends embrace and slap or pat each other on the back when greeting.

✔ Expect to eat supper well after 9 or 10 o'clock, when the restaurants open. This meal often extends well into the next morning.
✔ Take a small gift if invited to dinner.
✔ "*Sande*" is the traditional Portuguese toast. It means "health to all of us."

Traps

✗ First names are reserved for close friends and relatives.

Spain

Spain's history of finding new trade routes to and from new world markets is as vibrant today as it was in Christopher Columbus's day. Spain's economy has rebounded, having been spurred by liberalized trade and foreign and domestic investments since becoming a member of the European Economic Area Treaty and the European Union (EU).

Tips

✔ Make and keep appointments.
✔ Expect to need a third party to make introductions—otherwise you might remain unable to connect with power circles. That party is commonly called an "*enchufado*," meaning well-connected.
✔ Titles are not used when addressing a Spanish executive; however, the term "*señor*" or "*señora*" should always precede the family name.
✔ Men of distinction, business, professional men, and university graduates often use the term "*Don*" when addressing each other.
✔ Business cards should be offered on greeting.
✔ Use the handshake, but don't be surprised to see hugs (*abrazos*) among men who are friends or even only business associates.
✔ Spanish attitudes about punctuality are changing. Once, it was almost impolite to arrive on time, but now most business meetings begin reasonably on time.
✔ Put away your clock and join in this entirely different cultural application of time. You will start later and have the main meal in the middle of the day. You should expect to work later.
✔ The "*siesta*" is a break in the middle of the day when most stores and businesses close, usually from about 1.30 p.m. until about 4.30 p.m. Most people go home to join their families, and even take a short nap. Others spend the time in restaurants with their friends.
✔ Be prepared for late lunches and dinners.
✔ Since the day is already shifted, expect to eat supper well after 9 or 10 o'clock, when the restaurants open. This meal often extends well into the next morning.

✔ The Spanish have a saying that "one cannot do business with someone with whom one has not dined."

✔ Spaniards expect the person with whom they negotiate to be a person who has the authority to make financial decisions.

✔ Take a small gift if invited to dinner. But don't make it extravagant—it could be misinterpreted as a bribe.

✔ Tip in restaurants and taxis.

Traps

✗ Do not confuse the Basques with the Catalonians, or vice versa. Great offense can be taken.

Sweden

Once a major military power, Sweden has remained neutral for more than 180 years, concentrating instead on science, invention, and one of the highest living standards in the world. Sweden has achieved a remarkable economic standard under a mixed socio-capitalistic system, with high technology and extensive welfare benefits. It is an economic force despite its low population base. It has a modern distribution system, excellent internal and external communications, and a highly skilled labor force. Already a member of the European Free Trade Association (EFTA), the European Economic Area Treaty, and the European Union (EU), the government continues to harmonize its economic policies with those organizations. Sweden's international air and maritime ports are among the most modern in the world, and its telecommunications services are highly developed.

Tips

✔ Swedes may seem shy, uninterested and are seldom the first to break the ice, but once it is broken they are genuinely friendly.

✔ Sweden is a nation of progressive, even liberal, thinking about society and politics. Read up on the latest innovations and don't be afraid to use these as topics of conversation.

✔ Make sure you know something of the cultural differences between Sweden and the other Scandinavian countries, Norway and Denmark. Other terms you should be familiar with are "*Norden,*" which adds Finland and Iceland to the Scandinavian list, and "*Fennoscandia,*" a term often used to describe Finland and the Scandinavian Peninsula.

✔ Indulge in the famous *smorgasbord,* an assortment of cold and hot foods placed on a table for self-service. Eat the foods in the order your host

suggests, which is usually fish, followed by cold meats, then hot dishes, then finally desserts.
✔ Make appointments and be punctual.
✔ Bring flowers for the hostess.
✔ Expect almost all Swedes to speak English.
✔ Learn a few words, like "*damer*" (woman) and "*herrar*" (man).
✔ Do not touch your drink until the toast then make certain you offer a responding toast. Wait until your host toasts you. Toasts are initiated by seniority.
✔ The Swedes traditional toast is "*skoal.*" Watch your host carefully and replicate his or her "*skoal*" motion.
✔ Don't tip. It is usually included with the bill.
✔ Tip taxi drivers (about 10 percent).

Traps

✗ Don't drive while intoxicated, it is a very serious offense in Sweden (even two beers will put you over the limit). It is wise to designate a driver who will not drink.

Switzerland

Switzerland is one of the most prosperous and stable economies in the world. Swiss per capita output, general living standards, education and science, health care and diet remain unsurpassed in the world. It is Europe's pre-eminent commercial banker, and is a member of the European Free Trade Association (EFTA) and the European Economic Area Treaty, but not the European Union (EU).

Tips

✔ Expect a very formal and punctual people.
✔ Third-party introductions are needed.
✔ Arrange business appointments in advance
✔ Exchange business cards.
✔ Dress for the weather, but be formally attired.
✔ Expect to shake hands.
✔ Rank and status are important. Rank and titles are routinely used.
✔ Three main languages are spoken: French, German and Italian.
✔ Think conservative.
✔ Business lunches or dinners are rare. The Swiss often entertain after a deal.

✔ Flowers or a small gift are appropriate if invited to a home for dinner.
✔ A tip of about 15 percent is included in most hotel, restaurant, and bar bills.
✔ Tip taxis.

Traps

✗ It is quite rude to be more than five minutes late.

The United Kingdom

Of course, three countries comprise Great Britain: England, Scotland, and Wales. When Northern Ireland is added, the four become the island nation called the United Kingdom (UK). The UK is one of the world's great trading powers and financial centers, its socio-capitalistic economy ranking among the three or four strongest in Europe. The UK is a member of the European Economic Area Treaty and the European Union (EU). Free-trade zones exist at most of the major marine port cities.

Common cultural characteristics

✔ The British generally dress and talk conservatively.
✔ Expect English to be spoken differently in each country, and in different regions.
✔ When searching for a non-controversial subject, try sport, animals, or the weather. It may be better not to discuss politics.
✔ In military or Establishment circles titles are cherished and may be used even among old acquaintances. More modern industries are much less formal, sometimes using first names. Follow their lead.
✔ Do not vent your emotions, save it for the privacy of the hotel room.
✔ Expect attention to detail.
✔ When business meetings are finished, the British often change the mood with a joke.
✔ Scotch is the whiskey you drink. If you mean Bourbon don't ask for whiskey.
✔ Dinners are often similar to "dining-ins," often formal, and seldom at home. Invitations to formal dinners may specify "black tie," which means dinner jackets and long dresses.
✔ In general, business entertaining is likely to take place in restaurants and to be informal.
✔ Business is seldom discussed after the business day.

England

England is only one of the four political divisions that make up the United Kingdom, yet it has tremendous influence worldwide. It is the origin of English, which is rapidly becoming the world's common tongue.

Tips

✔ See the Common cultural characteristics on p. 143.
✔ Make appointments and be on time.
✔ Expect to be greeted with a handshake.
✔ First names are rarely used in Establishment English businesses, but may be in more modern industries.
✔ Expect Establishment business to still be done through the old-boy network, but modern businesses to work strictly on merit.

Traps

✗ See the Common cultural characteristics on p. 143.
✗ Don't move too quickly. It could be seen as offensive.
✗ Don't talk politics.

Northern Ireland

This country is about one-third the size of the Republic of Ireland, but is part of the United Kingdom.

Tips

✔ See the Common cultural characteristics on p. 143.
✔ Expect to be greeted with a handshake.
✔ Exchange business cards.
✔ Dress and act formal until the relationship warms.
✔ Take a small gift if invited to the home.
✔ Tip about 10–15 percent in restaurants, if a tip is not included in the bill.
✔ Tip taxi drivers.

Traps

✗ See the Common cultural characteristics on p. 143.
✗ Don't expect anyone to accept currency issued by The Republic of Ireland.
✗ Avoid debate about the political or religious struggles.

Scotland

Washed by the Atlantic Ocean on the west and north and the North Sea on the east, Scotland is the northern part of the island of Great Britain and a constituent part of the United Kingdom. Large, newly discovered crude petroleum reserves are being exploited in the North Sea and this industry is bringing new wealth to the country's northern ports. Fishing continues to be a major industry off the east coast, while manufacturing is located mainly in the central lowlands and along the east coast. The once important ship-building industry has recently declined greatly, while new industries of electronics and consumer goods have been developed.

Tips

- ✔ See the Common cultural characteristics on p. 143.
- ✔ Expect to be greeted with a handshake.
- ✔ Exchange business cards.
- ✔ Dress and act formal until the relationship warms.
- ✔ Listen to how they address each other—let that be your lead.
- ✔ Make appointments and be on time.
- ✔ Topics of conversation should include this country's rich heritage and its history of interaction with England—it is fascinating.
- ✔ Business people should not expect to be invited home—most entertaining is done in pubs and restaurants.
- ✔ Take a small gift if invited to an Scottish home.
- ✔ Tip about 10–15 percent in restaurants, if the tip is not included in the bill.
- ✔ Tip taxi drivers.

Traps

- ✗ See the Common cultural characteristics on p. 143.
- ✗ Don't call the Scottish "English," or the country "England." You can call them British or Scottish.
- ✗ Don't talk politics.

Wales

This is the smallest of the countries in the United Kingdom but a place where earliest humans lived, possibly more than 12,000 years ago. Lying in the west of England, it constitutes one of four entities of the Great Britain. The largest industrial centers—Swansea, Cardiff, and Newport—are in the south, using coal obtained from the mountain valleys of the interior.

Tips

✔ See the Common cultural characteristics on p. 143.
✔ Expect to be greeted with a handshake.
✔ Exchange business cards.
✔ Dress and act formal until the relationship warms.
✔ Expect these people to be kind and warmly hospitable.
✔ Welsh is taught in the schools along with English.
✔ Take a small gift if invited to a Welsh house.
✔ Tip about 10–15 percent in restaurants, if the tip is not included in the bill.
✔ Tip taxi drivers.

Traps

✗ See the Common cultural characteristics on p. 143.
✗ Don't call the Welsh "English," or their country "England." You can call them British or Welsh.
✗ Don't talk politics.

CHAPTER THIRTEEN

Central Europe

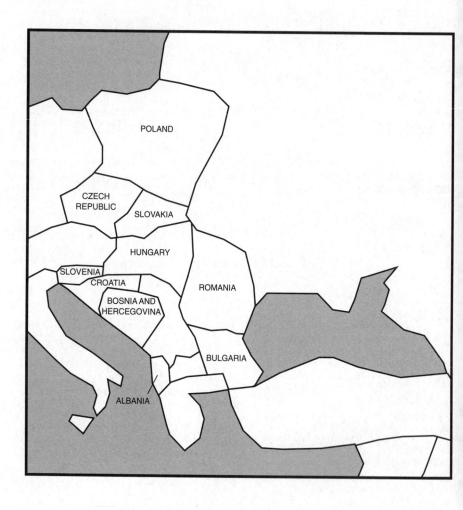

Albania

For over forty years, as a Stalinist-type economy, Albania operated on the principle of central planning and state ownership of the means of production. In 1992 the new democratic government announced a program of shock therapy to stabilize the economy, privatize, and establish a market economy. The Albanians also passed legislation allowing foreign investment, but not ownership of real estate. This nation possesses excellent mineral resources and as it moves ahead with privatization, the agricultural sector is steadily regaining its previous self-sufficiency.

Tips

✔ Make business appointments far in advance and be punctual.
✔ In Albania shaking your head from side to side means "yes," and nodding up and down means "no."
✔ An Albanian's word, called "*besa*," is his bond. Therefore Albanians are reluctant to promise anything unless they are certain they can keep their word.
✔ It is extremely important that you don't make promises you cannot or don't intend to keep.
✔ There are very few, if any, lawyers in this country.
✔ Albanians are known for being gracious hosts.
✔ Topics of conversation include Mother Teresa (she was an ethnic Albanian), sports, and geography.
✔ Talk about the country's recent economic transformation.
✔ Take plenty of pictures of the colorfully clothed people and their country of beautiful lakes, streams, and rivers.
✔ Don't expect running water at all times in this nation of changing economics.
✔ Don't expect to find Western-style toilets outside of major towns. The Turkish (squat) style predominates.
✔ Be prepared for people to smoke.

✔ Gifts are welcome if you are invited to a home.
✔ Tip 5–10 percent in restaurants.

Traps

✗ Do not talk politics.
✗ Do not try to take pictures of military or police installations.

Bosnia and Hercegovina

Bosnia and Hercegovinia rank among the poorest republics in the old Yugoslav federation. This state continues to be set back economically by bitter inter-ethnic warfare that has caused production to plummet, unemployment and inflation to soar, and human misery to multiply. Although the war appears to be over, the country will take years to recover from the destruction that the civil war brought. The only economy left is agriculture, which is in the hands of small, private, inefficient, traditional farms.

Tips

✔ Be punctual for your business appointments.
✔ Don't expect everyone to speak English—German is a more common second language.
✔ Talk about sports and literature (particularly Ivo Andric a Bosnian who won the Nobel Prize for Literature in 1961).
✔ Small gift exchanges are welcome, but don't overdo this and embarrass your host.
✔ Tip 5–10 percent in restaurants in addition to the service charge.

Traps

✗ Avoid talking politics.
✗ Stop and follow instructions if stopped at a checkpoint.
✗ Do not photograph military or police installations.

Bulgaria

Though one of the smallest economies in Eastern Europe, Bulgaria is making great strides toward renovating its aging industrial plant and keeping abreast of rapidly unfolding technological developments. By giving workers shares in their enterprises, and thus motivating its workers, Bulgaria is able to pursue a mass privatization program to overcome the country's economic problems. There are international airports in Sofia, Varna, and Burgas, and domestic service in seven other cities. The two main maritime ports are on the Black Sea at Varna and Burgas, and are connected mainly by inland waterways. There are six free-trade zones, offering five-year tax holidays for some companies.

Tips

✔ Address men or women by their last name.
✔ Head gestures mean the reverse of what they mean in our culture. A shake of the head means "yes," and a nod means "no."
✔ Candy, flowers, or wine make excellent gifts if you are invited to a home.

Traps

✗ Don't discuss politics, religion, or social conditions.

Croatia

Before the dissolution of Yugoslavia, the Republic of Croatia, after Slovenia, was the most prosperous and industrialized area. Croatia is now among the poorest republics in the old Yugoslav federation. This state continues to be set back economically by bitter inter-ethnic warfare that caused a dramatic decline in production, high unemployment and inflation, and enormous human misery.

Tips

✔ Be punctual for your business appointments.
✔ Don't expect many to speak English—German is a more common second language.
✔ Sport is a safe topic of conversation.
✔ Small gift exchanges are welcome, but don't overdo this and embarrass your host.
✔ Tip in restaurants.

Traps

✗ Avoid discussing politics
✗ Don't photograph military or police installations.

The Czech Republic

Czechoslovakia was the healthiest and most industrial nation, by Eastern European standards, before World War II; therefore it has a capitalist memory. Even so, it suffers from an aging capital plant, lagging technology, and a deficiency in energy and raw materials. With the dissolution of the old state into the Czech Republic and Slovakia on January 1, 1993, the two independent nations launched sweeping programs to convert their almost entirely state-owned and state-controlled economies to market systems. With any new free-market system there are growing pains and this nation, which has privatized over 3,000 large enterprises, welcomes all kinds of investment. The Czech Republic is landlocked but aggressive, and wants Western goods. It has international airports in Prague, Ostrava, Brno, and Karlovy Vary, and ocean cargo is sent by truck or rail to the German ports of Hamburg and Rostock or the Polish ports of Gyynia, Gdansk, and Szczecin. There are free-trade zones in Bor, Prague, and Zlin, all of which are linked by rail and road.

Tips

✔ Be punctual for your business appointments.
✔ Don't expect everyone to speak English. Many people speak German, and Russian was the compulsory second language for many years.
✔ Learn a few words Czech, such as "*prosim*" ("PRAW-sim"), which means "please," "*dekyju*" ("DYE-koo-yi"), which means "thank you," and "*prominte*" ("PRAW-miny-tay"), which means "excuse me."
✔ Safe topics of conversation include sports, economics, and the arts.
✔ Small gift exchanges are welcome, but don't overdo it and embarrass your host.
✔ Do not tip, but it's OK to round up the bill in restaurants.

Traps

✗ Avoid talking politics.
✗ Be careful not to photograph military or police installations.

Hungary

The Republic of Hungary is located in the "Heart of Europe," where the Danube River divides the city of Budapest. A competitive nation with big debt, Hungary is racing for Western markets. Because it got a head start in its transition from a command economy during the Communist era its economic reforms have attracted significant foreign investment;

however, the country is having some difficulty with inflation, so that some businesses keep currency in foreign banks. The Ferihegy International Airport is 10 miles from the center of Budapest and there is regular service to and from Europe, North Africa, and the Middle East. Ocean cargo enters this landlocked nation through the surrounding countries.

Tips

✔ Make your appointments well in advance and be on time.

✔ Expect formality.

✔ A handshake is the normal greeting, but do kiss the friends you have made on both cheeks when departing.

✔ Address your counterpart by the family name followed by "*Ur*" (Mr.), for example *Kus Ur*.

✔ Married women are addressed as "*kedves asszonyom*" (My dear madam). A married woman's family name is rarely used.

✔ An unmarried woman is introduced using her family name plus "*kisasszony*" (Miss), for example *kus kisasszony*.

✔ It is OK to kiss the extended hand of a woman.

✔ Learn and speak a few Hungarian words. They will like you for it.

✔ Business cards are exchanged but often not until the end of a meeting.

✔ It is OK to exchange a modest logo gift. Something that tells the history of your firm is welcomed.

✔ Expect to be entertained in restaurants for business lunches.

✔ Expect a high density of McDonald's fast-food outlets.

✔ If invited to a home, an appropriate gift might be flowers for the woman and wine or Western liquor for the man.

✔ Expect toasting to occur before, during, and after the meal.

✔ The formal Hungarian toast is "*egeszsegedre*" ("egg-a-shay-grr-dra"), which means "to your health."

✔ Be sure to talk about art, as this nation has had many world-famous composers and writers.

✔ Take pictures of the colorful folk costumes.

✔ Tip waiters and taxi drivers 10–15 percent.

✔ At restaurants the tip should not be left on the table.

✔ Tip the gypsy musicians.

Traps

✗ Avoid discussing politics.

✗ Do not photograph military or paramilitary personnel or installations.

✗ Don't clink your beer glasses when toasting.

✗ Don't drink and drive.

Poland

Poland underwent shock therapy by the Solidarity-led government from a Soviet-style economy with state ownership and control of the productive assets to a market economy. This included slashing subsidies, decontrolling prices, and tightening the money supply. As a result consumer goods shortages and lines disappeared. The Polish economy is now in the midst of a sustained recovery. There are international airports at Warsaw, Krakow, and Gdansk. Poland has access to maritime commerce through the Baltic Sea ports of Gdynia, Gdansk, and Szczecin. There are thirteen free-trade zones, most of which are suited for industrial production. They are connected by a well-developed road and railway system. Transportation by domestic air is excellent and convenient.

Tips

✔ Carry your passport (or a copy) with you at all times.

✔ Set up your appointments well in advance and be on time.

✔ Expect to be greeted with a handshake.

✔ A business woman should not be surprised if a Polish man kisses her hand upon introduction or when saying goodbye.

✔ Foreign men are not expected to kiss a Polish woman's hand; a handshake will do.

✔ Business cards are the norm and are generally given to each person present in a meeting. It is not necessary to have cards printed in Polish.

✔ Poles are outgoing and friendly, but visitors who don't speak Polish or German may need a translator. Few Poles speak English fluently, though this is changing.

✔ Poles like it when you try their language even if you mangle it beyond recognition.

✔ Dress in formal business attire—suit and tie for men, suit or a dress for women.

✔ This is an aggressive nation racing to trade, so be creative and careful.

✔ The Polish drink hard liquor and lots of it, even while doing business.

✔ Flowers, always in an odd number, are the most common gift among friends and acquaintances.

✔ Sunday is the traditional day for visiting family and friends in Poland.

✔ Be careful of your conversation. It's OK to talk about the United States and your family, but don't talk about World War II.

✔ Tip taxi drivers 10 percent, but don't tip in restaurants—a 10 percent service charge is normally included in the bill.

Traps

✗ Do not drink the water.
✗ Don't discuss World War II.

Romania

Romania started its transition from a command to a market economy in 1989, and has made considerable progress even though it had little or no experience of partial reforms, such as those undertaken by other Central European economies during the 1980s. Romanians have successfully renewed their most-favored nation status with most industrialized nations. Today much of the legislative framework and reform agenda is in place and Romania is on the right road to a healthy market economy. Western goods are scarce in Romania. The country suffers from an aging capital plant, but it is making progress toward privatization. Private enterprises form an increasingly important portion of the economy, largely in services, handicrafts, and small-scale industry. There are international airports at Bucharest-O-topeni, Kogainiceanu-Constanta, Timisoara, and Arad. Romania has several sea ports on the Danube river and the Black Sea. Free-trade zones at Sulina, Braila, and Constanta have the capacity for manufacturing.

Tips

✔ Make appointments well in advance.
✔ Romanians are generally very punctual, you should be too.
✔ Try some Romanian words; they appreciate it.
✔ Don't be surprised if Romanian sounds familiar. It is a Romance language and has many similarities with French, Italian, and Spanish.
✔ Trade with the West has been commonplace since the 1960s, so expect a high level of understanding of and appreciation for free enterprise.
✔ Expect negotiators to be clever business people.
✔ Do not expect to be invited to a Romanian home. Should it happen, take flowers for the hostess and a small gift for the family.
✔ Sport, art, music, and travel are good topics of conversation. This is the land of Dracula, Ilie "Nasty" Nastase (former professional tennis player), and Olympic star gymnast Nadia Comaneci.
✔ Tip about 10 percent in restaurants if a charge hasn't already been added to the bill.
✔ Tip taxis about 10 percent.

Traps

✗ Don't take pictures of military installations or personnel.

Slovakia

The dissolution of Czechoslovakia into two independent states—the Czech Republic and Slovakia—on 1 January, 1993, has complicated the task of moving toward a more open and decentralized economy. Situated in the middle of Central Europe, Slovakia is marketing itself as the ideal foreign base of operations for companies looking to gain a foothold in the region. Despite political feuding, rules allowing for freer circulation of the Slovak crown and plans to push privatization forward are promising. GDP growth has been stronger in each of the past several years and inflation continues to drop steadily. Trade groups have formed to attract investment and bolster ailing industries. Slovakia is landlocked and moves its goods through ports on the Danube river. There are several international airports and there is a free-trade zone at Kosice.

Tips

✔ Be punctual for your business appointments.
✔ Have someone teach you the words for "hello," "please," "thank-you," "excuse me," etc. They will like you more for trying.
✔ Everyone does not speak English, but they do speak several other European languages.
✔ Don't drink anything before driving.
✔ Sport is a safe topic of conversation.
✔ If invited to a private home take a gift of flowers for the hostess.
✔ It is customary for the host to pour everyone a shot of Slivovice, the powerful plum brandy. If you don't drink, cover your glass. If you do drink, cover your glass or it will be refilled each time you empty it.
✔ Small gift exchanges are welcome, but don't overdo it and embarrass your host.
✔ Do not tip, but round up the bill to an even amount.

Traps

✗ Avoid discussing politics.
✗ Be careful not to photograph military or police installations.

Slovenia

Slovenia is by far the most prosperous of the former Yugoslav republics. Its per capita income of about $7,000 is more than twice the average of other Central and Eastern European nations, and not far below the levels of neighboring Austria and Italy. In 1994 Slovenia's GDP grew by an impressive 5.5 percent, making it one of the fastest-growing economies in Europe. Bright spots for encouraging foreign investment are a relatively well-educated workforce, a developed infrastructure, and a Western business attitude. The rail link between Western Europe and Greece, Turkey, and the Near and Middle East runs through Slovenia. There are several international airports, and excellent rail and highway links to main cities and maritime ports.

Tips

✔ Make your appointments well in advance and be on time, even though Slovenes put less priority on punctuality than others.

✔ Pedestrians in this country are disciplined and can be seen waiting to cross a main street even if the street is momentarily empty. When the green WALK sign appears, people cross.

✔ Expect names to be in transition from the old to the new, or is it back to the old?

✔ Slovenes are similar in character to their Alpine neighbors, the Swiss and the Austrians—precise, respectful of rules, hard-working, and productive.

✔ You may be invited to a home in this country, so check out gift giving customs. Wine and flowers are always welcome. The men like whiskey.

✔ Conversation topics are less constrained in this country, because they get away to Western nations often for business. In the beginning, sport, family, and travel are still recommended topics.

✔ Tipping is OK in restaurants; give more for good service.

Traps

✘ Don't discuss politics, religion, or social conditions.

✘ Be careful not to photograph military or police installations.

CHAPTER FOURTEEN

Eastern Europe

Right or wrong, I have included in this section the nations east of Poland and Romania, most of which were members of the former Soviet Union.

The Baltics

The Baltic nations of Estonia, Latvia, and Lithuania are different but have many similarities with each other. For instance, they are principally Roman Catholic in their religious beliefs, highly nationalistic, and cultural. They are conservative in their values of family and traditions, and they like their freedom. Much of the behaviors experienced by visiting business people will seem alike; however, do learn the differences because each nation has its own strengths, weaknesses, and economic history.

Estonia

This is a nation that is reform-oriented and business-minded, with an industrial infrastructure. It is considered an entrepôt of high-tech services and industry. As of the mid-1990s Estonia ranked first among the fifteen former Soviet republics in moving from a command economy to a modern market economy. Its commitment to privatization, adoption of an independent currency (Kroon), and establishment of an extremely open trading regime have made Estonia one of the success stories of the region. Lured by a liberal trade policy that has reoriented trading patterns towards Western partners, a stable currency, and laws that encourage foreign investment, foreign businesses are testing the Estonian waters. The major share of this country's workforce engages in manufacturing both capital and consumer goods based on raw materials and intermediate products from other former Soviet republics. Estonia's products are of high quality by ex-Soviet standards and are exported to other republics. Estonia is fast attempting to improve quality so as to take advantage of its close export ties to Nordic and Western European countries. Tallinn is the major link to Russia in the east as well as Nordic and Western Europe. Main rail lines connect deep-water ports and international airports.

Tips

✔ Take warm clothing—it's a cold climate.
✔ Be punctual for business meetings.
✔ Business cards are a must—give one to everyone.
✔ Commercial hours are Monday through Friday, 9 a.m.–6 p.m.
✔ Try a few words in their language. Estonians are very proud of the Finno-Ugric tongue.
✔ Use your own language—English or German or whatever—before using Russian.
✔ Estonians have a reputation for being aloof; however, they greet visitors warmly and enjoy telling about their colorful history.
✔ Because of its close proximity to Finland, expect Estonia to be more Western than many.
✔ You should expect to find women in business.
✔ Don't skip lunch expecting a large late dinner. Lunch is the main meal and supper, a light meal, might be served well after 9 p.m.
✔ Expect to be entertained in restaurants and/or bars.
✔ Tip for good service—about 10–15 percent.

Traps

✗ Don't speak loudly in public places—it's associated with drunkenness.
✗ Be careful not to be drawn into discussions about Russia. Estonians can be testy about their freedom from that country.
✗ Estonians like their vodka so be careful of heavy drinking.

Latvia

This nation has historically been the corridor for Russia to Western Europe. It is the most industrial of the Baltics. With a rapidly expanding private sector, a commercial boom sweeping the nation's capital, and loosening of restrictions on foreign investment, Latvia is emerging as a promising market. The country is moving to privatize by attracting foreign investors for full ownership and repatriation of profits. Aside from its arable land and small forests, Latvia lacks natural resources. However, its most valuable economic asset is its workforce, which is better educated and disciplined than in most of the former Soviet republics. Industrial production is highly diversified, with products ranging from agricultural machinery to consumer goods. Latvia's international airport at Riga is the largest in the Baltic region, and its container port in the same location is the major terminal between St. Petersburg and Poland.

Tips

✔ Expect this to be a cold climate.
✔ Be punctual.
✔ A handshake will do as a greeting.
✔ The Latvians are rather formal people.
✔ Business hours are Monday through Friday, 9 a.m.–5 p.m.
✔ Expect to find women in business.
✔ Expect to find enthusiasm for things Western.
✔ Bring inexpensive gifts. Anything Western will do: coffee, T-shirts, ball caps, etc.
✔ English is everyone's second language, so try it first.
✔ Try a bit of the Latvian language: *"sveiki"* ("svay-key") is "hello," *"ata"* ("ah-tah") is "goodbye," *"ludzu"* ("lood-zuh") is "please," *"paldies"* ("pahl-dee-iss") is "thank-you."
✔ Expect open entertaining in restaurants and bars. Latvians are often hard drinkers.
✔ Let the men pour drinks—it is considered impolite for a woman to do so.
✔ Tip 10–15 percent in restaurants where service charge is not added.
✔ Tip taxi drivers about 10–15 percent.

Traps

✗ Don't call people *"tovarich"* (comrade). It is Russian and out of date.
✗ The Russian language is generally not popular, although many people speak it.

Lithuania

This country is moving toward a Scandinavian-style economy. Lithuania has above-average living standards and technology compared to the old USSR, but among the Baltics it lags behind Estonia and Latvia in economic development. Since declaring independence in 1990, Lithuania has implemented reforms aimed at eliminating vestiges of the command economy. The country has no natural resources aside from its arable land and it has only a limited comprehension of market economy. Nevertheless it is learning fast and privatization is underway. Lithuania has established a special agency to attract Western investment. Lithuania's location is strategic because it benefits from its ice-free port at Klaipeda on the Baltic Sea, and its rail and highway hub at Vilnius, which provides land communication between Eastern and Western Europe.

Tips

✔ Make appointments and be punctual.
✔ Expect a handshake as a greeting.
✔ Expect Lithuanians to be conservative in their negotiations.
✔ Women may be present during entertainment and in business.
✔ Try some Lithuanian: *"labas"* means "hello;" *"viso gero"* means "good-bye;" *"prasau"* ("prash-OW") means "please;" *"aciu"* ("ach-YOO") means "thank-you."
✔ Safe topics of conversation might include their basketball team and rock music.
✔ Lithuania is the most nationalistic of the three Baltic states.
✔ They are close to the Polish because they were part of the early Polish Empire.
✔ Expect to be entertained in restaurants and bars, but look out for the vodka.
✔ If invited to someone's home, take flowers, but not an odd number.
✔ Tip 5–10 percent.
✔ Bargain for taxi rides and tip only for good service.

Traps

✗ Don't drink the local water.
✗ Don't speak Russian unless it is the only language you can communicate in.

North Eastern Europe

The nations of Belarus (Byelorussia), Moldova, Russia, and Ukraine are sometimes considered the northern group of the former Soviet Union. Each is rich in its own history and culture, yet each has a great connection to the others.

Belarus

Literally translated "White Russia," Belarus (Byelorussia) took the brunt of the Nazi invasion of World War II. Although Belarus formally declared its independence from the Soviet Union on July 27, 1991, the people remain friendly to Russians and their culture. Because of its critical dependence on Russia and the other members of the Commonwealth of Independent States (CIS) for fuels and raw materials, Belarus has maintained a policy of gradual economic reform, stressing continuity and stability over mass restructuring in order to minimize social disruption.

Once mainly agricultural, the country now supplies important producer and consumer goods—and is sometimes the sole producer to the other states. It is especially noted for production of tractors, large trucks, machine tools and automation equipment. Belarus does not have direct access to the sea, but has a relatively well-developed rail and road network linking its strategic location both east and west. Belarus has observer status in the World Trade Organization (WTO).

Tips

✔ Expect to be greeted with a handshake.

✔ Be punctual.

✔ When addressing someone use both their first name and their patronymic middle name (modification of their father's first name). For instance, Alexander, son of Mikhail, would be addressed as Alexander Mikhailovitch.

✔ Belarussian business people keep their word.

✔ Learn the Cyrillic alphabet.

✔ Expect the religion to be Orthodox Christian.

✔ Expect the Belarussians to value friendship.

✔ Topics of conversation might include gymnastics (Vitaly Scherbo won six gold medals in 1992) and the Chernobyl disaster.

✔ This is a more traditional, conservative country, so expect less drinking.

✔ Expect taxi drivers to want to be paid in hard currency. Tip about 10 percent (or a pack of cigarettes).

Traps

✗ You should take toilet paper.

Moldova

This is the next-to-smallest of the former soviet republics, but is the most densely populated. Living standards are below average for the area because Moldova has no major mineral resources and only 20 percent of the population is engaged in the industrial sector. Although Moldova took to *perestroika* more than twenty years before it was pronounced in the Soviet Union, this country is having difficulty moving toward a market economy. Moldova declared independence from the former USSR on August 27, 1991, but its main problem is its dependence on the former republics for coal, oil, gas, steel, and major consumer durables. Privatization is moving ahead incrementally—small enterprises began in 1993 and medium to large in 1994. In all, some 1,500 enterprises, or about 35 percent of the countries state assets, became eligible.

Tips

✔ You should make appointments well in advance.

✔ Moldovans are generally very punctual; you should be too.

✔ Expect to be greeted with a handshake.

✔ Expect the Moldovans to value friendship.

✔ Expect Moldova to be close to Romania in culture and language.

✔ Moldovans are a very young and forward thinking people.

✔ This nation is dominated by the Eastern Orthodox religion (98.5 percent).

✔ Expect a warm and open heart as well as a warmer climate.

✔ Do not expect to be entertained in a Moldovan home. Should it happen, take flowers for the hostess and a small gift for the family.

✔ Moldovans enjoy laughing, singing, and drinking in restaurants and bars—they like their wine, which has won many medals in international competition.

✔ Sport, art, music, and travel are good topics of conversation.

✔ Tip 10–15 percent in restaurants and taxis.

Traps

✗ Avoid taking sides in the continuing political conflicts between Romania, the independent Moldovans, and the Russians, who may still stand guard.

Russia

Russia is a nation of about 160 million people living in the largest country in the world. It is a vast land mass spanning eleven time zones, almost twice as large as the United States. This land ranges from the highest mountains in Europe to some of the lowest spots in the world, and from Arctic tundra to seemingly endless plains. Its cities are home to some of the finest art and architecture in the world, and its countryside is untamed and beautiful. It is really a country of many customs and languages. According to an old Russian saying, "Russia is not a country, it is a world." It is the most politically powerful nation in Eastern Europe and is the place where Mikhail Gorbachev began a series of reforms collectively known as *glasnost* (openness) and *perestroika* (restructuring). Among sweeping economic reforms and broad privatization there are great shortages. Even with its diverse industrial base and extraordinary resources it continues to experience great difficulties moving from its old centrally planned economy to a modern market economy. The privatization of about 14,000 state-owned medium- to large-scale enterprises and other entities through voucher auctions has been the cornerstone for building a market economy. Approximately 90 percent of small shops and restaurants have been privatized. Many joint-venture opportunities exist, and investors may buy hard currency and repatriate profits and dividends. Goods imported into Russia face three levies: import tariff, value-added tax, and excise tax. Exported goods must adhere to a harmonized system for export licensing and quotas. There are free economic zones in the major cities of Kaliningrad, Larelia, Nakhodka, and Moscow, all connected by adequate road and rail networks. Marine ports are, in the east, Vladivostok, Nakhodka, Magadan, and Petropavlovsk; in the west, St. Petersburg and Kaliningrad have access to the Baltic Sea. Murmansk provides access to the Atlantic Ocean.

Tips

- ✔ Plan your trip and make appointments well in advance; be punctual.
- ✔ Russians expect to receive formal requests to and for meetings. Phone calls are not enough, but faxes are.
- ✔ Specify the name and title of all those attending and identify the purpose of the meeting.
- ✔ Russia is one of the last bastions of Old World Europe. It has not given up formal aristocratic manners and tastes.
- ✔ Titles are important. Russians have a history of elitism so do be sensitive to rank, titles and honors.
- ✔ Business hours are Monday through Friday, 9 a.m.–6 p.m.
- ✔ Dress conservatively.
- ✔ Many hotels offer business centers with direct-dial international telephones, fax machines, and photocopiers.
- ✔ The greeting will be a handshake, but kisses and hugs are occasionally seen among friends.
- ✔ Never shake hands over a threshold—it's considered bad luck.
- ✔ Expect Russians to know the English language. English is acceptable for business dealings but Russian is better. Hire a translator/interpreter if necessary.
- ✔ Take plenty of business cards with the information printed on both sides, in Russian and your own language.
- ✔ Do use all your titles on your business cards—business titles such as "sales representative" and your academic degrees—because Russians like to do business with experts.
- ✔ Specify your academic degrees, such as Bachelor of Science, Master of Arts, Ph.D. of Finance, on both side of your cards, in Russian and your first language (or English).
- ✔ Address Russians with their titles and last names, such as: "Chairman Mironov," Major Klimov," or "General Designer Medvedov."
- ✔ To address a Russian by his first name, unless you are invited to do so, is an insult.

✔ When addressing a Russian use both their first name and their patronymic middle name (modification of their father's first name). For instance, Alexander, son of Mikhail, would be addressed as Alexander Mikhailovitch.

✔ Try a few Russian words—it will be appreciated and they will be impressed.

✔ If you speak Russian, be sure to use the formal *vy* form, not the informal *ty* (these forms are analogous to *vous* and *tu* in French).

✔ Learn the Cyrillic alphabet. It's well worth the effort. You will be able to read many signs phonetically. For instance' "*PECTOPAH*" is pronounced "restoran"—a place to eat.

✔ Use visual aids to make presentations, but you may have to take your own projector and other equipment with you, with an adapter for 220 volt, 50 Hz.

✔ Do not expect short meetings. Russian meetings move deliberately—they do not like to be rushed.

✔ Expect small talk before getting to the business agenda.

✔ Expect two types of meetings: the one-on-one negotiation which lasts about one hour; and the more intense official visit lasting four or five hours, which could include a meeting, a factory tour, official lunch or dinner, and perhaps another formal meeting.

✔ Send senior people to represent your firm. The lead person should match the seniority of the Russian official. To send a project manager, no matter how technically competent, is a breach of protocol.

✔ Simple courtesy goes a long way.

✔ You should expect relationships to be more important than contracts.

✔ Be prepared to give a presentation of your objectives—they want to get to know you and your company and then the context of your visit. What are your objectives? Why are you interested in working with them?

✔ Hospitality is important to the Russian tradition. If you are the host you are expected to provide meals and accommodation. If you are the guest the Russians will provide.

✔ Russians tend to entertain lavishly even if it means skimping on their own meals the rest of the week or month. To Russians, meals are an important part of building a relationship.

✔ Russians are remarkable people, who are resilient after generations of hardships. They are truly warm and hospitable.

✔ Expect Russians to be very reserved and formal at first; they warm up gradually, but eventually can become quite intimate in their personal as well as their business relationships. As a result business relationships sometimes acquire a closeness that some foreigners, particularly Americans, find stifling and invasive.

✔ Russians are sports fans, so don't hesitate to use sport as a topic of conversation, but in this land often more famous for its talented people than

its industry, they also like in-depth discussions of history, painting, literature, or music.

✔ They like their politics, but you should be careful if you become involved
in a discussion.

✔ You should accept and exchange gifts: mementos of your country, flags,
etc. are normal.

✔ At the end of a formal visit, Russians like to exchange gifts. Something
small is appropriate like a pin or pen with the company logo or country
handicraft. Be assured that flowers are an appropriate gift for men as well
as women.

✔ In turn, you may expect a gift of bread and salt—an age-old Russian
custom.

✔ If you are invited to a Russian home give a bottle of drink to men, flowers
to men and women, and a toy or chocolates to children.

✔ Be careful of expressing what you admire. If you admire something in
their homes, they may feel obligated to give it to you.

✔ Be prepared to remove your shoes when invited to a Russian apartment
(you'll probably be furnished with slippers).

✔ You should expect heavy drinking. Russians like their vodka served in
small glasses and "chug-a-lugged."

✔ You do not have to down every glass the Russians put in front of you—a
little sip will do.

✔ You may be expected to make a toast—a long toast is not required, but it
should be sincere. A good toast might be "to the future and continued
friendship" or "to our future prosperity."

✔ Russians are highly educated as a result of their public education.

✔ Credit cards are not always accepted—take cash but keep it in a money
belt.

✔ Tipping is encouraged. About 10–15 percent in restaurants, hotels, and
taxis.

Traps

✗ Be careful about exchanging money with an ordinary citizen. The laws
are changing, but the penalty could be the cancellation of your visa. Do
exchange at official offices.

✗ When talking to Russians you do not know well avoid discussions of sex,
religion, or politics.

✗ Russia can have an unpleasant mixture of bad service, inflated costs, and
mysterious surcharges. Be patient, even though it might seem like everyone wants to take part in the latest hustle.

✗ Don't drink vodka on an empty stomach.

Ukraine

This is the second most important and powerful new nation. It supplied about half of the former Soviet Union's agriculture and a substantial proportion of its industrial production. It is very industrialized, with many large cities. However, Ukraine lagged behind Russia and some of the other newly independent states in opening its economy. More recently the government has liberalized prices and erected a legal framework for privatizing state enterprises, particularly the small and medium-sized companies. The principle international airport is in Boryspil, near Kiev. Major trading ports are Yalta, Yevpatoriya in Crimea, and Odessa. Key distribution points are Kiev, Khartov, Dnepropetrovsk, Odessa, Donetsk, and Lviv.

Tips

✔ Expect Ukranian people to be open and warm.

✔ Expect to shake hands, but Ukrainians often hug after you make friends.

✔ When addressing Ukrainians use both their first name and their patronymic middle name (modification of their father's first name). For instance, Alexander, son of Mikhail, would be addressed as Alexander Mikhailovitch.

✔ Learn a few phrases of the Ukrainian language, such as: "*pryvit*," which means "hello," and "*budmo*," which means "hey" (to your health).

✔ About 70 percent of the words in the Ukrainian and Russian languages are the same.

✔ The religion of this nation is dominated by Eastern Orthodox Christian; however there are also Jews, Catholics, and adherents of other religions.

✔ Ukraine is among the richest nations in natural resources. It is the bread basket for Russia.

✔ You may be entertained at home as well as in restaurants and bars.

✔ Be prepared to remove your shoes if invited into a home.

✔ If you learn the Cyrillic alphabet you'll be able to read some of the signs phonetically—like "*METPO*" which is pronounced "metro" and means "subway."

✔ Expect the people to be very well educated.

✔ Ukrainians are sports fans, so don't hesitate to use sport as a topic of conversation, but in this land, often more famous for its talented people than its industry, they also like in-depth discussions of history, painting, literature, or music.

✔ Ukraine is also the land of Chernobyl, which remains a tourist attraction and a topic of conversation.

✔ Ukraine is more Westernized than Russia.

✔ Don't expect an easy negotiation. Ukrainians are foxy and pride themselves in driving fair, but hard bargains.

✔ You should expect to find women in business.
✔ Tip about 10 percent in restaurants, hotels, and taxis.

Traps

✗ Don't use the old way of referring to the country as "the Ukraine." The definite article implies that it is still a province of Russia, while the name alone means it's independent.
✗ Never refer to Ukraine as Russia.

South Eastern Europe

Just as there are great similarities among the Baltics, there are also parallels among the seven new nations of the underbelly of Russia. Originating on the steppes of Mongolia these nations are all Muslim except for Armenia and Georgia. Consequently, they are all very traditional.

Armenia

The culture of this landlocked nation in the Caucasus Mountain region is among the oldest of the world. Armenia—the country's name in their language is "Hayastan"—goes back to the days of Babylon and is the place where the Ark is supposed to have settled after the great flood. Because it is a Christian country among many Muslims it has been a tragic page of persecution in world history. Under the old centrally planned Soviet system Armenia had built up textile, machine-building, and other industries, and became a key supplier to sister republics. In turn, Azerbaijan and Georgia supplied most of Armenia's supplies of raw materials and energy. However, Armenia continues to be gripped by the long-standing conflict with Azerbaijan over the disputed enclave of the Nagorno-Karabakh Autonomous Oblast, an enclave of mostly Armenians within the boundaries of Azerbaijan. The government of Armenia is firmly committed to turning the country from a centralized planned economy into a democracy with a free-market society; however, until the conflict is resolved, foreign investors remain wary.

Tips

✔ Armenia is a place of growing business opportunity.
✔ The people are traditional.
✔ Greet with a handshake.
✔ Exchange business cards.

✔ Take plenty of small items for gifts (key chains, pens with logos, T-shirts, etc.).
✔ Tipping is optional. Round up the bill in a restaurant.

Traps

✗ Don't take sides in political discussion, especially ones dealing with Azerbaijan or Turkey.

Azerbaijan

Azerbaijan is a country with a mostly Muslim population of about 7 million. It is less developed industrially than the other transcaucasian states of Armenia or Georgia. Its major industries include petrochemicals and plastics manufacturing (oil-based), fuel (oil extraction and refining), iron and steel, light industry (clothing production, textiles, etc.), and machine-building. It also grows cotton, grapes, and silk, and has the potential to be a large oil producer—it has one of the world's largest reserves of oil. Civil unrest caused by the armed conflict between Christian Armenians and Muslim Azeris has led to economic chaos. Foreign traders and investors are biding their time until a peaceful solution can be sorted out. Azerbaijan is moving slowly toward its goal of a decentralized market economy.

Tips

✔ You should shake hands on greeting.
✔ Expect to be entertained in the office.
✔ Offer your business cards on first meeting
✔ Although it is a nation of no lawyers, you should expect contracts.
✔ Expect the men to be jealous of their women.
✔ Expect women to be present when entertaining.
✔ Expect them to honor their elders.
✔ They may even serve alcohol early in the morning, even during business meetings.
✔ Take lots of small items as gifts.
✔ Tip about 10 percent in restaurants and taxis.

Traps

✗ Don't talk politics, especially about Armenians.
✗ Azerbaijan has a forgery problem, so take unblemished currency bills with you.

Georgia

Georgia is a special country with a very old culture and roots in the Old Testament. Located in the southern Caucasus region, it is a country of mountainous valleys. Georgia is expected to continue embracing open-door economic policies. It has pressed ahead with privatizations, a new foreign investment law, and a new German-style commercial code. One of the most important laws requires all companies to introduce Western accounting methods. The international airport located at Tblisi is connected by excellent rail and highway links with all major cities and marine ports. Georgia's western boundary is on the Black Sea, with several ports—Batumi, Sukhumi, and Poti (the busiest and most prominent among them).

Tips

✔ The religion is Eastern Orthodox Christian.
✔ Don't expect deluxe accommodation.
✔ A handshake is the usual form of greeting.
✔ Exchange gifts and business cards.
✔ Gifts should be small items. Georgians like things with logos from your company or handicraft from your home country.
✔ Relationships are more important than contracts.
✔ You should expect negotiations to be slow and careful. Georgians drive a hard but fair bargain.
✔ Expect the language to be Georgian, with Russian as the second.
✔ Learn Cyrillic (Russian) phonetics. Its not difficult, especially if you are familiar with Greek phonetics. Knowing the Cyrillic pronunciation will help in reading signs and finding your way around.
✔ Expect very warm-hearted, hospitable people.
✔ You are likely to be entertained in the home.
✔ Georgian men are jealous of their women.
✔ you should expect lots of drinking and very long toasts.
✔ If you are invited to a feast don't raise your glass before the *tomada* (toast-master) has made his toast.
✔ Your return toast should include a simple short speech of thanks.
✔ Tip 10 percent in restaurants and taxis.

Traps

✗ Don't call Georgians Russian. Neither the language nor the national culture is Russian.
✗ It is considered bad taste to get drunk.
✗ Don't take sides in political discussions.

Kazakhstan

This is a country with a population of about 16.6 million. It is the second largest in the area, (next to Russia) of the fifteen former Soviet republics. Kazakhstan is a large oil and coal producer with enormous untapped fossil-fuel reserves as well as plentiful supplies of other minerals and metals, but it is also very agricultural—it grew one-third of the former Soviet Union's wheat. Its industrial sector rests on extraction and processing of natural resources and also on a relatively large machine-building sector specializing in construction and agricultural equipment. Kazakhstan is highly dependent on trade with Russia, exchanging its natural resources for finished consumer goods. The government has continued its push toward privatization and freed many prices. The country seeks to import investment, technology, and management skills. Kazakhstan's international airport at Almaty is connected by a road and rail network with links to Russia and China.

Tips

✔ Kazakhs make up about 40 percent of the population; however, a slight majority of the population is Russian.
✔ Learn their alphabet so that you can read signs.
✔ You should expect to shake hands in greeting.
✔ Business hours are Monday through Friday, 9 a.m.–6 p.m.
✔ Kazakhs generally entertain in the office.
✔ Expect great respect for elders.
✔ Take lots of inexpensive gifts, like cosmetics, household items, modern gadgets, etc.
✔ Expect to drink tea, not heavy drink.

Traps

✗ Many Kazakhs can trace their genealogy back for generations and they know to which of the three "hordes" they belong: the "Great Horde," the "Middle Horde," or the "Little Horde." Horde allegiances are a subtext of Kazak life and are of interest when hiring staff or doing business.

The Kyrgyz Republic

With a population of only about 4.5 million, this nation, which is located in a mountainous region, is remote and poorly connected to world markets. It is one of the smallest and poorest of the countries of the former Soviet Union. Its obsolescent industrial sector is concentrated around Bishkek. However, the people mine coal, mercury ore, produce cotton, and the country is a net exporter of electricity. Painful but steady progress is being made toward reform, mainly privatizing business, granting lifelong tenure to farmers, and freeing most prices.

Tips

✔ Slightly less than half of the population is ethnic Kyrgyzsi. Russians make up about one-third, and the rest are Uzbeks (about 12 percent), Kazakhs, and Tajiks. Relations among the groups are harmonious, with many intermarriages.

✔ Expect to be greeted by a handshake, but they may also use the *namaste* greeting.

✔ You would do well to demonstrate a knowledge of the culture.

✔ Bring lots of inexpensive gifts, like cosmetics, household items, modern gadgets, etc.

✔ Expect to drink green tea.

✔ Show respect for the elders.

✔ The little white felt hat worn by nearly all Kyrgyzsi men is called "*akkalpak.*" To be given one is an honor.

✔ The big white turban ("*echelek*") worn by many women signifies that they are married.

✔ This is horse country, so horses, not politics, are the hot topic of conversation for you.

✔ Tip 10–15 percent in restaurants, hotels, and taxis.

Traps

✗ Do not give attention to women.

✗ Take toilet paper.

Tajikistan

This nation of about 5.1 million population has the lowest living standards of the republics of the Confederation of Independent States (CIS) and faces struggling economic prospects. Historically, it produced about 11 percent of the former Soviet Union's cotton. Tajikistan is undergoing profound political and economic change. It is a newly independent nation still in the process of sorting out its internal relations, as well as external relations with neighboring states. Constant political turmoil and the continued dominance by former Communist officials have impeded the introduction of meaningful reforms.

Tips

✔ This is the most orthodox of the Muslim republics.

✔ The official language is Tajik, a dialect similar to Farsi and Dari.

✔ Approximately 40 percent of the population and most business people and government officials speak Russian.

✔ Expect to be greeted by a handshake, but they may also use the *namaste* greeting.

✔ Tajiks are among the oldest surviving nationalities of Eastern Europe. Related to the Persians, they have inhabited the region since the tenth century.

✔ Expect strong nationalism.

✔ Expect the men to wear the square hat called the *"Tiubuityeaika."* To be given one as a gift is an honor.

✔ This is a very traditional, closed society.

✔ You should be respectful of their elders.

✔ This society was once very polygamous.

✔ Expect the men to be very protective of their women.

✔ A few women work, but don't expect to find them in business for themselves.

✔ Tajiks drink tea, not hard drink.

Traps

✘ Communists, who have been elected, may still be in power.

✘ Ask permission before taking anyone's picture. It is considered rude not to.

✘ Do not tip. It is considered an insult.

Turkmenistan

Turkmenistan is largely desert country, with nomadic cattle raising, intensive agriculture in irrigated oases, and huge gas and oil resources. To move away from Moscow-based central planning toward a system of decision-making by private entrepreneurs, Turkmenistan faces enormous problems of economic adjustment. The country is attempting to attract foreign investment and open new gas channels through Iran and Turkey. It has the largest sulfur deposits in the world and is the largest cotton producer. The western region of Turkmenistan is irrigated from the huge Karakumskiy Canal.

Tips

✔ More than seventy different nationalities reside in Turkmenistan.

✔ This country is rich in historical tradition, with marvelous architectural cathedrals and buildings.

✔ National dress is among the most gorgeous anywhere.

✔ Expect to be greeted by a handshake.

✔ Exchange inexpensive gifts.

✔ Learn a few words of Turkmen—it will be greatly appreciated. For example, "*niredeh*" means "where is," "*mekhmankhana*" is "hotel," "*ashkhana*" means "restaurant," and "*tangyr*" means "thank-you."

✔ If you are entertained at home there will be no women in sight.

✔ Topics of conversation might include sports, horsemanship, and wrestling in particular. The Turkmen are famous for horse breeding and training.

✔ Young women with two braids and a small scarf are unmarried; those with one braid and a big kerchief have been wed.

✔ The people to be very education-oriented.

Traps

✗ Do not tip. It is considered an insult.

Uzbekistan

Uzbekistan is a dry, landlocked country, of which 10 percent consists of intensely cultivated, irrigated river valleys. It is one of the poorest states of the former Soviet Union, with 60 percent of its population living in overpopulated rural communities. The population is about 19.9 million. It is the world's third largest producer of cotton (only the U.S.A. and China produce more) and grows 67 percent for the former Soviet Union. Uzbekistan also has important natural resources, including gold, uranium, and natural gas. Since independence the government has sought to prop up the Soviet-style economy with subsidies and tight controls, along with an acceleration of a reform agenda and privatization.

Tips

✔ This may be the region's most fascinating country. It has the two ancient Silk Road cities of Bukara and Khiva, as well as Samarkand, the historic capital of fifteenth century Mongol conqueror Tamerlane. Learn some of its history because it will stand you well among the people.

✔ Ethnic Uzbeks make up two-thirds of the population. Tartars, Russians,

Kazakhs, and Tajiks make up the remainder. There are also 200,000 North Koreans living in the country.

✔ A handshake will do as a greeting.
✔ Expect the education level of this country to be lower than that of others in the region.
✔ Religion plays a major part in their lives.
✔ Much business is based on personal and family connections.
✔ Learn some Uzbek or Russian.
✔ Tip about 10 percent in restaurants, hotels, and taxis.

Traps

✗ Take toilet paper.
✗ This nation is still very Communist-oriented.

CHAPTER FIFTEEN

The Middle East

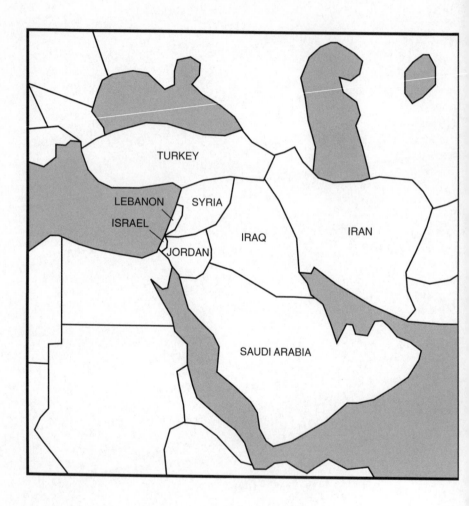

This group of states is composed of Iran, Iraq, Israel, Jordan, Lebanon, Syria, and Turkey.

In this region, except for Israel and much of Turkey, which is less orthodox, you can expect business to cease five times a day for Islamic prayers. Non-muslim visitors need not face Mecca, but should out of respect. The ninth month of the Islamic calendar is called Ramadan, and during this period all work stops before noon. Thursday or Friday is the Muslim day of rest.

It is common in all these states to eat with the right hand, and not to eat pork or drink alcohol.

Iran

This is a nation tired of revolution and war, and trying to rebuild. There is a growing need for foreign business and hard currency, which has brought about a change of focus toward greater strengthening of the county's economic situation and less religious fervor. This has opened the door for more business with industrialized nations previously excluded by fierce anti-Western rhetoric. Iran's economy is a mixture of central planning, state ownership of oil and other large enterprises, village agriculture, and small-scale private trading and service ventures. An oil windfall in 1990, combined with a substantial increase in imports, contributed to Iran's recent economic growth. Iran has also begun implementing a number of economic reforms to reduce government intervention (including subsidies) and has allocated substantial resources to development projects in the hope of stimulating the economy.

Tips

✔ Appointments are essential in private-sector business; however, they are less important in the public sector.
✔ Punctuality is less important in this country than in others.
✔ Dress conservatively. Men should wear long-sleeved shirts and pants (a

tie is not necessary). Women should tie a scarf around their hair, and wear neckwear and a full-length skirt (or a long-sleeved shirt and pants underneath a dark, loose-fitting, below-the-knee overcoat).

✔ Women should not wear make-up.

✔ Use the handshake for welcoming and greetings. Hugging and kissing are done only between friends. Instead of actually kissing, cheeks are touched during the greeting embrace.

✔ Don't shake hands with members of the opposite sex.

✔ Exchange business cards on first meeting.

✔ Iranians do not expect foreigners to speak their language, Farsi (Persian); nevertheless, do use these common words: *"selam"* for "hello," and *"merci"* or *"mutshakeram"* for "thank-you."

✔ The work week is Saturday through Thursday. Businesses are closed every Thursday (normally for a half-day) and all day Friday.

✔ Government working hours are 8.00 a.m.–3.00 p.m. with one hour for lunch.

✔ Private-sector hours vary and depend entirely on the owner.

✔ Accept tea when it is offered; it's a customary rite of hospitality.

✔ Iranians are extremely friendly and hospitable. They are interested in foreign people and like to invite them home.

✔ Business is often discussed over meals in restaurants.

✔ Meals are usually big gatherings where the main dishes are rice and chelo kebob.

✔ It is not traditional to exchange gifts in business relations, but they are not refused.

✔ Take a small gift when invited to dinner (candy or flowers).

✔ All women, including those in the business sector, must cover their hair and wear conservative skirts and blouses. Most Iranian women, especially followers of Khomeini also wear a *"chador"* (a long black dress).

✔ Once within the home, traditional clothing is often discarded in exchange for Western clothes.

✔ Take off your shoes when entering a carpeted area.

✔ Alcohol is prohibited, but some people—in violation of the law—drink it at home. It is not served at hotels.

✔ Tipping is not generally expected, although a 10–15 percent service charge is normally included in the hotel bill.

✔ Round up the bill and leave small change as a tip in restaurants.

Traps

✗ Avoid conversation about politics and war, particularly the U.S.A., Israel, and Iraq.

✗ Duel citizens of Iran and any other country risk having the passport of the other country confiscated. It is better to travel to Iran on your Iranian passport.

✗ Iran is a predominantly Shiite Muslim nation. Obey every law, for often what are misdemeanors in other nations are capital crimes in Iran, resulting in harsh Islamic penalties.

✗ Don't show affection in public for a member of the opposite sex.

✗ Don't slouch, stretch your legs, or show the soles of your shoes when in company.

Iraq

Iraq is seeking business to rebuild the nation after two disastrous wars; an eight-year war with Iran was followed almost immediately by war with the international coalition of allies to free Kuwait. Before the Gulf War Iraq was one of the most developed countries in the region. Today it is impoverished and oppressed. The Ba'athist government engages in extensive central planning and management of industrial production and foreign trade. There is some private enterprise, but mostly small-scale industry and agriculture. The economy has been dominated by the oil sector, which has traditionally provided about 95 percent of foreign-exchange earnings. In the 1980s financial problems caused by massive expenditures in the war with Iran and damage to oil export facilities by Iran led the government to implement austerity measures, and to borrow heavily and later reschedule foreign-debt payments. The industrial sector, although accorded high priority by the government, is under financial constraints. The UN-sponsored economic embargo has reduced exports and imports, and has contributed to shortages of spare parts and a sharp rise in prices.

Tips

✔ Make appointments and try to be there 10–15 minutes early to give the impression that you care.

✔ Initiate your greeting with a handshake, then follow up with small talk about how much you like your stay, the food, the climate, or historical places.

✔ Have business cards printed in Arabic.

✔ It is OK to use first names, but in the beginning call people by their full name—include job titles when talking with officials.

✔ Expect to be invited to lunch or dinner in a restaurant.

✔ Prepare yourself for traditional food, especially at lunchtime, which is the main meal and may be anytime between 1 p.m. and 5 p.m. You will most likely be served lamb cooked or fried in heavy corn oil.

- ✔ It is not a good idea to give presents to government officers—they become offended. Private-sector people can accept and exchange gifts.
- ✔ The work week is Saturday through Thursday. Businesses are closed every Thursday (normally for a half-day) and all day Friday.
- ✔ Working hours are 9 a.m.–2 p.m. (government); lunch 2 p.m.–4 p.m.; and after lunch 4 p.m.–8 p.m.
- ✔ Do not smoke in an office.
- ✔ Tip 10–15 percent unless a service charge is included in the bill.
- ✔ Do not tip taxi drivers—they don't expect it.
- ✔ A predominantly Shiite population (55 percent) and Kurds (about 21 percent) are ruled by the Sunni Muslims (about 33 percent).

Traps

- ✗ Alcohol is available, but it is illegal to drive under the influence–jail can result.
- ✗ Don't go near the Presidential Palaces—guards have been known to shoot and ask questions later.
- ✗ Don't enter any mosque unless you have been invited to do so.

Israel

Israel has a market economy with substantial government participation, which depends on imports of crude oil and natural resources. It has intensively developed its agricultural and industrial sectors over the past twenty years. Diamonds, magnesium, high-technology equipment, and agricultural products (fruits and vegetables) are leading exports. Israel usually posts balance-of-payments deficits, which are covered by large transfer payments from abroad and by foreign loans. To earn needed foreign exchange Israel has been targeting high-technology niches in international markets. The Ben-Gurion international airport near Tel Aviv is the main conduit for air cargo. There are free-trade zones located at Haifa and Eilat.

Tips

- ✔ When planning a trip for business purposes, make appointments in advance.
- ✔ Carry your passport with you at all times.
- ✔ This is a less formal land where the people often shift to first names after initial formal greetings.

✔ Don't put a lot of stock in titles; they're more casual about this than even the Americans.
✔ English is the language of business.
✔ *"Shalom"* is the greeting word, and a handshake is expected. They often will also say "hello" when they meet.
✔ Israel is very cosmopolitan.
✔ Dress is usually very casual. Men wear open-collar shirts. Sometimes they wear a coat with no tie.
✔ There are many women in business.
✔ The Hebrew word *giveret* means Miss.
✔ Business is often conducted over a meal.
✔ In most restaurants you may be asked to select Western or Middle Eastern food.
✔ Expect business to be straightforward and to stress the bottom line—much like with Americans.
✔ Customs in this Jewish state differ from those of its surrounding Arab neighbors. Whereas Friday, and in some cases Thursday, is the day of rest in Arab states, from nightfall Friday until nightfall Saturday is The Sabbath in Israel. Therefore the work week is from Sunday through Friday.
✔ Business hours are Monday through Friday, 8 a.m.–4 p.m.
✔ Politics, American and Israeli, is often a topic of conversation.
✔ Don't mention families during business meetings.
✔ Gifts are unnecessary, but tokens such as a toy for children or flowers for women are a nice touch.
✔ Tipping is not common.

Traps

✗ Don't photograph soldiers or military installations—it's against the law.
✗ Don't arrive late for a flight—airport security is the tightest in the world.

Jordan

The Persian Gulf crisis which began in August 1990 aggravated Jordan's already serious economic problems. Economic recovery depends on substantial foreign investment and aid, debt relief, and economic reform. Thus the government has restructured its tax and intellectual property rights laws and loosened investment restrictions. Through increased trade liberalization, ambitious investment plans, and closer business relations with neighboring countries and Europe, Jordan is clearing the way for greater foreign commerce activity. Jordan's five-year plan calls for lowering trade barriers and large investments in transportation, communications, and natural resources. There are international airports at

Amman, Aqaba, and Zisya. The highway system is one of the best in the Middle East and is linked to neighboring countries. There are free-trade zones in Zarka and Aqaba.

Tips

✔ Appointments are necessary. Foreign businessmen should be punctual.
✔ Dress conservatively.
✔ Women should not wear shorts, short skirts, halter tops, etc.
✔ Jordan has the highest literacy rate in the Middle East; you should therefore expect the people you deal with in the business sector to be highly educated.
✔ Be aware that about 75 percent of the population of this country are Palestinians who have become citizens of Jordan or were born in Jordan.
✔ Jordanians are very courteous, friendly, and hospitable.
✔ Talk about family and traditional issues such as recreation and sightseeing.
✔ Foreign business people are usually invited for dinner at either a restaurant or home, where business is a satisfactory topic.
✔ Jordanians expect presents, but this is an opportunity to promote your products with samples for gifts.
✔ Expect to be made comfortable by your Jordanian counterpart. You will be placed in an excellent hotel and taken sightseeing and to restaurants. Jordanians give you great importance if they see you are sincere.
✔ Working hours are 9 a.m.–1 p.m.; lunch for 2 hours; then work again from 3 p.m. until 7 p.m.
✔ A 10 percent service charge is normally included in hotel and restaurant bills.
✔ Tip taxi drivers and porters (about 8–10 percent).

Traps

✗ Be aware that Jordan imposes high border tariffs on such luxury items as televisions and cars. For instance, imported cars have as much as 300 percent duties.
✗ People in this country do not like to talk about politics with foreigners.
✗ Be aware that you may encounter some anti-Western feelings.

Lebanon

Business in this country is recovering after a long period of disruption. Lebanon's 1975 civil war cut national output by half, and all but ended Lebanon's position as a Middle Eastern entrepôt and banking hub. A tentative peace agreed to in October 1990 has enabled the central government to begin restoring control in Beirut (the Paris of the Middle East), collect taxes, and regain access to key port and government facilities. The battered economy has also been propped up by a financially sound banking system and resilient small and medium-sized manufacturers. Industrial production, agricultural output, and exports have showed substantial gains. Further rebuilding rests with the new business-oriented government.

Tips

✔ Expect this country to return to its traditional place as one of the business capitals of the world.
✔ Engage in small talk before getting down to business.
✔ Be careful how you sit—don't show the soles of your shoes.
✔ Don't display affection in public.
✔ You should accept food and drink (especially tea) when it is offered—it is impolite to refuse.
✔ Unlike other Arab countries, Lebanon has a Christian/Arab government; 50 percent of the population is Christian and 50 percent is Muslim.
✔ Give gifts, but not liquor or tobacco.
✔ Remove your shoes when entering a mosque.
✔ Tip (about 10–15 percent) if a service charge is not added to your bill.
✔ Tipping taxi drivers is not common.

Traps

✗ Don't be drawn into discussions about politics or religion.

Syria

Syria's state-dominated Ba'athist economy benefited from the Gulf war. Because of increased oil production and decreased economic deregulation, its economic growth averaged nearly 12 percent in 1990/91. Yet, due to low wages, living conditions in Syria are very low. In 1992 the government spurred economic development by loosening controls on domestic and foreign investment while maintaining strict political controls. Syria's economy is still saddled with a large number of poorly performing public-sector firms, and industrial and agricultural productivity is poor. The international airport is in Damascus and the one at Aleppo is being upgraded. There are free-trade zones at Aleppo, Damascus, Latakia, and Tartous. Telecommunications are in the process of receiving significant upgrades.

Tips

✔ Make appointments and be punctual, but don't be surprised by lack of punctuality in others.

✔ Dress conservatively.

✔ Expect a handshake and say "*marha-bah, kief halak*" when greeting people.

✔ Unless she offers, don't shake hands with a woman.

✔ French is the second language.

✔ The psychological space of men is much closer than for most Westerners.

✔ The work week is Saturday through Thursday. Businesses are closed every Thursday (normally for a half-day) and all day Friday.

✔ Don't be surprised when everything stops five times a day for prayers.

✔ Shaking the head side-to-side means "I don't understand." Shaking the head upwards and saying "tut" means "no."

✔ If you are given an invitation you should take a gift (not liquor).

✔ In a social setting don't accept food the first time it's offered—its impolite not to decline at least once.

✔ Feel free to talk politics, but don't say negative things about the country or its ruler, even if asked.

✔ Tipping is everywhere. Tip about 10 percent for most services.

Traps

✗ Don't admire a specific thing in a person's home, he may feel obliged to give it to you.

✗ Don't show the soles of your shoes—it's offensive.

✗ Don't point at people or use your hands to give directions—it is considered rude.

✗ Don't pass anything with your left hand.

Turkey

The Republic of Turkey, founded in 1923 in the aftermath of World War I and the fall of the Ottoman Empire by Mustafa Kemal Atatürk, rests at the nexus of Europe and Asia. The country was founded as a secular parliamentary democracy adhering to the principle of the separation of church and state. From its inception Turkey has looked West, became a member of various European and world bodies, seeking acceptance as a full member of the European Union (EU). Because of its geographic location and the assimilation of diverse cultures over its long history, its people are equally at ease with European, Middle Eastern, and Asian visitors. Its 1997 census counted 63 million, of whom 50 percent are under 20 years of age.

The United States has designated Turkey as one of the world's "big emerging markets" (BEMs). Manufacturing (27 percent), agriculture (15 percent), and transportation and telecommunications (12 percent) are the leading sectors in Turkey's GDP. In 1996 Turkey's dynamic market recorded $14.5 billion in exports, $27.7 billion in imports, and $6.0 billion in tourism. A member of the European Custom Union, which thus far favors Europe in its trade balance, Turkey is seeking elimination of trade barriers and greater commercial investments. As part of its structural reforms Turkey has embarked in a major privatization program which aims to raise $4.5 billion and $10 billion in 1997 and 1998, respectively. Global companies are exploring investment and joint-venture opportunities in power generation and distribution, telecommunications, and the automotive and tourism sectors. Further legislation to facilitate foreign investments and repatriation of profits and to provide concessions to investors is high on the government's priority list.

Tourism and construction, which account for 3 percent and 6 percent of GDP, respectively, are two major growth sectors. There are five first-class five-star hotels in Istanbul, with views of the Bosphorus, and scores of well-appointed four-star locations. There are currently over 30,000 holiday rooms under construction by foreign firms throughout Turkey's 5,000-mile coastline, which affords quality beaches and yachting locations. Turkey expects its 600,000 beds to be increased to 1 million by the year 2000. Leading 1996 tourists were Germans (2.1 million), Russians (1.6 million), and Americans (330,000).

Agriculture remains Turkey's most important economic sector. The government has launched a multi-billion-dollar development plan in the southeast region of the country. It will include building a dozen dams on the Tigris and Euphrates rivers to generate power and irrigate large tracts of farmland. By eliminating duties on industrial imports and applying the European Custom Union's common tariffs the country is moving toward periods of excellent growth. Turkey is a member of the European Economic Area Treaty, but not the EU, which it would like to join. Turkey's main air and maritime ports are connected by a standard-gage railroad and an extensive highway system.

Istanbul, formerly Constantinople and Byzantium, rests on both the continents of Europe and Asia on the banks of the Bosphorus. The city is a vast commercial center with an established stock exchange and a population of 9.2 million. Ankara is a modern capital city of 3.7 million people, and is only one hour by air from Istanbul. World-class hotels, modern international airports serviced by all major international airlines, and a network of superhighways make Turkey business- and tourism-friendly.

Tips

✔ Protocol is important.

✔ Appointments are necessary and should be arranged in advance; be punctual.

✔ Firm handshakes are customary.

✔ Dress conservatively.

✔ Cards are always exchanged.

✔ Visitors meet with counterparts of equal position in their companies.

✔ Accept whatever is offered—tea, coffee, soft drinks, etc.

✔ Reputations are jealously guarded.

✔ It is important to get references on the Turkish side in advance and have some person of like standing present your credentials prior to initial contacts. (Note: Someone with an unethical reputation is referred to as a "JR," as in *Dallas*'s J. R. Ewing.)

✔ Invitations to dinner and luncheon are usual and should be graciously accepted. Do not offer to pay, as this would be offensive.

✔ It is appropriate for the visitor to return the compliment on a subsequent visit or if the negotiations are of an extended duration.

✔ Invitations to the host's home are not uncommon and would be tendered by a contemporary of the guest/visitor.

✔ If you are invited home for a meal the host will push food toward you and insist you eat more than normal. It is their way of showing hospitality.

✔ Turkish cuisine is world famous. Try the sish kebob, doners, baklawa, and of course the Turkish coffee.

✔ Businessmen in Turkey are treated with the hospitality afforded to guests.

✔ Common courtesies will not go unnoticed.

✔ Tardiness may be construed as an affront or as gamesmanship.

✔ Ice breakers include the 3 "Fs," discussion of football (soccer), food, and family.

✔ Turks are close knit and proud of their family, hometown, and country. It is useful to know where the host comes from.

✔ There are great similarities between Greek and Turkish food. Fish and lamb are well prepared.

✔ English is spoken in most milieus, but there are instances when an interpreter is invaluable.

✔ Turks will normally address each other by their first name followed by "*Bey*," but foreigners with a "Mr." followed by a last name. It is best to stay with the "Mr." until a first-name basis is established, and then the first name is followed with a "*Bey*." It may seem awkward but it is best to err on the side of formality.

✔ Because of its location and its historical background, Turkey has always attracted many foreigners. Istanbul, which connects the two continents of Asia and Europe, is the heart of business.

✔ Turkey stresses business and economic development, both domestic and international.
✔ Turkey is considered one of the more competitive markets of the future.
✔ Regardless of sex, wear clothing that covers your shoulders, arms, and legs—that means no shorts or sleeveless shirts.
✔ To use a few Turkish words eases the atmosphere, even if those few are the limit of your vocabulary. Try *"merhaba"* for "hello," and *"merci"* or *"tesekkur ederim"* for "thank-you."
✔ Tip about 5 percent in expensive restaurants, even if a service charge has been added.

Traps

✗ Turkish people are sensitive about being confused with Arab nations, particularly in regard to religion. Unlike the Arab countries, religion in Turkey is free and is not emphasized—do not mix religion with business relations.
✗ Turkish people are proud of their heritage and not to be confused with other nationalities. There are approximately thirty-seven ethnic groups (Anatolian Turks, Jews, Greeks, Armenians, Kurds, Chechens, Tartars Georgians, etc., etc.) in Turkey. All call themselves Turks. Do not call them Arabs.
✗ Relationships with the EU were strained in December 1997 by the EU decision to exclude Turkey from the eleven-country list of suitable candidates to join the EU.

CHAPTER SIXTEEN

The Gulf States

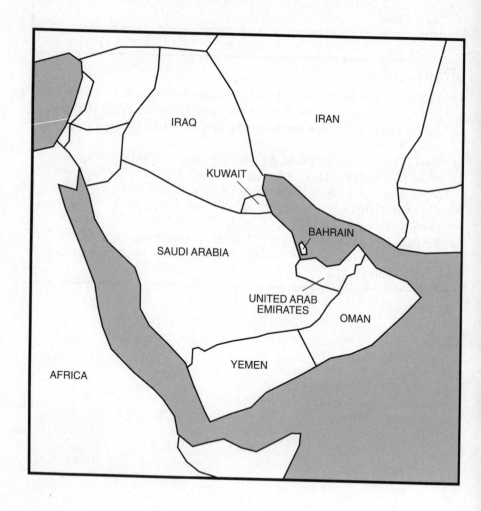

This group of countries comprises Bahrain, Kuwait, Oman, Saudi Arabia, United Arab Emirates, and Yemen. These countries have several cultural characteristics, which are presented here as a group of traits. Individual cultural differences are specified separately, country by country.

In this region you can expect business to cease five times a day for Islamic prayers. Non-muslim visitors need not face Mecca, but should do so out of respect. The ninth month of the Islamic calendar is called Ramadan and during this period all work stops before noon. Thursday or Friday is the Muslim day of rest. It is common in all these states to eat with the right hand, and not to eat pork or drink alcohol. Holidays in the Muslim world vary because it follows the Islamic calendar, which is based on the moon rather than the sun. Be sure to do your research before finalizing business schedules.

Common cultural characteristics

- Essentially, the people of these nations all come from the same tribe; therefore they have many common cultural characteristics.
- Expect people to be very conservative, especially in their external appearance.
- Don't expect religion in these nations to be separate from politics. Politics is religion and vice versa.
- Expect presents and gifts as a sign of appreciation.
- If you receive a gift you should give one in return.
- Expect the working hours to be regulated by prayers. Everyone goes home and businesses are closed during prayers, which occur five times a day. Every workplace has a small praying area or mosque.
- Alcoholic beverages are prohibited.
- Lunch is the main meal of the day.
- If you are served lamb (the most prestigious meat) or turkey you are being treated as very special.
- Women are treated significantly differently than in the West. They remain in the background, and are forbidden to drive or ride bicycles.

- Make appointments, but do not expect that the meeting will happen on time.
- Expect to do business with contracts, even though in earlier times one's word, a handshake, and the reading of the Koran represented a promise.
- Do not admire someone's personal property or children. If you do it could be considered as giving them the evil eye.
- During a business meeting, expect to be served coffee, tea, and later coffee again. The drinking cups are generally very small, and the server will continue to pour until you shake the cup forwards and backwards, signifying that you have had your fill. The second serving of coffee signals the end of the meeting, whether the contract is concluded or not.
- To keep wealth in the family, intra-family marriage is common, especially in Saudi Arabia. First-cousin marriages are most common, and relationships between families are very strong.
- Do not be surprised to find two men kissing and hugging. This is a sign of strong friendship and has no sexual connotation at all.
- Expect a higher-class person to kiss a lower-class person twice on the cheek. If the person is especially loyal or valuable, he or she will receive an additional kiss right after the second kiss.

Bahrain

Located on an island in the Persian Gulf, this small kingdom's petroleum production and processing account for about 80 percent of export receipts, 60 percent of government revenues, and 31 percent of GDP. Economic conditions have fluctuated with the changing fortunes of oil since 1985. Bahrain (meaning "two seas"), with its highly developed communication and transport facilities, is home to numerous multinational firms with business in the Gulf. Bahrain is also an important center for trade in textiles, metals, pottery and agricultural products. A large share of exports is made up of petroleum products made from imported crude. In its fight to become a regional banker Bahrain is allowing foreign companies in targeted industries greater freedom to sell and market their goods and services, especially financial and high-technology. Bahrain international airport handles about 24,000 flights annually. Mina Sulman and Sitra are the principal maritime ports. There is a free-trade zone at Mina Sulman that provides storage, cargo handling, repair, and assembly. They are connected to a major highway system, but there is no rail service.

Tips

✔ See the common cultural characteristics on pp. 191–2.

✔ Make appointments, but do not expect that the meeting will happen on time.
✔ Dress conservatively.
✔ Business cards are important.
✔ Expect Westerners to be greeted with a handshake.
✔ Expect to do business with contracts.
✔ Government business hours are Saturday through Thursday, 7 a.m.–1 p.m.
✔ Banking hours are Saturday through Wednesday 7:30 a.m.–12 p.m; Thursday 7:30 a.m.–11:00 a.m.
✔ Private industry hours are Saturday through Thursday 7 a.m.–12 p.m. and 2:30 p.m.–5 p.m.
✔ Women in Bahrain have the right to own and sell property, and to hold high, responsible positions. This is in contrast to women's diminished (public) status in other countries in the region.
✔ There is a very high literacy rate. Attendance at primary schools is 100 percent.
✔ Drinking alcohol is permitted.
✔ Remove your shoes prior to entering a mosque.
✔ Leave a tip of about 10 percent in restaurants if a service charge is not included.
✔ Tip taxis.

Traps

✗ See the common cultural characteristics on pp. 191–2.
✗ Don't drink, smoke, or eat in public during Ramadan.
✗ Don't wear shorts or swimming attire anywhere except poolside or at the beach.
✗ Don't photograph women without first obtaining their permission.

Kuwait

Kuwait is a small and relatively open economy with proven crude oil reserves of about 94 billion barrels—10 percent of world reserves. It is rebuilding its war-ravaged petroleum sector, which accounts for over half of GDP and over 90 percent of export and government revenue. As a result of income from oil, Kuwait has the second-highest per capita income (greater than $30,000 per year) in the world after the United Arab Republic.

Tips

✔ See the common cultural characteristics on pp. 191–2.

✔ Dress conservatively.

✔ You should present business cards.

✔ Handshakes are for the initial greeting of Westerners, but soon thereafter you will receive kisses on the cheek.

✔ Although the people are not formal and often use first names, they do like to use titles such as Doctor or Engineer.

✔ In spite of the high incomes, expect to find this country in serious need of social and economic development.

✔ The quality and reputation of your products is very important. Kuwaitis like to buy expensive goods.

✔ Local contacts (third parties) are vital to make introductions, interpret, and assist in making deals.

✔ Dishdash is the name of the long white robes worn by men.

✔ Giving high-priced gifts is very common.

✔ Loyalty is held in high regard.

✔ Expect the topics of conversation to be casual, such as where they spent their last vacation and what they purchased while away.

✔ Expect rice, lamb, and seafood to be the main dishes.

✔ Expect ceremonial coffee to be served frequently in small cups. If you don't want any more, shake the cup lightly when the waiter comes or he will continue to fill it.

✔ Tip about 10 percent.

✔ Expect a high hotel tax.

Traps

✗ See the common cultural characteristics on pp. 191–2.

✗ Be careful about political discussions. They often become diatribes about the conflict between Arabs, Iraqis, Palestinians, and Jews.

✗ Do not use your left hand for anything—not to pick up food, not to shake hands, not to hand anything over.

✗ Don't take liquor—they can arrest you.

Oman

The economic performance of Oman is closely tied to the fortunes of the oil industry. Petroleum accounts for more than 85 percent of export earnings, about 80 percent of government revenues, and roughly 40 percent of GDP. Oman has proved oil reserves of 4 billion barrels, equivalent to about twenty years' supply at the current rate of extraction. Agriculture is carried on at a subsistence level; the general population depends on imported food, and practically all consumer and capital goods are imported.

Tips

✔ See the common cultural characteristics on pp. 191–2.
✔ Handshakes are for the initial greeting of Westerners, but soon thereafter you will receive kisses on the cheek.
✔ Exchange business cards.
✔ Dress modestly and conservatively outside swimming/beach areas.
✔ Men should not wear shorts or sleeveless shirts.
✔ Women's dresses should cover the arms and knees.
✔ Although an Omani may wear a Western-style suit and tie when out of the country, he must wear his national dress (long white robe with turban) in Oman.
✔ If he is a sheik, government official, or tribal elder he will wear a ceremonial dagger.
✔ Expect long lunch hours during the heat of the day, 1.30–4.00 p.m.
✔ You should accept any refreshments offered by the host.
✔ Expect ceremonial coffee to be served frequently in small cups. If you don't want any more, shake the cup lightly when the waiter comes or he will continue to fill it.
✔ Don't be surprised if you are invited home.
✔ Take off your shoes prior to entering someone's home.
✔ Be respectful of age.
✔ Tip 10–15 percent in restaurants.

Traps

✗ See the common cultural characteristics on pp. 191–2.
✗ Do not use your left hand for anything—not to pick up food, not to shake hands, not to hand anything to anyone.
✗ Don't expose the soles of your feet or shoes—it's considered a grave insult.
✗ Alcoholic beverages are forbidden.
✗ Don't take photos of people unless you ask permission.

Saudi Arabia

Saudi Arabia, the largest Middle Eastern country, has some 26 percent of the world's reserves of petroleum and ranks as the largest exporter of petroleum. It plays a leading role in the Organization of Petroleum Exporting Countries (OPEC). Its petroleum sector accounts for roughly 75 percent of Saudi Arabia's budget revenues, 35 percent of GDP, and almost all export earnings. The government is encouraging private economic activity and attempting to turn the country into a modern industrial state that retains traditional Islamic values. Four million foreign workers play an important role in the Saudi economy, particularly in the oil and banking sectors. King Khalid international airport in Riyadh is the principle port for cargo. There are no free-trade zones. Its main maritime ports are at Jiddah and Dammam, and there are several others at Yanbu, Gizan, and Jubail. Saudi Arabia has the only rail system in the Arabian peninsula. The telecommunications network is modern, with extensive microwave and coaxial and fiber-optic cable systems. It is a member of the Global System for Mobile Communications (GSM) digital telephone network, allowing visitors to use GSM-connected cellular telephones within the country.

Tips

✔ See the common cultural characteristics on pp. 191–2.
✔ On greeting and saying goodbye, you may say "*salamu-ee-laykoom*," (phonetically), which translates roughly as "God be with you."
✔ Handshakes (with men) are for initial greetings of Westerners, but soon thereafter you will receive kisses on the cheek.
✔ Dress conservatively and modestly. Wear a coat and tie when first meeting a business associate.
✔ Women should wear clothes that cover the knees and elbows—such as loose-fitting dresses.
✔ Saudi Arabia has many restrictions for women.
✔ Make appointments but determine if the time is based on Western time or traditional Arab time, where the new day begins at sunset.
✔ The Saudi calendar is only 355 days because it is based on the moon and not the sun.
✔ Even though the Saudi lifestyle is generally laid back, you should be punctual for business meetings.
✔ Be prepared to exchange business cards—have them printed both in Arabic and your own language.
✔ Business hours are Monday through Friday; government: 7:30 a.m.–2:30 p.m.; Banks: 8 a.m.–noon and 5–8 p.m., commercial 8 a.m.–noon and 3–6 p.m.
✔ Don't rush into business. Saudis like to establish a relationship first.
✔ You should expect to exchange gifts.
✔ Don't be surprised if your hand is held by a man when standing in conversation or when walking. He's just being friendly.
✔ The phrase "*sha'allah*" may be used to respond to any question or statement. It means "God willing."
✔ Eat as much as you can when invited to a Saudi's home. It shows appreciation—take a second helping but after that you may graciously decline more.
✔ Tipping is not necessary or common, since service is usually included in the bill.

Traps

✗ See the common cultural characteristics on pp. 191–2.
✗ Do not use your left hand for anything—not to pick up food, not to shake hands, not to hand anything to anyone.
✗ Don't expose the soles of your feet or shoes—it's considered a grave insult.
✗ Don't wear shoes on carpeted areas.
✗ Alcoholic beverages and narcotics are forbidden.
✗ Don't take photos of people unless you ask permission.
✗ To refuse a gift is considered very offensive.
✗ Sharia ("path to follow"), based on the Koran (Islamic scripture), is the governing creed in the legal, political, religious, and everyday life of Saudi citizens. Islamic law is strictly enforced.

United Arab Emirates (UAE)

The UAE has an open economy and the highest per capita income in the world outside the nations of the Organization for Economic Cooperation and Development (OECD). This wealth is based on oil and gas, and the fortunes of the economy fluctuate with the prices of these commodities. Since 1973 the UAE has undergone a profound transformation, from an impoverished region of small desert principalities to a modern state with a high standard of living. At present levels of production, crude oil reserves should last for over 100 years.

Tips

✔ See the common cultural characteristics on pp. 191–2.
✔ The lifestyle and the people of this country are very similar to those of the other Gulf States, especially Kuwait.
✔ It is a country that is modernizing at a furious rate.
✔ Dress conservatively.
✔ Women should wear clothes that cover their elbows and knees and are loose-fitting.
✔ Don't be surprised to see women wearing black mask-like veils over their faces.
✔ The work week is Saturday morning until noon on Thursday.
✔ Government offices are only open in the morning.
✔ In addition to service charge, tip about 10 percent for exceptional service in restaurants.
✔ Do not tip taxi drivers.

Traps

✗ See the common cultural characteristics on pp. 191–2.
✗ Do not take pictures of military installations.
✗ Don't take photos of people unless you ask permission.
✗ Do not use your left hand for anything—not to pick up food, not to shake hands, not to hand anything over.
✗ Don't expose the soles of your feet or shoes—it's considered a grave insult.
✗ Alcoholic beverages and narcotics are forbidden.
✗ To refuse a gift is considered very offensive.
✗ Sharia ("path to follow"), based on the Koran (Islamic scripture), is the governing creed in the legal, political, religious, and everyday life of UAE citizens. Islamic law is strictly enforced.

Yemen

Yemen is considered among the least developed countries of the world. Whereas the northern city Sanaa is the political capital of a united Yemen, the southern city Aden, with its refinery and port facilities, is the economic and commercial capital. Future economic development depends heavily on Western-assisted development of promising oil resources. Former South Yemen's willingness to merge stemmed partly from the steady decline in Soviet economic support. The low level of domestic industry and agriculture has made northern Yemen dependent on imports for virtually all of its essential needs. Large trade deficits have been compensated for by remittances from Yemenis working abroad and by foreign aid. Once self-sufficient in food production, northern Yemen has become a major importer. Land once used for export crops—cotton, fruit, and vegetables—has been turned over to growing "qat," a mildly narcotic shrub chewed by Yemenis and which has no significant export market. Economic growth in former South Yemen has been constrained by a lack of incentives, partly stemming from centralized control over production decisions, investment allocation, and import choices.

Tips

✔ See the common cultural characteristics on pp. 191–2.
✔ Dress conservatively.
✔ Women should wear clothes that cover their elbows and knees and are loose-fitting.
✔ You should expect to see men carrying guns. They are generally not dangerous—they like to be well armed.

✔ Hire a guide when traveling.
✔ The tea and coffee are very sweet and often flavored with spices.
✔ Tip 10–15 percent to taxi drivers and in restaurants.

Traps

✗ See the common cultural characteristics on pp. 191–2.
✗ Don't drink the water or even brush your teeth with it.
✗ Do not take pictures of military installations.
✗ Don't take photos of people unless you ask permission.
✗ Do not use your left hand for anything—not to pick up food, not to shake hands, not to hand anything to anyone.
✗ Don't expose the soles of your feet or shoes—it's considered a grave insult.
✗ Alcoholic beverages and narcotics are forbidden.
✗ To refuse a gift is considered very offensive.
✗ Sharia ("path to follow"), based on the Koran (Islamic scripture), is the governing creed in the legal, political, religious, and everyday life of these citizens. Islamic law is strictly enforced.

CHAPTER SEVENTEEN

Africa

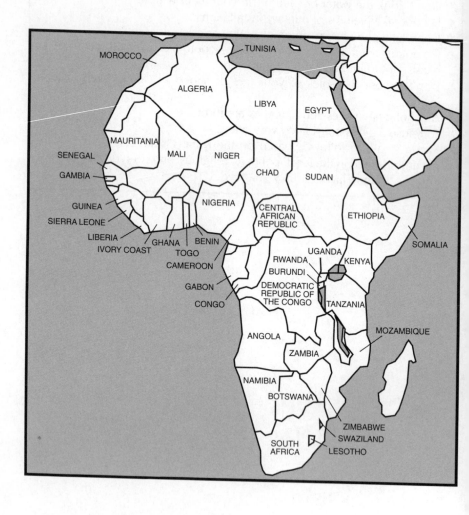

This, the second largest continent, is rich in natural resources and has always been the source of minerals and raw materials such as diamonds, cobalt, copper, gold, manganese, and uranium. But the nations of this great continent are just coming into their own as industrial traders.

More than 800 languages are spoken in Africa; therefore there are at least 800 different cultures. Nevertheless most business continues to take place in the urban areas and there, for the sake of business, the various cultures become fused.

While it is dangerous to generalize, this section is organized into five regions: North Africa, Central Africa, East Africa, West Africa, and Southern Africa. These groupings lend themselves to logical cultural statements that are useful to the foreign business person.

Do keep in mind that all the new countries were once old European colonies; therefore throughout Africa there are strong remnants of those cultures interlaced with the new. There are lingering sensitivities about colonization so be careful to avoid those discussions in conversation. In general, international politics and the positive achievements of the country you are visiting are good topics.

North Africa

This grouping of states has several cultural characteristics which can be presented as a group of traits. Individual protocol differences are specified separately. In this region you can expect business to cease five times a day for Islamic prayers. Non-Muslim visitors need not face Mecca, but should do so out of respect. The ninth month of the Islamic calendar is called Ramadan and during this period all work stops before noon. Thursday or Friday is the Muslim day of rest. It is common in all these states to eat with the right hand, but not to eat pork or drink alcohol.

Common cultural characteristics

- Make appointments, but do not try to schedule them when they fall on their national holidays.
- Don't hug. It is not accepted.
- Don't stare at people.
- Talk slowly and avoid being loud.
- Don't pass anything with the left hand.
- Don't show the soles of your feet.
- Do not be shy about asking your host to pose for a group photo, but avoid taking pictures of buildings, people or places without checking with your host.
- Don't be in a hurry in business meetings.
- Expect most business people in this region to be very trusting of foreigners.
- Do not attend a business meeting with alcohol on your breath.
- You should accept invitations for meals at home, which are often made at short notice.
- Respect that women sit before men.
- Respect their currencies.
- Avoid talking politics.
- Respect family traditions and practices.
- Be patient with bureaucratic hassles. It may take longer than expected to get your money out of the country.

Algeria

Oil and natural gas form the backbone of the Algerian economy. Hydrocarbons account for nearly all export receipts. The current government has continued efforts to admit private enterprise to the hydrocarbon industry, but has put reform, including privatization of some public-sector companies and an overhaul of the banking and financial system, on hold.

Tips

- ✔ See the Common cultural characteristics on p. 202.
- ✔ Dress as much like a local as possible. Wear dark-colored clothes.
- ✔ Make appointments.
- ✔ Knowledge of French or Arabic is helpful. Otherwise, hire an interpreter.
- ✔ Weekends begin Thursday afternoon and last through Friday.
- ✔ Holidays are based on the lunar calendar and vary from year to year.
- ✔ Don't expect friendships to form quickly.
- ✔ Expect relationships to proceed slowly and formally.

✔ Women should dress and behave modestly.
✔ Women should never travel alone.
✔ Tip about 15 percent.

Traps

✗ See the common cultural characteristics on p. 202.
✗ This country is going through a period of guerrilla warfare and is very dangerous. Foreigners must keep a low profile—don't draw attention to yourself in any way.
✗ Declare all your possessions on entry.
✗ Don't eat, drink, or smoke in public during Ramadan, the religious holiday.

Egypt

Egypt, the land of the pyramids, has one of the largest public sectors of all the North African states—most industrial plants are owned by the government. Over-regulation tends to hold back technical modernization and foreign investment. However, as Egypt and its Middle Eastern neighbors pursue regional peace, foreign companies are pitching in to help meet their economic development goals. The main airports are at Heliopolis, near Cairo, and at Alexandria. Egypt's marine ports are Port Said and Suez, and a free industrial zone is located in Northern Sinai, all of which are serviced by inland waterways. The telecommunications system is undergoing intensive upgrading.

Tips

✔ See the common cultural characteristics on p. 202.
✔ Time is less important in this country than it is for most foreigners; nevertheless, do make appointments.
✔ On greeting, expect a handshake, but also a hug and kiss on one or both cheeks.
✔ Dress coolly but conservatively—no shorts, tank tops, or short dresses.
✔ Exchange business cards.
✔ Register with the police within seven days of arrival. For a small fee most hotels will take care of it for you.
✔ Office hours are 8 a.m. to noon; lunch break is for 2–3 hours during which people usually go home, then return to the office and work 2 p.m.–6 p.m.
✔ This is a land of hospitable people.
✔ Expect the major meal of the day to be lunch. Business meetings often take place over lunch.

✔ Do not expect to be invited home for lunch, but if you are, take a gift and be aware that the meal will be served in one large bowl, from which everyone will eat.

✔ It is considered bad manners to decline an invitation; however, you can do so without offending if you make a good excuse.

✔ Egyptians do not like to say "no." Instead, expect that they will postpone things by saying "we will see."

✔ Be careful of gifts. Know the receiver well before offering a gift; otherwise it could be perceived as an attempt to bribe.

✔ Keep a pocketbook full of small change or notes ready to pay *baksheesh*, which is a small payment, like a tip, to get something done and is not considered wrong in the culture.

✔ Tip or pay *baksheesh* about 10 percent in restaurants and taxis.

✔ Take off your shoes before going into a mosque.

Traps

✗ See the Common cultural characteristics on p. 202.

✗ Declare all your possessions on entry.

✗ Don't eat, drink, or smoke in public during Ramadan, the religious holiday.

✗ Avoid discussions of religion, law, or politics in conversation.

✗ Ask before taking someone's photo.

Libya

Libya is one of the most ancient of countries—it existed before the Romans ruled it, and prior to that there were the Phoenicians, Carthaginians, and Greeks. Today it is an Islamic, socialist-oriented economy which depends primarily upon revenues from an oil sector that contributes practically all export earnings and about one-third of GDP. Per capita GDP of about $5,410 is the highest in Africa. Import restrictions and inefficient resource allocations have led to shortages of basic goods and foodstuffs; therefore Libya imports about 75 percent of its food requirements. Austerity budgets and a lack of trained technicians have undermined the government's ability to implement a number of planned infrastructure development projects. The non-oil manufacturing and construction sectors have expanded from processing mostly agricultural products to include petrochemicals, iron, steel, and aluminum.

Tips

✔ See the common cultural characteristics on p. 202.

✔ Dress coolly, but conservatively. The world's highest recorded temperature was here.
✔ Make appointments, even if your trading partner does not adhere to them.
✔ On greeting, expect a handshake, but also a hug and kiss on one or both cheeks.
✔ You should observe Arab social customs and conventions.
✔ Don't take neckties, but do wear long pants.
✔ Women should wear either pants or long dresses.
✔ If invited, take a gift for the host, not the hostess.
✔ Expect only men to be present when you are being entertained.
✔ Expect long, late lunch hours.
✔ Expect Libyan women to be very liberated. They hold many senior science and academic positions.
✔ Do not tip—a 10–20 percent service charge is generally added to your hotel and restaurant bills.

Traps

✗ See the common cultural characteristics on p. 202.
✗ An intense and difficult relationship still exists with the West, particularly the United States.
✗ Never turn down offers of food or drink. You don't have to eat or drink, but it is considered rude to say no.

Morocco

Morocco's economy has recovered moderately as a result of the resolution of a trade dispute with India over phosphoric acid sales, a rebound in textile sales to the European Union (EU), and lower prices for food imports. In 1992 the Moroccan government embarked on privatizing 112 state-owned companies. It now plans to shift its program into higher gear in a bid to reverse recent set-backs to the largely agricultural economy. The most important ports in terms of cargo volumes are Casablanca, Mohammedia, Jor Lasfa, and Safi. Morocco has a good telecommunications system and several international airports. Morocco is an associate member of the EU.

Tips

✔ See the common cultural characteristics on p. 202.
✔ Dress coolly, but conservatively.
✔ Make appointments, even if your trading partner does not adhere to them.

✔ On greeting, expect a handshake, but also a hug and kiss on one or both cheeks.

✔ Moroccans speak Berber and Arabic, but a little French will go a long way.

✔ Try some Arabic; they will like you for the effort. "Hello" is "*salaam wa laykoom;*" "goodbye" is "*ma'salaama;*" "please" is "*afak;*" "thank-you" is "*shukran;*" "how much" is "*suq;*" and "that's too much" is "*ghalee.*"

✔ Tip about 10 percent in restaurants, cafes, and taxis.

Traps

✗ See the common cultural characteristics on p. 202.

✗ Ask permission before taking pictures of anyone.

✗ Do not make public displays of affection.

Tunisia

This economy depends primarily on petroleum, phosphates, tourism, and exports of light manufactures. The economy came back strongly in the 1990s as a result of good harvests, continued export growth, and higher domestic investment. High unemployment forced Tunis to slow the pace of economic reform. Nonetheless, the government appears committed to implementing its International Monetary Fund-supported structural adjustment program and to servicing its foreign debt.

Tips

✔ See the Common cultural characteristics on p. 202.

✔ Dress coolly, but conservatively.

✔ Make appointments.

✔ On greeting, expect a handshake, but also a hug and kiss on one or both cheeks.

✔ Exchange business cards.

✔ Because of the high midday heat, do your business before 1 p.m. and after 5 p.m.

✔ Expect a long, late, lunch-hour siesta.

✔ Expect women to enjoy all political and civil rights, but not necessarily all social rights. For instance, they are not welcome in local bars or cafes—only tourist places.

✔ If when asked a question a Tunisian throws back his or her head, it means "no."

✔ Tipping is not required.

Traps

✗ See the common cultural characteristics on p. 202.
✗ Ask permission before taking pictures of anyone.
✗ Do not make public displays of affection.

Central Africa

This grouping of states has several cultural characteristics which can be presented as a group of traits. Individual cultural differences are specified separately, country by country.

Common cultural characteristics

- Expect to be greeted with a handshake; hugging is highly unusual.
- Remember that old people talk, sit, walk in, and walk out first.
- Make and keep appointments; be on time, but don't be surprised if appointments are canceled without notice. Be patient.
- Public holidays are observed by everyone, particularly independence days.
- Be careful to get names and pronunciation correct.
- Show respect to flags and national currencies. They are national symbols of remarkable respect.
- Stop walking when the national anthem is played.
- Don't mix pleasure with business.
- In conversation, don't betray a shared confidence, don't tease, don't curse, and don't pretend to know it all.
- For women, don't over-talk men.
- Check with your embassy to learn how to identify police, public transportation, etc.

Central African Republic

Geographically landlocked, this country is mainly a well-watered savanna plain, where more than 70 percent of this country's population live in the countryside; therefore subsistence agriculture, including forestry, is the backbone of the Central African Republic's economy. Agricultural products accounts for about 60 percent of export earnings and the diamond industry for 30 percent. Important constraints on economic development include the CAR's landlocked position, a poor transportation system, and a weak human resource base. Multilateral and bilateral development assistance, particularly from France, plays a major role in providing capital for new investment.

Tips

✔ See the common cultural characteristics on p. 207.
✔ On entering a room, you should expect to shake hands with everyone.
✔ Dress coolly, but conservatively.
✔ Don't wear shorts; wear loose-fitting long garments.
✔ Expect a very formal business environment.
✔ Christianity is the dominant religion.
✔ Tip about 10 percent.

Traps

✗ See the common cultural characteristics on p. 207.
✗ Don't take pictures of people or military installations without asking.

Chad

The climate, geographic location, and lack of infrastructure and natural resources make Chad one of the most underdeveloped countries in the world. Its economy has been burdened by the ravages of civil war, conflict with Libya, drought, and food shortages. Over 80 percent of the workforce is employed in subsistence farming and fishing. Industry is based almost entirely on the processing of agricultural products, including cotton, sugar cane, and cattle. Chad is highly dependent on foreign aid. Oil companies are exploring areas north of Lake Chad and in the Doba basin in the south.

Tips

✔ See the Common cultural characteristics on p. 207.
✔ Expect everything to stop five times a day for prayers.
✔ Make appointments.
✔ Exchange business cards.
✔ Always remove your sunglasses when speaking to someone.
✔ Dress conservatively.
✔ Women should not wear shorts, pants, or sleeveless shirts.
✔ Men should wear long pants.
✔ Tipping is not expected in restaurants. Exception are those that are French, where 10 percent is fair.

Traps

✗ See the common cultural characteristics on p. 207.
✗ Carry your passport with you at all times.
✗ Never eat with your left hand.
✗ Never motion your hand toward someone with a gesture that looks like you are turning a door knob—this is the worst insult possible in Chad.

Congo

Congo's economy is a mixture of village agriculture and handicrafts, a beginning industrial sector based largely on oil, supporting services, and a government characterized by budget problems and overstaffing. A reform program supported by the International Monetary Fund (IMF) and World Bank ran into difficulties because of problems in changing to a democratic political regime and a heavy debt-servicing burden. Oil has supplanted forestry as the mainstay of the economy, providing about two-thirds of government revenues and exports. The government, responding to pressure from businessmen and the electorate, is reducing bureaucracy and government regulation.

Tips

✔ See the common cultural characteristics on p. 207.
✔ The people are very friendly.
✔ Wear light-weight clothing because to is often hot and humid.
✔ Don't be disappointed if things don't go exactly according to schedule.
✔ Tip 10 percent in restaurants and hotels.
✔ Don't tip porters.

Traps

✗ See the common cultural characteristics on p. 207.
✗ Don't confuse the Congo (previously ruled by the French) with Belgian Congo, which is now called Democratic Republic of the Congo (Zaire).
✗ Always ask permission before taking photographs.

Democratic Republic of the Congo (Zaire)

This country is not ready for business until it is over its genocidal war- ring. Zaire's hyper-inflation, large government deficit, and plunging min- eral production have made the country one of the world's poorest. Most formal transactions are conducted in hard currency as indigenous bank-notes have lost almost all value, and a barter economy now flourishes in all but the largest cities. The government has not been able to meet its financial obligations to the International Monetary Fund (IMF) or put in place the financial measures advocated by the IMF. Although short-term prospects for improvement are dim, improved political stability would boost the country's long-term potential to exploit its vast wealth of mineral and agricultural resources effectively.

Tips

✔ See the common cultural characteristics on p. 207.
✔ Register at your local embassy immediately on arrival.
✔ Exchange business cards.
✔ Dress conservatively
✔ Men should not wear short pants.
✔ Women should dress modestly.
✔ Tip about 10 percent in restaurants.

Traps

✗ See the common cultural characteristics on p. 207.
✗ Don't be too confused by the name of this country. Today it is called the Democratic Republic of the Congo (formerly Zaire and the Belgian Congo). The Republic of the Congo is just across the Congo river.
✗ Always ask permission before taking photographs.

Gabon

Gabon, located in Central Africa along the equator, is rich in natural resources and is one of the most secure and stable countries on the continent. The economy, previously dependent on timber and manganese, is now dominated by the oil sector. In 1981–85, oil accounted for about 45 percent of GDP, 80 percent of export earnings, and 65 percent of government revenues. The high oil prices of the early 1980s contributed to a substantial increase in per capita national income, stimulated domestic demand, reinforced migration from rural to urban areas, and raised the level of real wages to among the highest in sub-Saharan Africa.

Tips

✔ See the common cultural characteristics on p. 207.
✔ The population includes more than forty separate tribal groups with distinct customs and languages.

✔ Shake hands.
✔ Exchange business cards.
✔ Including a tie in your wardrobe is unnecessary—it is a very hot place.
✔ Take a jacket; several of the better restaurants require them.
✔ Carry your passport and health certificate.
✔ Tip about 10 percent unless it is included in your bills.

Traps

✗ See the common cultural characteristics on p. 207.
✗ Always ask permission before taking photographs.

East Africa

This grouping of states has several cultural characteristics which can be presented as a group of traits. Individual cultural differences are specified separately, country by country.

Common cultural characteristics

■ Make appointments and be on time.
■ Be careful of protocol procedures, proper addresses, and titles. When in doubt consult your embassy.
■ Avoid complimenting business associates. Compliments are not popular.
■ Don't try to impress your business contacts. Avoid limousines and chauffeurs.
■ Honesty and truth are highly valued as a basis of a good business relationship.
■ Be respectful of tribal traditions. Check with your host when in doubt.
■ Respect national flags. To do otherwise is a reminder of colonial times.
■ Expect to be served food and drink without being asked. Graciously accept that which is served. It is a sign of appreciation.
■ Avoid dominating the conversation.
■ Avoid interrupting during a conversation.
■ Always ask permission before taking photographs.
■ When invited for a meal, do not offer to share or pay the bill.
■ Don't hug when meeting your host; use the handshake.
■ Make sure you don't smell of alcohol at business meetings.
■ Never disguise your full identity.
■ Don't rest your feet on tables and chairs–it is a sign of bad manners.
■ Don't be too inquisitive.

Burundi

This country is not ready for business until it is over its genocidal warring. A landlocked, resource-poor country in an early stage of economic development, Burundi is predominately agricultural, with only a few basic industries. Its economic health depends on the coffee crop, which accounts for an average of 90 percent of foreign-exchange earnings each year. The ability to pay for imports therefore continues to rest largely on the vagaries of the climate and the international coffee market. As part of its economic reform agenda, Burundi launched, with International Monetary Fund (IMF) and World Bank support, an effort to diversify its agricultural exports and attract foreign investment in industry. Several state-owned coffee companies have been privatized.

Tips

✔ See the Common cultural characteristics on p. 211.
✔ Expect ethnic tensions.
✔ Do not expect anyone to speak English. You can get by with French or hire an interpreter.
✔ You should expect a two-hour lunch break, generally from about noon until 2 p.m.
✔ Tip 10–15 percent, if this is not included in the bill.

Traps

✗ See the Common cultural characteristics on p. 211.

Ethiopia

With the independence of Eritrea in 1993, Ethiopia continues to face difficult economic problems as one of the poorest and least developed countries in Africa, yet it seems to be on the way to recovery after more than two decades of war. Its economy is based on subsistence agriculture, which accounts for about 45 percent of GDP, 90 percent of exports, and 80 percent of total employment; coffee generates 60 percent of export earnings. The manufacturing sector is heavily dependent on inputs from the agricultural sector. Over 90 percent of large-scale industry, but less than 10 percent of agriculture, is state run; the government is considering selling off a portion of state-owned plants. In 1991 the lack of law and order, particularly in the south, interfered with economic development and growth. Since 1992, because of some easing of civil strife and aid from the outside world, the economy has substantially improved.

Tips

✔ See the Common cultural characteristics on p. 211.
✔ Register at your embassy on arrival.
✔ Wear comfortable, conservative clothes.
✔ Take a coat and tie. They may be needed in the better restaurants.
✔ Exchange business cards.
✔ Expect business to be conducted on standard time, using the Western calendar, even though their local calendar is different. They use the pre-Julian, which has twelve months of thirty days (the remaining five or six days form a thirteenth month), and their new year begins on 11 September.
✔ Although business is conducted in English, more than seventy languages and 200 dialects are spoken in this country.
✔ Address people using Mr., Mrs., or Miss before their first name.
✔ Find out when the rainy season begins and ends (usually April and May), and if you go during that period prepare for mud.
✔ Expect long lunch hours, 12 noon–2 p.m.
✔ Tip about 10 percent.

Traps

✗ See the Common cultural characteristics on p. 211.
✗ Carry your papers with you at all times.

Kenya

Kenya's 3.6 percent annual population growth rate—one of the highest in the world—presents a serious problem for the country's economy. GDP growth in the near term has kept slightly ahead of population, averaging 4.9 percent annually. Undependable weather conditions and a shortage of arable land hamper long-term growth in agriculture, the leading economic sector. There are international airports at Nairobi, Mombassa, and Kisumu, as well as several export-processing zones. Telecommunications are considered among the best in Africa.

Tips

✔ See the Common cultural characteristics on p. 211.
✔ You should pronounce the name of the country as KHEN-yah, not KEEN-yah; the latter is the colonial pronunciation.
✔ You should expect a residual British culture.
✔ Take a coat and tie, particularly when doing business in Nairobi and its better hotels and restaurants.

✔ Business hours are: government: Monday through Friday, 8 a.m.–1 p.m., 2 p.m.–5 p.m.; Banks: Monday through Friday, 9:30 a.m.–3 p.m. Commerce: Monday through Friday, 8 a.m.–Noon, 2 p.m.–6 p.m.
✔ Tip waiters and taxi drivers 10 percent.
✔ Find out the dates of the rainy season, which begins and ends usually April and May. If you go during that period prepare for mud.

Traps

✗ See the Common cultural characteristics on p. 211.
✗ Don't photograph military installations.

Rwanda

This country is not ready for business until it is over its genocidal warring. Almost 50 percent of Rwanda's GDP comes from the agricultural sector; coffee and tea make up 80–90 percent of total exports. The amount of fertile land is limited, however, and deforestation and soil erosion have created problems. The industrial sector in Rwanda is small, contributing only 17 percent to GDP. Manufacturing focuses mainly on the processing of agricultural products. The Rwandan economy remains dependent on coffee exports and foreign aid.

Tips

✔ See the Common cultural characteristics on p. 211.
✔ Check in with your embassy immediately.
✔ Conduct business in one of the better hotels.

Traps

✗ See the Common cultural characteristics on p. 211.
✗ Don't photograph military installations.

Somalia

This country is not ready for business until it is over its warring clan conflicts. One of the world's poorest and least developed countries, Somalia has few resources. Moreover, much of the economy has been devastated by the civil war. Agriculture is the most important sector, with livestock accounting for about 40 percent of GDP and about 65 percent of export earnings. Nomads and semi-nomads who are dependent upon livestock for their livelihoods make up more than half of the population. Crop production generates only 10 percent of GDP and employs about 20 percent of the workforce. The main export crop is bananas; sugar, sorghum, and corn are grown for the domestic market. The small industrial sector is based on the processing of agricultural products and accounts for less than 10 percent of GDP. Somalia is the only non-Arab member of the League of Arab Nations.

Tips

✔ See the Common cultural characteristics on p. 211.
✔ Wear conservative Western dress—men should not wear shorts.
✔ Shake hands.
✔ Tip 10 percent.

Traps

✗ See the Common cultural characteristics on p. 211.
✗ Don't photograph military installations.

Sudan

Sudan is not ready for business until it is over its civil war. The country is buffeted by civil war, chronic political instability, adverse weather, high inflation, a drop in remittances from abroad, and counterproductive economic policies. The economy is dominated by government entities that account for more than 70 percent of new investment. The private sector's main areas of activity are agriculture and trading, with most private industrial investment predating 1980. The economy's base is agriculture, which employs 80 percent of the workforce. Industry mainly processes agricultural items. In 1990 the International Monetary Fund (IMF) took the unusual step of declaring Sudan noncooperative because of its nonpayment of arrears to the Fund. Despite subsequent government efforts to implement reforms urged by the IMF and the World Bank, the economy remains stagnant as entrepreneurs lack the incentive to take economic risks.

Tips

✔ See the Common cultural characteristics on p. 211.
✔ On arrival, immediately check in with your embassy and register with the police.

✔ Follow currency regulations.
✔ Carry your passport and other papers with you at all times.
✔ Do not wear shorts.
✔ Women should not go bare shouldered.
✔ Do not tip unless it is not added as a service charge to your bill (which it will almost certainly be).

Traps

✘ See the Common cultural characteristics on p. 211.
✘ Don't photograph military installations.

Tanzania

Tanzania is one of the poorest countries in the world. The economy is heavily dependent on agriculture, which accounts for about 58 percent of GDP, provides 85 percent of exports, and employs 90 percent of the workforce. Industry accounts for 8 percent of GDP, and is mainly limited to processing agricultural products and light consumer goods. An economic recovery program announced in the mid-1980s has generated notable increases in agricultural production and financial support for the program by bilateral donors. The World Bank, the International Monetary Fund (IMF), and bilateral donors have provided funds to rehabilitate Tanzania's deteriorated economic infrastructure. Subsequent growth featured a pickup in industrial production and a substantial increase in output of minerals, led by gold. Inland waterways and two railways connect the country's several air and maritime ports.

Tips

✔ See the Common cultural characteristics on p. 211.
✔ You should dress conservatively—no shorts for men or women except if you go on safari.
✔ Currency control is important, so declare your money and keep your receipts.
✔ You should expect a residual German culture.
✔ Shake hands.
✔ Exchange business cards.
✔ Tipping is not required, but do tip about 10 percent in good restaurants.

Traps

✗ See the Common cultural characteristics on p. 211.

✗ Don't photograph military installations.

Uganda

Uganda has substantial natural resources, including fertile soils, regular rainfall, and sizable mineral deposits of copper and cobalt. After independence in 1962 the economy was devastated by widespread political instability, mismanagement, and civil war, which kept Ugandans poor, with a per capita income of about $300. In recent years, the economy has turned in a solid performance based on continued investment in the rehabilitation of infrastructure, improved incentives for production and exports, and gradually improving domestic security. Agriculture is the most important sector of the economy, employing over 80 percent of the workforce. Coffee is the major export crop and accounts for the bulk of export revenues.

Tips

✔ See the Common cultural characteristics on p. 211.

✔ Currency control is important, so declare your money and keep your receipts.

✔ Carry your passport and other papers, such as health certificates, with you at all times.

✔ Shake hands.

✔ Exchange business cards.

✔ Make appointments but don't expect things to happen on time.

✔ You should expect most Ugandans to speak English.

✔ Expect to be entertained in restaurants.

✔ If invited to a home, take a gift.

✔ Tip 10 percent unless it's included as a service charge.

Traps

✗ See the Common cultural characteristics on p. 211.

✗ Don't photograph military installations.

West Africa

This grouping of states has several cultural characteristics which can be presented as a group of traits. Individual cultural differences are specified separately, country by country.

Common cultural characteristics

- Greetings by handshake, not hugs, are the order of the day.
- Use both hands when shaking hands with old people, i.e. left hand grasps the right wrist or forearm as you shake with the right hand.
- Expect a flexible schedule with regard to appointments. Even confirmed appointments can be canceled at the last minute, even without your consent.
- Don't be surprised if business meetings are held in the home.
- Carry a gift when you are invited home.
- Cursing is considered rude and can alienate your business contacts.
- Be straightforward–honesty pays well in this region.
- Don't wear short pants to an office or home meeting.
- Old people are highly respected.
- Expect old people to be seated first.
- Expect women to be first in walking, entering, sitting and exiting.
- Accept whatever is offered—it is a way of expressing appreciation and it is considered impolite not to accept.
- Wash your hands before a meal in anticipation of eating finger food.
- Don't lick your fingers or make noise when eating.
- Pay a lot of attention to family eating styles and the order in which people eat.
- Don't ask your host to split the bill. In these countries when they invite, they pay. When you invite, you pay. No half-half.
- Refrain from discussing political matters.
- Always ask permission before taking photographs and don't photograph military installations.

Benin

Benin, until recently, was one of the least developed countries in the world; however, the discovery of 4 billion cubic meters of gas has stimulated a new outlook. With a stable democracy in place, the government is undertaking to improve its poorly developed infrastructure and make sweeping market-oriented reforms. Agriculture accounts for about 35 percent of GDP, employs about 60 percent of the labor force, and generates a major share of foreign-exchange earnings. Port facilities and the international airport near Cortonou are being upgraded to serve as a hub for Benin's many landlocked neighbors.

Tips

✔ See the Common cultural characteristics on p. 218.
✔ Expect a greater equality of sexes here than in other countries of the region.
✔ Some French language will be helpful in business dealings.
✔ Tip about 10 percent.

Traps

✗ See the Common cultural characteristics on p. 218.

Cameroon

Because of its offshore oil resources, Cameroon has one of the highest per capita incomes in tropical Africa. Still it faces many of the same serious problems as other underdeveloped countries, such as political instability, a top-heavy civil service, and a generally unfavorable climate for business enterprise. With support from the International Monetary Fund (IMF) and World Bank, the Cameroon government has begun to introduce reforms designed to spur business investment, increase efficiency in agriculture, and recapitalize the nation's banks.

Tips

✔ See the Common cultural characteristics on p. 218.
✔ Always carry your passport and other papers.
✔ Currency control is important, so declare your money and keep your receipts.
✔ Topics of conversation might include sports, particularly football (soccer) —their team, known as the Indomitable Lions, made it to the World Cup quarter finals in 1990.

Traps

✗ See the Common cultural characteristics on p. 218.

The Gambia

Although very politically stable, it has no important mineral or other natural resources and has a limited agricultural base. It is one of the world's poorest countries. About 75 percent of the population is engaged in crop production and livestock raising, which contribute 30 percent to GDP. Small-scale manufacturing activity—processing peanuts, fish, and hides—accounts for less than 10 percent of GDP. Tourism is a growing industry. The Gambia imports one-third of its food, all fuel, and most manufactured goods. Exports are concentrated on peanut products (about 75 percent of the total value).

Tips

- ✔ See the Common cultural characteristics on p. 218.
- ✔ Always carry your passport and other papers.
- ✔ Currency control is important, so declare your money and keep your receipts.
- ✔ Always pass things with your right hand.
- ✔ Tip 10 percent.

Tips and Traps

- ✗ See the Common cultural characteristics on p. 218.

Ghana

Supported by substantial international assistance, Ghana has been implementing a steady economic rebuilding program since 1983, including moves toward privatization and relaxation of government controls. Ghana is heavily dependent on cocoa, gold, and timber exports, and is encouraging foreign trade and investment. Ghana opened a stock exchange in 1990.

Tips

- ✔ See the Common cultural characteristics on p. 218.
- ✔ Always carry your passport and other papers.
- ✔ Currency control is important, so declare your money and keep your receipts.
- ✔ Never pass things or eat with the left hand.
- ✔ Don't wear shorts.
- ✔ You should shake hands when greeting.

> ✔ Sport is a good topic of conversation, particularly boxing—Ghana has had six world champions. They also like football (soccer).

Traps

✗ See the Common cultural characteristics on p. 218.

Guinea

Although it possesses many natural resources and considerable potential for agricultural development, Guinea is one of the poorest countries in the world, yet, thanks to its rich mineral and other natural resources, is now one of the few African nations where the standard of living is on the rise. The agricultural sector contributes about 40 percent to GDP and employs more than 80 percent of the workforce, while industry accounts for 27 percent of GDP. Guinea possesses over 25 percent of the world's bauxite reserves, as well as excellent diamonds, uranium, gold, and manganese. Exports of bauxite and alumina accounted for about 70 percent of total exports in 1989.

Tips

✔ See the Common cultural characteristics on p. 218.
✔ This former French colony should not be confused with Guinea-Bissau or Equatorial Guinea.
✔ Take plenty of rain gear if you visit during the rainy season.
✔ Expect long lunch hours—from somewhat before noon until 3 p.m.
✔ Always carry your passport and other papers.
✔ Currency control is important, so declare your currency and keep your receipts.
✔ Typically there is no need to tip because a service charge is added.

Traps

✗ See the Common cultural characteristics on p. 218.

Ivory Coast

This country's commodity-driven economy depends on the coffee and cocoa market. However, a plan supported by the International Monetary Fund (IMF) is underway to privatize and curb government spending. Major air and maritime ports are near Abidjan and San Pedro. Telecommunications are well developed by African standards.

Tips

✔ See the Common cultural characteristics on p. 218.
✔ Always carry your passport (or a copy) and other papers.
✔ Currency control is important, so declare your currency and keep your receipts.
✔ This country has more than 60 different ethnic groups.
✔ Expect Ivorians to prefer the country be called by its French name, *Côte d'Ivoire*.
✔ Tip 15 percent if the service charge is not already added to the bill.

Traps

✗ See the Common cultural characteristics on p. 218.

Liberia

This country is not ready for business until it is over its civil warring and other conflicts. Political instability threatens prospects for economic reconstruction and repatriation of some 750,000 Liberian refugees who have fled to neighboring countries. The political impasse between the interim government and rebel leaders prevented restoration of normal economic life, including the re-establishment of a strong central government with effective economic development programs. Richly endowed with water, mineral resources, forests, and a climate favorable to agriculture, Liberia is a producer and exporter of basic products. Manufacturing, mainly foreign-owned, is small in scope. Liberia is also known for having few or no restrictions (almost no inspection requirements nor safety standards) for registering merchant ships.

Tips

✔ See the Common cultural characteristics on p. 218.
✔ Always carry your passport (or a copy) and other papers.
✔ Currency control is important, so declare your currency and keep your receipts.
✔ Tip about 10 percent.

Traps

✗ See the Common cultural characteristics on p. 218.
✗ Don't drink the water.

Mali

Landlocked Mali is the largest country in West Africa, but among the poorest countries in the world. About 70 percent of its land area is desert or semi-desert. Economic activity is largely confined to the riverine area irrigated by the Niger. About 10 percent of the population live as nomads and some 80 percent of the labor force is engaged in agriculture and fishing. Industrial activity is concentrated on processing farm commodities. In consultation with international lending agencies, the government has adopted a structural adjustment program, aiming at annual GDP growth of 4.6 percent, inflation of no more than 2.5 percent on average, and a substantial reduction in the external current-account deficit.

Tips

✔ See the Common cultural characteristics on p. 218.
✔ Always carry your passport (or a copy) and other papers.
✔ Currency control is important, so declare your currency and keep your receipts.
✔ Expect the French language to be dominant and little English to be spoken.
✔ Malians are fun and friendly people.
✔ Dress comfortably for the heat, but don't wear shorts.
✔ Greet with a handshake.
✔ Be respectful of elders.
✔ Tip about 10 percent, but not to taxi drivers.

Traps

✗ See the Common cultural characteristics on p. 218.
✗ Don't use your left hand to eat or pass anything—it is considered rude.

Mauritania

A majority of the population still depends on agriculture and livestock for its livelihood, even though most of the nomads and many subsistence farmers were forced into the cities by recurrent droughts. Mauritania has extensive deposits of iron ore, which account for almost 50 percent of total exports. The nation's coastal waters are among the richest fishing areas in the world. The country's first deep-water port opened near Nouakchott in 1986. The government has begun the second stage of an economic reform program in consultation with the World Bank, the International Monetary Fund (IMF), and major donor countries.

Tips

✔ See the Common cultural characteristics on p. 218.
✔ Always carry your passport (or a copy) and other papers.
✔ Currency control is important, so declare your currency and keep your receipts.
✔ Expect the French language to be dominant and little English to be spoken.
✔ Be prepared for the unspoken caste system of this country.
✔ Dress conservatively. Dress comfortably for the heat, but don't wear shorts.
✔ Greet with a handshake.
✔ Be respectful of elders.
✔ Register with your embassy immediately.
✔ Tip waiters and taxi drivers about 10 percent.

Traps

✗ See the Common cultural characteristics on p. 218.
✗ Don't use your left hand to eat or pass anything—it is considered rude.

Niger

Niger is one of fourteen landlocked countries in Africa and the world's sixth largest uranium producer. The economy also depends heavily on exploitation of these large uranium deposits. About 90 percent of the population is engaged in farming and stock raising, activities that generate almost half the national income. France is a major customer, while Germany, Japan, and Spain also make regular purchases.

Tips

✔ See the Common cultural characteristics on p. 218.
✔ This is a hot country so dress in loose and comfortable clothes.
✔ Do not wear shorts.
✔ Women especially should dress modestly—no halter tops and cover your shoulders.
✔ Don't use your left hand to eat or pass things.
✔ You should pronounce Niger "nee Jair."
✔ Currency control is important, so declare your currency and keep your receipts.
✔ Expect the French language to be dominant and little English to be spoken.
✔ Tip about 10 percent.

Traps

✗ See the Common cultural characteristics on p. 218.

Nigeria

This country is not ready for business until it has control and becomes a civil society. Crime and scams are a problem in Nigeria, and it is the world's major drug-smuggling and money-laundering center. Although Nigeria is Africa's leading oil-producing country, it remains very poor. Lagos, the capital, has set ambitious targets for expanding oil-production capacity and is offering foreign companies more attractive investment incentives. Government efforts to reduce Nigeria's dependence on oil exports and to sustain non-inflationary growth, however, have fallen short of their aims because of inadequate new investment funds.

Tips

✔ See the Common cultural characteristics on p. 218.
✔ Currency control is important, so declare your currency and keep your receipts.
✔ Always carry your passport (or a copy) and other papers.
✔ Dress conservatively.
✔ Dress comfortably for the heat, but don't wear shorts.
✔ Greet with a handshake.
✔ Be respectful of elders.
✔ Register with your embassy immediately.
✔ Most restaurants add a service charge; tip 10 percent if they don't.
✔ Tip taxi drivers about 10 percent.

Traps

✗ See the Common cultural characteristics on p. 218.
✗ Be prepared to pay bribes everywhere you go, even at road blocks—a pack of Western cigarettes will often do. If you don't pay you may be delayed or refused passage.
✗ Don't use your left hand to eat or pass things.

Senegal

This is a country ready to do business. It has been stable since independence and the government has relaxed trade and investment restrictions.

The agricultural sector accounts for about 12 percent of GDP and provides employment for about 80 percent of the labor force. About 40 percent of the total cultivated land is used to grow peanuts, an important export crop. Another principal economic resource is fishing, which brought in about 23 percent of total foreign-exchange earnings in 1990. Mining is dominated by the extraction of phosphate, but production has faltered because of reduced worldwide demand for fertilizers in recent years. Over the past ten years tourism has become increasingly important to the economy. There is an international airport and a free-trade zone at Dakar, the capital, as well as the second-largest maritime port in West Africa. Senegal enjoys most-favored nation trading status with the U.S.A. under the Generalized System of Preferences, and reduced rates with the European Union under the Lome Convention.

Tips

✔ See the Common cultural characteristics on p. 218.
✔ This is a hot country, so dress comfortably but conservatively.
✔ There is a growing population of well-educated people. Senegal is considered the center of African learning. The University of Dakar attracts students from all over the world.
✔ French is the official language.
✔ Expect lunch to be from about noon to 3 p.m.
✔ Tip about 10 percent if a service charge is not added to your bill.
✔ Do not tip taxi drivers.

Traps

✗ See the Common cultural characteristics on p. 218.
✗ Be prepared to pay bribes everywhere you go, even at road blocks—a pack of Western cigarettes will often do. If you don't pay you may be delayed or refused passage.
✗ Be careful of night travel as there is some street crime.

Sierra Leone

Recent stabilization of the government indicates a turnaround for this country and it seems to be ready to do business. However, the economic and social infrastructure of this country is not well developed. Subsistence agriculture dominates the economy, generating about one-third of GDP and employing about two-thirds of the working population. Manufacturing, which accounts for roughly 10 percent of GDP, consists mainly of the processing of raw materials and of light manufacturing for the domestic market. Diamond mining provides an important source of hard currency. The economy suffers from high unemployment, rising inflation, large trade deficits, and a growing dependency on foreign assistance. Liberian rebels in southern and eastern Sierra Leone have severely strained the economy and have undermined efforts to institute economic reforms.

Tips

✔ See the Common cultural characteristics on p. 218.
✔ Currency control is important, so declare your currency and keep your receipts.
✔ Always carry your passport (or a copy) and other papers.
✔ Dress conservatively.
✔ A service charge is usually added to your bill; if not, tip about 10 percent.
✔ Taxi drivers are not normally tipped.

Traps

✗ See the Common cultural characteristics on p. 218.
✗ When traveling be careful of land mines.

Togo

The economy is heavily dependent on subsistence agriculture, which accounts for about 33 percent of GDP and provides employment for 78 percent of the labor force. Primary agricultural exports are cocoa, coffee, and cotton, which together account for about 30 percent of total export earnings. Togo is self-sufficient in basic foodstuffs when harvests are normal. In the industrial sector phosphate mining is by far the most important activity, with phosphate exports accounting for about 40 percent of total foreign-exchange earnings. Togo serves as a regional commercial and trade center. The government, with International Monetary Fund (IMF) and World Bank support, has been implementing a number of economic reform measures to encourage foreign investment and bring revenues in line with expenditures.

Tips

✔ See the Common cultural characteristics on p. 218.
✔ Currency control is important, so declare your currency and keep your receipts.
✔ Always carry your passport (or a copy) and other papers.

✔ Dress conservatively.
✔ Expect a very young population of friendly people.
✔ A service charge is usually added to your bill; if not, tip about 10 percent.
✔ Taxi drivers are not normally tipped.

Traps

✗ See the Common cultural characteristics on p. 218.

Southern Africa

This grouping of states has several cultural characteristics which can be presented as a group of traits. Individual cultural differences are specified separately, country by country.

Common cultural characteristics

■ Make appointments and be on time, but remember to observe public holidays.
■ Don't hug when greeting—use the handshake.
■ In case you are met by both husband and wife, shake hands with the man first, then the wife.
■ Give old people greater respect.
■ Use both hands when shaking hands with old people, i.e. left hand grasps the right wrist or forearm as you shake with the right hand.
■ Remove your hat when talking to old people, seniors, and government officials.
■ Check with your embassy about the titles of leaders, chiefs, and other seniors.
■ Don't ask people what tribe they belong to.
■ Avoid smelling of liquor in public or at business meetings.
■ When invited for a meal pay great attention to eating instructions and habits.
■ Wash your hands before a meal–you may need to eat with your fingers.
■ Unless you are left handed, always use the right hand to greet others, to receive, or give something.
■ For women, do not cross your legs; use minimal eye contact.
■ You should expect to exchange gifts.
■ In conversation, avoid teasing, gossiping, rumors, and discussions of politics.
■ As a guest, don't refuse drink, fruit, or food when it is offered. It's polite to offer and to accept.
■ Be patient about government bureaucracy.

■ Don't attempt to bribe.
■ Always ask permission before taking photographs and don't photograph military installations.

Angola

This country, still feeling the effects of war, is approaching readiness to do business in the global economy. Subsistence agriculture provides the main livelihood for 80–90 percent of the population, but accounts for less than 15 percent of GDP. Oil production is vital to the economy, contributing about 60 percent of GDP. For the long run, Angola has the advantage of rich natural resources in addition to oil, notably gold, diamonds, and arable land.

Tips

✔ See the Common cultural characteristics on pp. 228–9.
✔ Follow to the letter Angolan laws and regulations.
✔ Currency control is important, so declare your currency and keep your receipts.
✔ Always carry your passport (or a copy) and other papers.
✔ Dress conservatively. The safari suit is standard dress.

Traps

✗ See the Common cultural characteristics on pp. 228–9.
✗ Don't tip! It is illegal.

Botswana

The economy has historically been based on cattle raising and crops. Agriculture today provides a livelihood for more than 80 percent of the population, but produces only about 50 percent of food needs. The mining industry, mostly on the strength of diamonds, has gone from generating 25 percent of GDP in 1980 to 50 percent in 1991. No other sector has experienced such growth, especially not agriculture, which is plagued by erratic rainfall and poor soils.

Tips

✔ See the Common cultural characteristics on pp. 228–9.
✔ Follow to the letter Botswanan laws and regulations.

- ✔ Currency control is important, so declare your currency and keep your receipts.
- ✔ Always carry your passport (or a copy) and other papers.
- ✔ Dress conservatively. The safari suit is standard dress.
- ✔ Take a jacket or sweater—it can get chilly in the evening.
- ✔ Tip about 10 percent.

Traps

✗ See the Common cultural characteristics on pp. 228–9.

Lesotho

Small, landlocked, mountainous, and completely surrounded by South Africa, Lesotho has no important natural resources other than water. Its economy is based on agriculture, light manufacturing, and remittances from laborers employed in South Africa. The great majority of households gain their livelihoods from subsistence farming and migrant labor. Manufacturing depends largely on farm products to support the milling, canning, leather, and jute industries; other industries include textile, clothing, and construction—in particular a major water-improvement project which will permit the sale of water to South Africa.

Tips

- ✔ See the Common cultural characteristics on pp. 228–9.
- ✔ Lesotho is pronounced "Le-SOO-too."
- ✔ Currency control is important, so declare your currency and keep your receipts.
- ✔ Always carry your passport (or a copy) and other papers.
- ✔ Dress conservatively. The safari suit is standard dress.
- ✔ Take a jacket or sweater—it can get chilly in the evening.
- ✔ Tip about 10 percent.

Traps

✗ See the Common cultural characteristics on pp. 228–9.

Mozambique

One of Africa's poorest countries, Mozambique has failed to exploit the economic potential of its sizable agricultural, hydropower, and transportation resources. The economy depends heavily on foreign assistance to keep afloat. The continuation of civil strife has dimmed chances of foreign investment.

Tips

✔ See the Common cultural characteristics on pp. 228–9.
✔ Currency control is important, so declare your currency and keep your receipts.
✔ Always carry your passport (or a copy) and other papers.
✔ Dress conservatively. The safari suit is standard dress.
✔ Take a jacket or sweater—it can get chilly in the evening.
✔ Address people by their titles, not their first names.
✔ There is a Portuguese residual culture.
✔ Tip about 10 percent.

Traps

✗ See the Common cultural characteristics on pp. 228–9.

Namibia

The Namibian economy is heavily dependent on the mining industry to extract and process minerals for export. Mining accounts for almost 25 percent of GDP. Namibia is the fourth largest exporter of non-fuel minerals in Africa and the world's fifth largest producer of uranium. Alluvial diamond deposits are among the richest in the world, making Namibia a primary source for gem-quality diamonds. Namibia also produces large quantities of lead, zinc, tin, silver, and tungsten. More than half the population depends on agriculture (largely subsistence agriculture) for its livelihood.

Tips

✔ See the Common cultural characteristics on pp. 228–9.
✔ Currency control is important, so declare your currency and keep your receipts.
✔ Always carry your passport (or a copy) and other papers.
✔ Dress conservatively. The safari suit is standard dress.
✔ Take a jacket or sweater—it can get chilly in the evening.
✔ Address people by their titles, not their first names.
✔ There is a German residual culture.
✔ Tip about 10 percent.

Traps

✗ See the Common cultural characteristics on pp. 228–9.

South Africa

For years apartheid kept some countries out of South Africa, but political reform and political stability have turned the country into a hot market. Many of the whites—one-seventh of the South African population—enjoy incomes, material comforts, and health and educational standards equal to those of Western Europe. In contrast, most of the remaining population suffer from the poverty patterns of the third world, including unemployment and lack of job skills. The main strength of the economy lies in its rich mineral resources, which provide two-thirds of exports. Economic developments in the future will be driven partly by the changing relations among the various ethnic groups. The shrinking economy in recent years has absorbed less than 10 percent of the more than 300,000 workers entering the labor force annually. Local economists estimate that the economy must grow between 5 percent and 6 percent in real terms annually to absorb all of the new entrants. There are international airports at Johannesburg and Cape Town, and marine ports at all of the major coastal cities. Telecommunications as well as road and rail services are extensive.

Tips

✔ See the Common cultural characteristics on pp. 228–9.
✔ Always carry your passport (or a copy) and other papers.
✔ Dress conservatively.
✔ Although the safari suit is popular during the day time, take a coat and tie—many of the better restaurants require them.
✔ Take a jacket or sweater—it can get chilly in the evening.
✔ Address people by their titles, not their first names.
✔ There are eleven official languages, but English is used for business.
✔ Business hours are Monday through Friday, 8 a.m.–5 p.m.
✔ If South Africans say they will do something "just now" it means they will do it later. If they say they will do it "now now" it means right away.
✔ Tip taxi drivers about 10 percent.
✔ If a service charge is not added, tip about 10–15 percent.
✔ Currency control is important, so declare your currency and keep your receipts.

Traps

✗ See the Common cultural characteristics on pp. 228–9.

Swaziland

The economy is based on subsistence agriculture, which occupies most of the labor force and contributes nearly 25 percent of GDP. Manufacturing, which includes a number of agro-processing factories, accounts for another quarter of GDP. Exports of sugar and forestry products are the main earners of hard currency. Surrounded by South Africa, except for a short border with Mozambique, Swaziland is heavily dependent on South Africa, from which it receives 75 percent of its imports and to which it sends about half of its exports.

Tips

✔ See the Common cultural characteristics on pp. 228–9.
✔ Always carry your passport (or a copy) and other papers.
✔ Dress conservatively. The safari suit is popular.
✔ Take a jacket or sweater—it can get chilly in the evening.
✔ Address people by their titles, not their first names.
✔ Tip about 10–15 percent if a service charge is not added.
✔ Don't tip taxi drivers.
✔ Currency control is important, so declare your currency and keep your receipts.

Traps

✗ See the Common cultural characteristics on pp. 228–9.

Zambia

The economy has been in decline for more than a decade, with falling imports and growing foreign debt. Some of the world's largest copper mines are found in this country; however, economic difficulties stem from a chronically depressed level of copper production. A high inflation rate has also added to Zambia's economic woes in recent years.

Tips

✔ See the Common cultural characteristics on pp. 228–9.

✔ Always carry your passport (or a copy) and other papers.
✔ Do dress conservatively. The safari suit is popular.
✔ Currency control is important, so declare your currency and keep your receipts.
✔ Tipping in hotels is illegal.

Traps

✗ See the Common cultural characteristics on pp. 228–9.

Zimbabwe

Agriculture employs three-quarters of the labor force and supplies almost 40 percent of exports. The manufacturing sector, based on agriculture and mining, produces a variety of goods and contributes 35 percent of GDP. Mining accounts for only 5 percent of both GDP and employment, but supplies of minerals and metals account for about 40 percent of exports.

Tips

✔ See the Common cultural characteristics on pp. 228–9.
✔ Always carry your passport (or a copy) and other papers.
✔ Dress conservatively.
✔ Although the safari suit is popular during the day time, take a coat and tie—many of the better restaurants require them.
✔ Address people by their titles, not their first names.
✔ Business hours are Monday through Friday, 8 a.m.–5 p.m.
✔ If a service charge is not added, tip about 10–15 percent.
✔ Tip taxi drivers about 10 percent.

Traps

✗ See the Common cultural characteristics on pp. 228–9.

■ APPENDICES ■

World commercial holidays

There are hundreds of holidays and other periods when business is discouraged in particular countries; therefore when planning your business travel it is wise to consult the following list of commercial holidays.

Keep in mind that this list of calendar dates, arranged alphabetically by country around the world, is intended only as a working guide. It may vary by several days due to calendar changes year to year, and in the case of the Muslim world by lunar sightings. Before scheduling final business arrangements, corroboration of specific days is suggested. There are Web sites which update world holidays each year. Examples are:

- http://www.pds.mail.com/holidays
- http://www.prninternational.com/holidays
- http://www.worldtime.com

In particular, it is worth noting that January 1 is not an official holiday in every country and that holidays may vary within a country according to the region, or sometimes the religion.

Albania—January 1–2 (New Year's); January 30 (Ramadan/Id al-Fitr); April 12 and 19 (Easter); April 28 (Islamic New Year); May 1 (Workers' Day); November 28 (Independence Day); November 28 (National Day); December 25 (Christmas).

Algeria—January 1 (New Year's); January 30–31 (Id al-Fitr); March 8 (Women's Day); April 8–9 (Id al-Adha); April 28 (Islamic New Year); May 1 (Labor Day); July 5 (Independence Day/Youth Day); July 7 (Muhammad's Birthday); November 1 (Revolution Day).

Angola—January 1 (New Year's); February 4 (Beginning of the Armed Struggle Day); February 24 (Carnival Tuesday); May 1 (Labor Day); September 17 (Heroes' Day); November 11 (Independence Day); December 25 (Christmas).

Argentina—January 1 (New Year's); April 9 (Holy Thursday); April 10 (Good Friday); May 1 (Labor Day); May 25 (Revolución de Mayo); June 13 (Malvinas Day); June 20 (Flag Day); July 9 (Independence Day); August 17 (Day of San Martín); October 12 (Day of the Race); December 8 (Our Lady of Luján); December 25 (Christmas).

Armenia—January 1 (New Year's); January 6 (Christmas—Epiphany); April 7 (Motherhood and Beauty Day); April 24 (Genocide Memorial Day); May 9 (Victory Day); May 28 (Independence Day); September 21 (Referendum Day); December 7 (Earthquake Memorial Day).

Australia—January 1 (New Year's); January 26 (Australia Day); April 10 (Good Friday); April 13 (Easter Monday); April 25 (Anzac Day); June 8 (Queen Elizabeth's Official Birthday); December 25 (Christmas); December 26 (Boxing Day).

Austria—January 1 (New Year's); January 6 (Epiphany); April 12 (Easter); April 13 (Easter Monday); May 1 (Labor Day); May 21 (Ascension Thursday); May 31 (Pentecost); June 1 (Pentecost Monday); June 11 (Corpus Christi); August 15 (Feast of the Assumption); October 26 (National Holiday); November 1 (All Saints' Day); December 8 (Immaculate Conception); December 25 (Christmas); December 26 (St. Stephen's Day).

Azerbaijan—January 1 (New Year's); January 20 (Day of the Martyrs); January 30 (Id al-Fitr); March 8 (Women's Day); March 20–21 (Novruz Bairamay); April 8 (Id al-Adha); May 28 (Republic Day); October 9 (Army and Navy Day); October 18 (National Independence Day); November 17 (Day of National Revival); December 31 (Day of Azeri Solidarity).

Bahrain—January 1 (New Year's); January 30–February 1 (Id al-Fitr); April 28 (Islamic New Year); April 8–10 (Id al-Adha); May 6–7 (Ashura); July 7 (Muhammad's Birthday); December 16 (Independence Day).

Bangladesh—April 8–9 (Id al-Adha); April 14 (Bengali New Year); May 1 (Labor Day); May 7 (Ashura); June 30 (Bank Holiday); July 7 (Muhammad's Birthday); October 1 (Durga Puja); November 7 (Solidarity Day); December 16 (Victory Day); December 25 (Christmas).

Belarus—January 1 (New Year's); January 7 (Christmas); March 8 (Women's Day); March 15 (Constitution Day); April 12 and 19 (Easter); April 13 and 20 (Easter Monday); April 28 (Radounitsa); May 1 (Labor Day); May 9 (Victory Day); July 3 (Independence Day); November 2 (Remembrance Day/All Saints' Day); November 7 (October Revolution Day); December 25 (Christmas).

Belgium—January 1 (New Year's); April 13 (Easter Monday); May 1 (Labor Day); May 21 (Ascension Thursday); June 1 (Pentecost Monday); July 21 (National Day); August 15 (Feast of the Assumption); November 1 (All Saints' Day); November 2 (All Souls' Day); November 11 (Armistice Day); November 15 (Royal Family Day); December 25 (Christmas); December 26 (St. Stephen's Day).

Belize—January 1 (New Year's); March 9 (Baron Bliss Day); May 1 (Labor Day); May 24 (Commonwealth Day); September 10 (National Day/St. George's Day); September 21 (Independence Day); October 12 (Columbus Day); November 19 (Garifuna Settlement Day); December 25 (Christmas); December 26 (Boxing Day).

Benin—January 1 (New Year's); January 30 (Id al-Fitr); April 13 (Easter Monday); May 1 (May Day); May 21 (Ascension Day); June 1 (Pentecost Monday); July 7 (Muhammad's Birthday); August 1 (National Day); August 15 (Feast of the Assumption); November 1 (All Saints' Day); November 30 (National Day); December 25 (Christmas).

Bolivia—January 1 (New Year's); February 23 (Rose Monday); February 24 (Shrove Tuesday); May 1 (Labor Day); June 11 (Corpus Christi); August 6 (Independence Day); November 2 (All Souls' Day); December 25 (Christmas).

Bosnia and Hercegovina—January 1 (New Year's); January 7 (Christmas); January 30 (Id al-Fitr); March 1 (Independence Day); April 8 (Id al-

Adha); April 12 (Easter); April 15 (Army Day); April 19 (Easter); May 1 (Labor Day); May 9 (Liberation Day); November 25 (National Day); December 25 (Christmas).

Botswana—January 1 (New Year's); April 10 (Good Friday); April 11 (Easter Saturday); April 13 (Easter Monday); May 21 (Ascension Thursday); July 1 (Sir Seretse Khama Day); July 20–21 (President's Day); September 30–October 1 (Independence Day); December 25 (Christmas); December 26 (Boxing Day).

Brazil—January 1 (New Year's); April 10 (Good Friday); April 21 (Tiradentes Day); May 4 (Labor Day); June 8 (Corpus Christi); September 7 (Independence Day); October 12 (Nossa Senhora de Aparecida); November 2 (All Souls' Day); November 16 (Republic Day); December 25 (Christmas).

Bulgaria—January 1 (New Year's); March 3 (Liberation Day); April 19 (Easter); April 20 (Easter Monday); May 1 (Labor Day); May 24 (Day of Slavonic Script); September 6 (Unification Day); December 24 (Christmas Eve); December 25 (Christmas).

Burundi—January 1 (New Year's); February 5 (Unity Day); May 1 (Labor Day); May 21 (Ascension Thursday); July 1 (Independence Day); August 15 (Feast of the Assumption); October 13 (Rwagasore Day); November 1 (All Saints' Day); December 25 (Christmas).

Cambodia—January 1 (New Year's); February 12 (Makha Puja); March 8 (International Women's Day); April 13–15 (New Year's); May 1 (International Labor Day); May 10 (Visakha Bochea); June 1 (International Children's Day); June 13 (Ploughing Ceremony); July 9 (Ashala Puja); September 22–24 (Ancestors' Day); September 24 (Constitutional Declaration Day);

October 6–8 (Fête des Eaux); October 6 (Ok Phansa); October 23 (Cambodia Peace Treaty Day); October 30–November 1 (King's Birthday); November 9 (National Independence Day); December 10 (Human Rights Day).

Cameroon—January 1 (New Year's); January 25 (Mt. Cameroon Race); January 30 (Id al-Fitr); February 11 (Youth Day); April 8 (Id al-Adha); April 10 (Good Friday); May 1 (Labor Day); May 20 (National Day); May 21 (Ascension Thursday); July 7 (Muhammad's Birthday); December 25 (Christmas).

Canada—January 1 (New Year's); April 10 (Good Friday); April 13 (Easter Monday); May 18 (Victoria Day); July 1 (Canada Day); September 7 (Labor Day); October 12 (Thanksgiving); November 11 (Remembrance Day/Armistice Day); December 25 (Christmas); December 26 (Boxing Day).

Central African Republic—January 1 (New Year's); March 29 (Boganda Day); April 13 (Easter Monday); May 1 (Labor Day); May 21 (Ascension Thursday); May 31 (Mother's Day); June 1 (Pentecost Monday); August 13 (Independence Proclamation Day); August 15 (Feast of the Assumption); November 1 (All Saints' Day); December 1 (National Day); December 25 (Christmas).

Chad—January 1 (New Year's); January 30 (Ramadan/Id al-Fitr); April 8 (Id al-Adha); April 10 (Good Friday); April 12 (Easter); April 13 (Easter Monday); May 1 (Labor Day); May 25 (Africa Day); May 31 (Pentecost); July 7 (Muhammad's Birthday); August 11 (Independence Day); November 28 (Republic Day); December 1 (Coup Anniversary); December 25 (Christmas).

Chile—January 1 (New Year's); April 9 (Holy Thursday); April 10 (Good

Friday); May 1 (Labor Day); May 21 (Naval Glories Day); June 11 (Corpus Christi); June 29 (St. Peter and Paul); August 15 (Feast of the Assumption); September 18 (Independence Day); September 19 (Armed Forces Day); October 12 (Day of the Race); November 1 (All Saints' Day); December 8 (Immaculate Conception); December 25 (Christmas).

China—January 1–2 (New Year's); January 28–30 (Chinese New Year); May 1 (Labor Day); October 1 (National Day).

Colombia—January 5 (New Year's); January 12 (Epiphany); March 30 (Feast of the Annunciation); April 9 (Holy Thursday); April 10 (Good Friday); May 1 (Labor Day); May 25 (Ascension Thursday); June 15 (Corpus Christi); June 22 (Sacred Heart); June 29 (St. Peter and Paul); July 20 (Independence Day); August 7 (Battle of Boyac); August 17 (Feast of the Assumption); October 12 (Columbus Day); November 2 (All Souls' Day); November 11 (Independence of Cartagena Day); December 14 (Immaculate Conception); December 25 (Christmas).

Congo—January 1 (New Year's); May 1 (Labor Day); June 10 (Day of National Reconciliation); August 15 (Independence Day); November 1 (All Saints' Day); December 25 (Christmas).

Costa Rica—January 1 (New Year's); March 19 (St. Joseph's Day); April 9 (Holy Thursday); April 10 (Good Friday); April 11 (Battle of Rivas); May 1 (Labor Day); June 11 (Corpus Christi); July 25 (Guanacaste Day); June 29 (St. Peter and Paul); August 2 (Virgen de los Angeles, Patron Saint); August 15 (Feast of the Assumption); August 15 (Mother's Day); September 15 (Independence Day); October 12 (Día de la Raza); December 8 (Immaculate Concep-

tion); December 24 (Christmas Eve); December 25 (Christmas); December 31 (New Year's Eve).

Croatia—January 1 (New Year's); January 7 (Christmas); January 19 (Epiphany); January 30 (Ramadan/Id al-Fitr); April 8 (Id al-Adha); April 13 and 20 (Easter Monday); May 1 (Labor Day); May 30 (Statehood Day); June 22 (Antifascist Struggle Commemoration Day); August 5 (Homeland Thanksgiving Day); August 15 (Feast of the Assumption); September 21 (Rosh Hashanah); September 30 (Yom Kippur); November 1 (All Saints' Day); December 25–26 (Christmas).

Cuba—January 1 (Revolution Day); May 1 (Labor Day); July 25–27 (Moncada Anniversary); July 26 (National Revolution Day); October 10 (Beginning of Independence Wars Day).

Czech Republic—January 1 (New Year's); April 12 (Easter); April 13 (Easter Monday); May 1 (Labor Day); May 8 (Day of Liberation from Fascism); July 5 (St. Cyril and Methodius); July 6 (Hus Day); October 28 (Independence Day); December 24 (Christmas Eve); December 25–26 (Christmas).

Democratic Republic of the Congo— January 1 (New Year's); January 4 (Martyrs of Independence); May 1 (Labor Day); May 20 (National Party Day); June 30 (Independence Day); November 17 (Armed Forces Day); December 25 (Christmas).

Denmark—January 1 (New Year's); April 9 (Holy Thursday); April 10 (Good Friday); April 12 (Easter); April 13 (Easter Monday); May 1 (Labor Day); May 8 (Great Prayer Day); May 21 (Ascension Thursday); May 31 (Pentecost); June 1 (Pentecost Monday); June 5 (Constitution Day); December 24 (Christmas Eve); December 25–26 (Christmas).

Ecuador—January 1 (New Year's); April 10 (Good Friday); May 1 (Labor Day); May 24 (Battle of Pichincha); July 25 (Foundation of Guyaquil Day); August 10 (Independence Day); October 9 (Guyaquil Independence Day); November 2 (All Souls' Day); November 3 (Cuenca Independence Day); December 25 (Christmas).

Egypt—January 30 (Id al-Fitr); April 8 (Id al-Adha); April 20 (Sham el Nessim/Easter Monday); April 25 (Liberation of Sinai Day); April 28 (Islamic New Year); May 1 (Labor Day); May 7 (Ashura); June 18 (Night of the Droplet); July 7 (Muhammad's Birthday); July 23 (Anniversary of the 1952 Revolution); October 6 (Armed Forces Day); November 21 (Mawlid Season, for one lunar month).

El Salvador—January 1 (New Year's); January 16 (National Day of Peace); April 9 (Holy Thursday); April 10 (Good Friday); May 1 (Labor Day); May 7 (Soldiers' Day); September 15 (Independence Day); October 12 (Columbus Day); November 2 (Memorial Day/All Saints' Day); November 5 (First Cry of Independence); December 24 (Christmas Eve); December 25 (Christmas); December 31 (New Year's Eve).

Estonia—January 1 (New Year's); February 24 (Independence Day); April 10 (Good Friday); May 1 (Labor Day); June 23 (Victory Day); June 24 (St. John's Day); November 16 (Day of National Rebirth); December 25 (Christmas); December 26 (St. Stephen's Day).

Ethiopia—January 7 (Christmas); January 19 (Epiphany); January 30 (Id al-Fitr); March 2 (Commemoration Day/Adawa Day); April 8 (Id al-Adha); April 17 (Good Friday); April 19 (Easter); May 1 (Labor Day); May 5 (Ethiopian Patriots' Victory Day); May 28 (Overthrow of the Derg Regime); July 7 (Muhammad's Birth-day); September 11 (New Year's); September 27 (Maskal).

Finland—January 1 (New Year's); January 6 (Epiphany); April 10 (Good Friday); April 12 (Easter); April 13 (Easter Monday); April 30 (May Day Eve/Vappu Eve); May 1 (May Day/Vappu); May 21 (Ascension Thursday); June 1 (Pentecost Monday); June 26–27 (Midsummer/Juhannus); November 1 (All Saints' Day); December 6 (Independence Day); December 24 (Christmas Eve); December 25–26 (Christmas).

France—January 1 (New Year's); April 12 (Easter); April 13 (Easter Monday); May 1 (Labor Day); May 8 (Liberation Day); May 21 (Ascension Thursday); May 31 (Pentecost); June 1 (Pentecost Monday); July 14 (Bastille Day); August 15 (Feast of the Assumption); November 1 (All Saints' Day/Toussaint); November 11 (Armistice Day); December 25 (Christmas).

Gabon—January 1 (New Year's); January 30 (Id al-Fitr); April 8 (Id al-Adha/Tabaski); April 13 (Easter Monday); May 1 (Labor Day); June 1 (Pentecost Monday); August 17–18 (Independence Day); November 1 (All Saints' Day); December 25 (Christmas).

Gambia—January 1 (New Year's); January 30 (Id al-Fitr); February 18 (Independence Day); April 8 (Id al-Adha/Tabaski); April 10 (Good Friday); April 12 (Easter); April 28 (Islamic New Year); May 1 (Labor Day); July 7 (Muhammad's Birthday); August 15 (Feast of the Assumption); December 25 (Christmas).

Georgia—January 1 (New Year's); January 7 (Christmas); January 19 (Epiphany); March 13 (Mother's Day); April 19 (Easter); May 26 (Independence Day); August 28 (Feast of the Assumption/Santa Marija); October 14 (Day of Svetitskhovlova); November 23 (St. George of Iberia).

Germany—January 1 (New Year's); January 6 (Epiphany); April 10 (Good Friday); April 12 (Easter); April 13 (Easter Monday); May 1 (Labor Day/May Day); May 21 (Ascension Thursday); May 31 (Pentecost); June 1 (Pentecost Monday); June 11 (Corpus Christi); August 15 (Feast of the Assumption); October 3 (Day of German Unity); November 1 (All Saints' Day); November 15 (National Day of Mourning); November 18 (Buß- und Bettag); November 22 (Totensonntag); December 25–26 (Christmas).

Ghana—January 1 (New Year's); January 30 (Id al-Fitr); March 6 (Independence Day); April 8 (Id al-Adha/Eid il Adel); April 10 (Good Friday); April 13 (Easter Monday); May 1 (May Day); July 1 (Republic Day); December 4 (Farmers' Day); December 25 (Christmas); December 26 (Boxing Day).

Greece—January 1 (New Year's); January 6 (Epiphany); March 2 (Lent Monday); March 25 (Independence Day); March 25 (Feast of the Annunciation); April 17 (Good Friday); April 19 (Easter); April 20 (Easter Monday); May 1 (Labor Day); May 28 (Ascension Thursday); June 8 (Pentecost Monday); August 15 (Feast of the Assumption); September 14 (Holy Cross Day); October 28 (Ochi Day); November 8 (Cretan National Day); December 25 (Christmas); December 26 (St. Stephen's Day).

Guatemala—January 1 (New Year's); April 9 (Holy Thursday); April 10 (Good Friday); May 1 (Labor Day); May 10 (Mother's Day); June 30 (Army Day); August 15 (Feast of the Assumption); September 15 (Independence Day); October 20 (Revolution Day); November 1 (All Saints' Day); December 24 (Christmas Eve); December 25 (Christmas); December 31 (New Year's Eve).

Guinea—January 1 (New Year's); January 30 (Id al-Fitr); April 3 (Military Power); April 8 (Id al-Adha/Tabaski); April 12 (Easter); May 1 (Labor Day); May 25 (Organization of African Unity Day); July 7 (Muhammad's Birthday); October 2 (National Day); December 25 (Christmas).

Honduras—January 1 (New Year's); April 9 (Holy Thursday); April 10 (Good Friday); April 14 (Day of the Americas); May 1 (Labor Day); September 15 (Independence Day); October 3 (Day of Francisco Morazán); October 3 (Soldier Day); October 12 (Discovery Day); October 21 (Armed Forces Day); December 25 (Christmas); December 31 (New Year's Eve).

Hong Kong—January 28–30 (Chinese New Year); April 5 (Ching Ming); April 10 (Good Friday); April 12 (Easter); April 13 (Easter Monday); May 30 (Dragon Boat Festival); July 1 (Half-year Day); August 25 (Liberation Day); September 5 (Mid-autumn Festival); October 18 (Cheung Yeung); December 25 (Christmas); December 26 (Boxing Day). (NB The holidays themselves may change because of the handover to China in 1997.)

Hungary—January 1 (New Year's); March 15 (National Day); April 12 (Easter); April 13 (Easter Monday); May 1 (Labor Day); May 31 (Pentecost); June 1 (Pentecost Monday); August 20 (St. Stephen's Day); October 23 (Uprising Day); December 25–26 (Christmas).

India—January 1 (New Year's); January 26 (Republic Day); January 30 (Id al-Fitr); February 1 (Kumbha Mela/Hardiwar); February 27 (Kumbha Mela/Hardiwar); March 28 (Kumbha Mela/Hardiwar); April 8 (Id al-Adha/Idu'z Zuha); April 9 (Mahavir Jayanti); April 10 (Good

Friday); April 24 (Kumbha Mela/ Hardiwar); May 7 (Ashura/Muharram); May 11 (Buddha Purnima); August 15 (Independence Day); October 1 (Dussera/Vijaya Damami/ Ramlila); October 2 (Gandhi's Birthday); October 19 (Deepavali/ Diwali); November 4 (Guru Nanak's Birthday); December 25 (Christmas).

Indonesia—January 1 (New Year's); January 28 (Chinese New Year); January 30–31 (Id al-Fitr); April 8 (Id al-Adha); April 10 (Good Friday); April 21 (Kartini Day); May 10 (Vaisakha Puja); May 21 (Ascension Thursday); July 7 (Muhammad's Birthday); August 17 (Independence Day); November 17 (Lailat al-Miraj); December 25 (Christmas).

Iran—January 21 (Martyrdom of Ali, First Imam); January 30 (Id al-Fitr); February 11 (Victory Day of the Revolution); February 23 (Martyrdom of the Sixth Imam); March 19 (National Day of Oil); March 21–24 (No Ruz); April 1 (Islamic Republic Day/National Day); April 2 (Sizdah Bidar); April 8 (Id al-Adha); April 16 (Aid al-Ghadir); May 6–7 (Ashura); June 4 (Anniversary of the Death of Imam Khomeini); June 5 (Fifteenth of Khordad); June 16 (Chhelum); June 24 (Anniversary of the Death of the Second Imam); June 24 (Anniversary of the Death of Muhammad); July 7–13 (Week of Unification); July 12 (Muhammad's Birthday); November 3 (Birthday of the First Imam); November 17 (al-Miraj); December 5 (Birthday of the Twelfth Imam).

Iraq—January 1 (New Year's); January 6 (Day of the Army); January 30–February 1 (Id al-Fitr); February 8 (Revolution by the Baath Party); April 8–11 (Id al-Adha); April 28 (Islamic New Year); May 1 (Labor Day); July 7 (Muhammad's Birthday); July 14 (Revolution Day); July 17

(National Day); August 8 (End of the Iran–Iraq War).

Ireland—January 1 (New Year's); March 17 (St. Patrick's Day); April 10 (Good Friday); April 12 (Easter); April 13 (Easter Monday); May 4 (May Holiday); June 1 (June Holiday); August 3 (August Holiday); October 26 (October Holiday); December 25 (Christmas); December 26 (St. Stephen's Day).

Israel—February 11 (Tu B'Shvat/Arbor Day); March 11 (Ta'anis Esther); March 12 and 15 (Purim); April 11–21 (Passover/Pesach); April 23 (Holocaust Remembrance Day); April 30 (Memorial Day); May 1 (Independence Day); May 14 (Lag B'Omer); May 24 (Jerusalem Day); May 31–June 1 (Shavuot); July 12 (Shiva Asar B'Tammuz); September 21–22 (Rosh Hashanah/New Year's); September 23 (Tzom Gedalya); September 30 (Yom Kippur); October 5–11 (Sukkot); October 12–13 (Shmini Atzeret); December 14–21 (Chanukah); December 29 (Asharah B'Tevet).

Italy—January 1 (New Year's); January 6 (Epiphany); April 12 (Easter); April 13 (Easter Monday); April 25 (Liberation Day); May 21 (Ascension Thursday); May 31 (Pentecost); August 15 (Feast of the Assumption); November 1 (All Saints' Day); December 8 (Immaculate Conception); December 25 (Christmas); December 26 (St. Stephen's Day).

Ivory Coast—January 1 (New Year's); January 30 (Ramadan/Id al-Fitr); April 8 (Id al-Adha/Tabaski); April 13 (Easter Monday); May 1 (Labor Day); June 1 (Pentecost Monday); July 7 (Muhammad's Birthday); August 7 (Independence Day); August 15 (Feast of the Assumption); November 1 (All Saints' Day); November 15 (National Peace Day); December 5 (Night of Destiny); December 7

(Anniversary of the Death of President Felix Boigny); December 25 (Christmas).

Japan—January 1 (New Year's); January 15 (Coming of Age Day); February 11 (National Foundation Day); April 29–May 5 (Golden Week); April 29 (Greenery Day); May 3 (Constitution Memorial Day); May 5 (Children's Day); September 15 (Old People's Day); October 10 (Sports Day); November 3 (Culture Day); November 23 (Labor Thanksgiving Day); December 23 (Emperor's Birthday); May 4 (Kokumin Kyusoku-no-Hi).

Jordan—January 1 (New Year's); January 30 (Id al-Fitr); April 8 (Id al-Adha); April 19 (Easter); April 28 (Islamic New Year); May 1 (Labor Day); May 25 (Independence Day); June 10 (Army Day); July 7 (Muhammad's Birthday); August 11 (King's Accession); November 14 (King's Birthday); November 17 (Lailat al-Miraj); December 21 (Ramadan); December 25 (Christmas).

Kazakhastan—January 1 (New Year's); March 8 (Women's Day); March 22 (Navruz); May 1 (Labor Day); August 31 (Constitution Day); October 25 (Independence Day).

Kenya—January 1 (New Year's); April 10 (Good Friday); April 13 (Easter Monday); May 1 (Labor Day); June 1 (Madaraka Day); October 10 (Moi Day); October 20 (Kenyatta Day); December 12 (Jamhuri and Uhuru Day); December 25 (Christmas); December 26 (Boxing Day).

Kuwait—January 1 (New Year's); January 30–February 1 (Id al-Fitr); February 25 (National Day); February 26 (Liberation Day); April 8–10 (Id al-Adha); April 28 (Islamic New Year); July 7 (Muhammad's Birthday); December 25 (Christmas).

Kyrgyz Republic—January 1 (New Year's); January 7 (Christmas); March 8 (Women's Holiday); March 21

(Nooruz); April 8 (Id al-Adha/Kurban Ait); May 1 (Workers' Day); May 5 (Constitution Day); May 9 (Victory Day); May 29 (Armed Forces Day); August 31 (Independence Day); April 8 (Orozo Ait/Id al-Adha).

Latvia—January 1 (New Year's); May 1 (Labor Day); June 24 (St. John's Day); November 18 (Independence Day); December 25 (Christmas); December 26 (St. Stephen's Day).

Lebanon—January 1 (New Year's); January 30–31 (Id al-Fitr); February 9 (St. Maron's Day); April 8–9 (Id al-Adha); April 10 (Good Friday); April 13 (Easter Monday); April 17 (Good Friday); April 20 (Easter Monday); April 28 (Islamic New Year); May 1 (Labor Day); May 7 (Ashura); August 15 (Feast of the Assumption); November 22 (Independence Day); December 25 (Christmas).

Lesotho—January 1 (New Year's); January 20 (Army Day); March 12 (Moeshoeshoe Day); March 21 (Tree Planting Day); April 10 (Good Friday); April 13 (Easter Monday); May 21 (Ascension Thursday); July 17 (King's Birthday); October 4 (Independence Day); October 5 (National Sports Day); December 25 (Christmas); December 26 (Boxing Day).

Liberia—January 1 (New Year's); February 11 (Armed Forces Day); March 10 (Decoration Day); March 15 (J. J. Roberts Day); April 10 (Fast and Prayer Day); May 14 (Unification and Integration Day); July 26 (Independence Day); August 24 (Flag Day); November 5 (Thanksgiving); November 29 (President Tubman's Birthday); December 25 (Christmas).

Libya—January 30 (Id al-Fitr); March 2 (Establishment of the Authority of the People); March 28 (Evacuation Day); April 8 (Id al-Adha); June 11 (Evacuation Day); July 7 (Muhammad's Birthday); July 23 (Egyptian Revolution Day);

September 1 (Day of the Revolution).

Lithuania—January 1 (New Year's); February 16 (Restoration of Lithuanian Statehood); April 12 (Easter); July 6 (Day of Statehood); November 1 (All Saints' Day); December 25 (Christmas); December 26 (St. Stephen's Day).

Malaysia—January 28 (Chinese New Year); January 30–31 (Id al-Fitr); April 5 (Ching Ming); April 8 (Id al-Adha); April 28 (Islamic New Year); May 1 (Labor Day); May 7 (Hari Hol Pahang); May 10 (Vesak Day); May 29 (Dayak Day); May 30–31 (Harvest Festival); June 6 (Head of State's Birthday); July 7 (Muhammad's Birthday); July 23 (Hungry Ghosts); August 31 (National Day/Merdeka Day); October 19 (Deepavali); October 20 (Diwali); December 5 (Lailat al-Bara/Nisfu Night); December 25 (Christmas/Hari Krismas).

Mali—January 1 (New Year's); January 20 (Army Day); January 30 (Id al-Fitr/Ramadan); April 8 (Id al-Adha/Tabaski); May 1 (Working Day); May 25 (Africa Day); July 7 (Muhammad's Birthday); September 22 (Independence Day); November 19 (Army Coup Day); December 25 (Christmas).

Mauritania—January 1 (New Year's); January 30 (Id al-Fitr); April 8 (Id al-Adha); April 28 (Islamic New Year); May 1 (Labor Day); July 7 (Muhammad's Birthday); November 28 (National Day).

Mexico—January 1 (New Year's); January 6 (Epiphany); February 5 (Constitution Day); February 24 (Flag Day); March 21 (Benito Juarez's Birthday); April 9 (Holy Thursday); April 10 (Good Friday); April 12 (Easter); May 1 (Labor Day); May 5 (Cinco de Mayo); September 1 (Presidential Message Day); September 15–16 (Independence Day); October 12 (Columbus Day); Nov-

ember 2 (Day of the Dead); November 20 (Anniversary of the Revolution); December 25 (Christmas).

Moldova—January 1 (New Year's); January 7–8 (Christmas); March 8 (International Women's Day); April 19 (Easter); April 20 (Easter Monday); May 1 (International Labor Day); May 9 (National Heroes' Day); August 27 (Independence Day); August 31 (National Language Day).

Morocco—January 1 (New Year's); January 11 (Independence Manifesto); January 30 (Id al-Fitr/Aid Seghir); March 3 (Throne Day); April 8 (Id al-Adha/Aid el-Kebir); April 28 (Islamic New Year); May 1 (Labor Day); May 23 (National Holiday); July 7 (Muhammad's Birthday); July 9 (Youth Day/King's Birthday); August 14 (Oued Ed-Dahab Day); August 20 (The King and People's Revolution); November 6 (Green March Day); November 18 (Independence Day).

Mozambique—January 1 (New Year's); February 3 (Heroes' Day); April 7 (Women's Day); May 1 (Workers' Day); June 25 (Independence Day); September 7 (Victory Day); September 25 (Armed Forces Day); October 19 (Samora Machel Day); December 25 (Christmas).

Namibia—January 1 (New Year's); March 21 (Independence Day); April 10 (Good Friday); April 13 (Easter Monday); May 1 (May Day/Labor Day); May 4 (Casinga Day); August 26 (Heroes' Day); December 10 (Human Rights Day); December 25 (Christmas); December 26 (Boxing Day/Family Day).

Netherlands—January 1 (New Year's); April 10 (Good Friday); April 12 (Easter); April 13 (Easter Monday); April 30 (Queen's Day); May 4 (Remembrance Day); May 5 (Liberation Day); May 21 (Ascension

Thursday); May 31 (Pentecost); June 1 (Whit Monday); December 25 (Christmas); December 26 (St. Stephen's Day).

New Zealand—January 1–2 (New Year's); February 6 (New Zealand Day); April 10 (Good Friday); April 13 (Easter Monday); April 25 (Anzac Day); June 1 (Queen Elizabeth's Official Birthday); October 26 (Labor Day); December 25 (Christmas); December 26 (Boxing Day).

Nicaragua—January 1 (New Year's); April 9 (Holy Thursday); April 10 (Good Friday); May 1 (Labor Day); July 19 (Triumph of the Revolution); September 14 (San Jacinto Day); September 15 (Independence Day); November 2 (All Souls' Day); December 8 (Immaculate Conception); December 25 (Christmas).

Niger—January 1 (New Year's); January 30 (Id al-Fitr); April 8 (Id al-Adha); April 13 (Easter Monday); July 7 (Muhammad's Birthday); August 3 (Independence Day); December 18 (Proclamation of the Republic Day); December 25 (Christmas).

Nigeria—January 1 (New Year's); January 30 (Id al-Fitr); April 8–9 (Id al-Adha); April 10 (Good Friday); April 13 (Easter Monday); May 1 (May Day); July 7 (Muhammad's Birthday); October 1 (National Day); December 25 (Christmas); December 26 (Boxing Day).

North Korea—April 25 (Armed Forces Day); September 9 (National Day); October 10 (Party Foundation Day); February 16 (Kim Jong-il's Birthday); April 15 (Kim Il-sun's Birthday).

Norway—January 1 (New Year's); April 9 (Holy Thursday); April 10 (Good Friday); April 12 (Easter); April 13 (Easter Monday); May 1 (Labor Day); May 17 (Constitution Day); May 21 (Ascension Thursday); May 31 (Pentecost); June 1 (Pentecost Monday); December 25–26 (Christmas).

Oman—January 30–February 2 (Id al-Fitr); April 8–10 (Id al-Adha); April 28 (Islamic New Year); July 7 (Muhammad's Birthday); November 17 (Lailat al-Miraj); November 18–19 (National Day).

Pakistan—January 30–February 1 (Id al-Fitr); March 23 (Pakistan Day); April 8–10 (Id al-Adha); May 1 (May Day); May 6–7 (Ashura); June 16 (Chhelum); June 30 (Special Bank Holiday); July 7 (Muhammad's Birthday); August 14 (Independence Day); September 6 (Defense of Pakistan Day); September 11 (Jinnah Day); November 9 (Iqbal Day); December 25 (Jinnah's Birthday).

Panama—January 1 (New Year's); January 9 (Martyrs' Day); February 24 (Shrove Tuesday); April 10 (Good Friday); May 1 (Labor Day); October 12 (Columbus Day); November 1 (National Anthem Day); November 2 (All Souls' Day); November 3 (Independence Day); November 4 (Flag Day); November 10 (First Cry of Independence); November 28 (Independence Day); December 8 (Mother's Day); December 20 (Day of Mourning); December 25 (Christmas).

Paraguay—January 1 (New Year's); February 3 (St. Blaise); March 1 (National Heroes' Day); April 9 (Holy Thursday); April 10 (Good Friday); May 1 (Labor Day); May 15 (Independence Day); May 15 (Mother's Day); June 12 (Day of Chaco Peace); August 15 (Foundation of Asunción Day); September 29 (Battle of Boquerón Day); December 8 (Our Lady of Caacupe); December 25 (Christmas).

Peru—January 1 (New Year's); April 9 (Holy Thursday); April 10 (Good Friday); May 1 (Labor Day); June 24 (Countryman's Day); June 29 (St. Peter and Paul); July 28 (Independence Day); August 30 (St. Rose of Lima); September 8 (Immaculate Conception); October 8 (Navy Day/Battle of Angamos); October 9 (Day of National Dignity); November 1 (All Saints' Day); December 8 (Immaculate Conception); December 24 (Christmas Eve); December 25 (Christmas); December 31 (New Year's Eve).

Philippines—January 1 (New Year's); February 26 (People Power Day); April 9 (Day of Valor); April 9 (Holy Thursday); April 10 (Good Friday); May 1 (Labor Day); June 12 (Independence Day); August 30 (Heroes' Day); November 1 (All Saints' Day); November 30 (Bonifacio Day); December 25 (Christmas); December 30 (Rizal Day); December 31 (New Year's Eve).

Poland—January 1 (New Year's); March 8 (Women's Day); April 12 (Easter); April 13 (Easter Monday); May 1 (Workers' Day); May 3 (Constitution Day); May 3 (Our Lady of Czestochowa); June 11 (Corpus Christi); August 15 (Assumption); November 1 (All Saints' Day); November 11 (Independence Day); December 25 (Christmas); December 26 (St. Stephen's Day).

Portugal—January 1 (New Year's); February 24 (Shrove Tuesday); February 25 (Ash Wednesday); April 5 (Palm Sunday); April 10 (Good Friday); April 25 (Liberty Day); May 1 (Labor Day); June 10 (Portugal and Camões Day); June 11 (Corpus Christi); August 15 (Feast of the Assumption); October 5 (Republic Day); November 1 (All Saints' Day); December 1 (Independence Day); December 8 (Immaculate Conception); December 24 (Christmas Eve); December 25 (Christmas).

Romania—January 1-2 (New Year's); April 12 (Easter); April 13 (Easter Monday); May 1 (Labor Day); December 1 (Romanian National Day);

December 25-26 (Christmas).

Russia—January 1-2 (New Year's); January 7 (Christmas); March 8 (Women's Day); May 1-2 (Labor Day); May 9 (Victory Day); June 12 (Independence Day); November 7 (Day of Accord and Reconciliation); November 7 (Anniversary of the October Revolution).

Rwanda—January 1 (New Year's); January 30 (Id al-Fitr); April 7 (Genocide Remembrance Day); May 1 (Labor Day); July 1 (Independence Day); July 4 (Liberation Day); August 15 (Feast of the Assumption); September 25 (Republic Day); December 25 (Christmas).

Saudi Arabia—January 30-February 6 (Id al-Fitr); April 8-22 (Id al-Adha); September 23 (National Day).

Senegal—January 1 (New Year's); January 30 (Id al-Fitr); April 4 (Independence Day); April 8 (Id al-Adha); April 13 (Easter Monday); April 28 (Islamic New Year); May 1 (Labor Day); May 21 (Ascension Thursday); June 1 (Pentecost Monday); July 7 (Muhammad's Birthday).

Sierra Leone—January 1 (New Year's); January 30 (Id al-Fitr); April 8 (Id al-Adha); April 10 (Good Friday); April 13 (Easter Monday); April 27 (Independence Day); April 28 (Islamic New Year); July 7 (Muhammad's Birthday); December 25 (Christmas); December 26 (Boxing Day).

Singapore—January 1 (New Year's); January 28-29 (New Year's); January 30 (Id al-Fitr); April 8 (Id al-Adha); April 10 (Good Friday); May 1 (Labor Day); May 10 (Vesak Day); August 9 (National Day); October 19 (Deepavali); December 25 (Christmas).

Slovakia—January 1 (New Year's); January 1 (Foundation of the Independent Slovak Republic); January 6 (Christmas Eve); April 10 (Good Friday); April 13 (Easter Monday); May 1

(Labor Day); May 8 (Victory Over Fascism Day); July 5 (St. Cyril and Methodius Day); August 29 (Slovak National Uprising Day); September 1 (Constitution Day); September 15 (Our Lady Mary of Sorrows); November 1 (All Saints' Day); December 24 (Christmas Eve); December 25–26 (Christmas).

Slovenia—January 1–2 (New Year's); February 8 (Preseren/Culture Day); April 12 (Easter); April 13 (Easter Monday); April 27 (Insurrection Day); May 1–2 (Labor Day); May 31 (Pentecost); June 25–26 (National Day); August 15 (Feast of the Assumption); October 31 (Reformation Day); November 1 (All Saints' Day); December 25 (Christmas); December 26 (Independence Day).

Somalia—January 1 (New Year's); January 30–31 (Id al-Fitr); April 8–9 (Id al-Adha); May 1 (Labor Day); October 21 (National Day).

South Africa—January 1 (New Year's); April 6 (Founders' Day); April 10 (Good Friday); April 13 (Easter Monday/Family Day); May 1 (Workers' Day); May 21 (Ascension Thursday); May 31 (Republic Day); October 10 (Kruger Day); December 16 (Day of the Vow); December 25 (Christmas); December 26 (Boxing Day/Day of Goodwill).

South Korea—January 1–2 (New Year's); January 28 (Chinese New Year); March 1 (Independence Day); April 5 (Arbor Day); May 3 (Buddha's Birthday); May 5 (Children's Day); June 6 (Memorial Day); July 17 (Constitution Day); August 15 (Liberation and Republic Day); September 5 (Chusok); October 3 (Foundation Day); December 25 (Christmas).

Spain—January 1 (New Year's); April 10 (Good Friday); April 12 (Easter); May 1 (Labor Day); August 15 (Feast of

the Assumption); November 1 (All Saints' Day); December 6 (Constitution Day); December 8 (Immaculate Conception); December 25 (Christmas).

Sri Lanka—January 12 (Full Moon Poya Day); January 14 (Tamil Thai-Pongal Day); January 30 (Id al-Fitr); February 4 (National Day); February 11 (Full Moon Poya Day); February 25 (Maha Shivarathri Day); March 13 (Full Moon Poya Day); April 8 (Id al-Adha); April 10 (Good Friday); April 11 (Full Moon Poya Day); April 13 (Sinhala and Tamil New Year's Eve); April 14 (Sinhala and Tamil New Year's); May 1 (May Day); May 11 (Full Moon Poya Day); May 12 (Day After Vesak Full Moon Poya Day); May 22 (National Heroes' Day); June 10 (Full Moon Poya Day); June 30 (Special Bank Holiday); July 7 (Muhammad's Birthday); July 9 (Full Moon Poya Day); August 8 (Full Moon Poya Day); September 6 (Full Moon Poya Day); September 26 (Bandaranaike Memorial Day); October 5 (Full Moon Poya Day); October 19 (Deepavali Festival Day); November 4 (Full Moon Poya Day); December 3 (Full Moon Poya Day); December 25 (Christmas); December 31 (Special Bank Holiday).

Sudan—January 1 (Independence Day); January 7 (Christmas); January 30 (Id al-Fitr); April 6 (Uprising Day); April 8 (Id al-Adha); April 20 (Sham an-Nassim (Easter Monday); April 28 (Islamic New Year); June 30 (Revolution Day); July 1 (Decentralization Day); July 7 (Muhammad's Birthday); December 25 (Christmas).

Swaziland—January 1 (New Year's); April 10 (Good Friday); April 13 (Easter Monday); April 19 (King's Birthday); April 25 (National Flag Day); May 21 (Ascension Thursday); July 22 (Public Holiday); September 6 (Somhlolo Day); December 25

(Christmas); December 26 (Boxing Day).

Sweden—January 1 (New Year's); January 6 (Epiphany); April 10 (Good Friday); April 12 (Easter); April 13 (Easter Monday); May 1 (May Day); May 21 (Ascension Thursday); May 31 (Pentecost); June 1 (Pentecost Monday); June 26–27 (Midsummer's Day); October 31 (All Saints' Day); December 24 (Christmas Eve); December 25–26 (Christmas).

Switzerland—January 1 (New Year's); April 10 (Good Friday); April 12 (Easter); April 13 (Easter Monday); May 21 (Ascension Thursday); May 31 (Pentecost); June 1 (Pentecost Monday); August 1 (National Day/ Swiss Confederation Day); December 25 (Christmas).

Syria—January 1 (New Year's); January 30–February 1 (Id al-Fitr); March 8 (March 8 Holiday); April 8–11 (Id al-Adha); April 12 (Easter); April 17 (Independence Day); April 19 (Easter); April 28 (Islamic New Year); May 1 (Labor Day); July 7 (Muhammad's Birthday); November 16 (Correction Day); December 25 (Christmas).

Taiwan—January 1–2 (Foundation Day); January 28 (Chinese New Year); February 28 (Two-Twenty-Eight Day); March 12 (Arbor Day); March 17 (Kuanyin's Birthday); March 29 (Youth Day); April 5 (Tomb Sweeping Festival); April 19 (Matsu's Birthday); May 30 (Dragon Boat Festival); July 23 (Hungry Ghosts); August 6 (Hungry Ghosts); September 5 (Mid-autumn Festival/ Moon Cake Day); September 28 (Teachers' Day/Confucius' Birthday); October 10 (Double Tenth Day); October 25 (Restoration Day); October 31 (Chiang Kaishek's Birthday); November 12 (Sun Yat-sen's Birthday); December 25 (Constitution Day).

Tajikistan—January 1 (New Year's); January 30 (Id al-Fitr); March 8 (Women's Day); March 21 (Navruz); May 9 (Victory Day); September 9 (Independence Day).

Tanzania—January 1 (New Year's); January 12 (Zanzibar Revolution Day); January 30 (Id al-Fitr); April 8 (Id al-Adha); April 10 (Good Friday); April 13 (Easter Monday); April 26 (Union Day/National Day); May 1 (Workers' Day); July 7 (Muhammad's Birthday); July 7 (Saba Saba); July 7 (International Trade Fair Day); August 8 (Farmers' Day/Nane Nane); December 9 (Independence Day); December 25 (Christmas); December 26 (Boxing Day).

Thailand—January 1 (New Year's); February 12 (Makha Puja/Makha Bucha); April 6 (Chakri Day); April 13–15 (New Year's); May 1 (Labor Day); May 5 (Coronation Day); May 10 (Visakha Puja/Wisakha Bucha); June 11 (Royal Ploughing Cere-mony); July 1 (Mid-year Day); July 9 (Ashala Puja/Asarnha Bucha); July 10 (Buddhist Lent begins); July 10 (Khao Phansa); August 12 (Queen's Birthday); October 4–6 (Loy Krath-ong); October 6 (Ok Phansa); October 23 (Chulalongkorn Day); December 5 (King's Birthday); December 10 (Constitution Day); December 31 (New Year's Eve).

Togo—January 1 (New Year's); January 13 (Liberation Day); January 24 (Economic Liberation Day); January 30 (Id al-Fitr/Ramadan); April 8 (Id al-Adha/Tabaski); April 27 (Inde-pendence Day); May 1 (Labor Day); May 21 (Ascension Thursday); May 31 (Pentecost); June 21 (Martyrs' Day); August 15 (Feast of the Assumption); November 1 (All Saints' Day); December 25 (Christmas).

Tunisia—January 1 (New Year's); January 30–31 (Id al-Fitr); March 20 (Independence Day); March 21

(Youth Day); April 8–9 (Id al-Adha); April 9 (Martyrs' Day); April 28 (Islamic New Year); May 1 (Labor Day); July 7 (Muhammad's Birthday); July 25 (Republic Day); August 13 (Women's Day); November 7 (November 7 Holiday).

Turkey—January 1 (New Year's); January 30–February 1 (Id al-Fitr/ Seker Bayrami); April 8–11 (Id al-Adha/Kuban Bayrami); April 23 (National Sovereignty Day); April 23 (Children's Day); May 19 (Youth and Sports Day); August 30 (Victory Day); October 29 (Republic Day).

Turkmenistan—January 1 (New Year's); January 12 (Memory Day); February 19 (Flag Day); March 21–22 (November Ruz Bairam); April 8–9 (Id al-Adha); May 9 (Victory Day); May 18 (Revival and Unity Day); October 4 (Earthquake Memorial Day); October 27–28 (Independence Day); December 12 (Neutrality Day).

Uganda—January 1 (New Year's); January 26 (NRM Day); January 30 (Id al-Fitr); March 8 (Women's Day); April 8 (Id al-Adha); April 10 (Good Friday); April 11 (Liberation Day); April 13 (Easter Monday); May 1 (Labor Day); June 3 (Martyrs' Day); June 9 (Heroes' Day); October 9 (Independence Day); December 25 (Christmas); December 26 (Boxing Day).

Ukraine—January 1 (New Year's); January 7 (Christmas); March 8 (International Women's Day); May 1–2 (Labor Day); May 9 (Victory Day); August 24 (Independence Day).

United Arab Emirates—January 1 (New Year's); January 30 (Id al-Fitr); April 8 (Id al-Adha); April 28 (Islamic New Year); May 7 (Ashura); July 7 (Muhammad's Birthday); November 17 (Lailat al-Miraj); December 2–3 (National Day).

United Kingdom—January 1 (New Year's); April 10 (Good Friday); April 13 (Easter Monday); May 4 (May Day); May 25 (Spring Bank Holiday); June 13 (Queen Elizabeth's Official Birthday); August 31 (Summer Bank Holiday); December 25 (Christmas); December 26 (Boxing Day).

United States of America—January 1 (New Year's); January 19 (Martin Luther King's Birthday); February 16 (President's Day); May 25 (Memorial Day); July 4 (Independence Day); September 7 (Labor Day); October 12 (Columbus Day); November 11 (Veterans' Day); November 26 (Thanksgiving Day); December 25 (Christmas).

Uruguay—January 1 (New Year's); January 6 (Day of the Child/Three Kings' Day); February 23–24 (Carnival); April 5–11 (Holy Week); April 19 (Landing of the Thirty-three Patriots); May 1 (Labor Day); May 18 (Battle of Las Piedras Day); June 19 (Artigas Day); July 18 (Constitution Day); August 25 (Independence Day); October 12 (Day of the Race); November 2 (All Souls' Day); December 8 (Beach Day); December 25 (Christmas).

Uzbekistan—January 1 (New Year's); January 30 (Id al-Fitr); March 8 (Women's Day); March 21 (Navruz); April 8 (Id al-Adha); May 1 (Labor Day); May 9 (Victory Day); September 1 (Independence Day); December 10 (Constitution Day).

Venezuela—January 1 (New Year's); February 23 (Rose Monday); February 24 (Shrove Tuesday); April 10 (Good Friday); April 19 (Independence Day); June 24 (Battle of Carabobo Day); July 5 (Independence Day); July 24 (Bolívar's Birthday); October 12 (Day of the Race); December 17 (Bolívar Day); October 12 (María Lionza Day); December 25 (Christmas).

Vietnam—January 28–February 3 (Chinese New Year); February 3

(Foundation of the Vietnamese Communist Party); April 30 (Liberation Day); May 1 (Workers' Day); May 19 (Ho Chi Minh's Birthday); August 6 (Trung Nguyen); September 2 (National Day); September 3 (Anniversary of the Death of Ho Chi Minh).

Yemen—January 1 (New Year's); January 30–February 2 (Id al-Fitr); April 8–12 (Id al-Adha); April 28 (Islamic New Year); May 1 (Labor Day); May 22 (National Day); July 7 (Muhammad's Birthday/Victory Day); September 26 (September Revolution); October 14 (October Revolution); November 17 (Lailat al-Miraj);

November 30 (Evacuation Day).

Zambia—January 1 (New Year's); April 10 (Good Friday); April 11 (Holy Saturday); May 1 (Labor Day); May 25 (Africa Freedom Day); July 6 (Heroes' Day); July 7 (Unity Day); October 24 (Independence Day); December 25 (Christmas).

Zimbabwe—January 1 (New Year's); April 10 (Good Friday); April 11 (Easter Saturday); April 12 (Easter); April 13 (Easter Monday); April 18 (Independence Day); May 25 (Africa Day); August 11 (Heroes' Day); August 12 (Defense Forces Day); December 25 (Christmas); December 26 (Boxing Day).

World currencies

COUNTRY	CURRENCY	SYMBOL
Albania	lek	Lk
Algeria	Algerian dinar	AD
Angola	new kwanza	NKz
Argentina	peso	$a
Armenia	dram	Dram
Australia	Australian dollar	A$
Austria	schilling	Sch
Azerbaijan	manat	Manat
Bahrain	Bahraini dinar	BD
Bangladesh	taka	Tk
Belarus	Belarusian rouble	BRb
Belgium	Belgian franc	Bfr
Belize	Belizean dollar	Bz$
Benin	CFA franc	CFAfr
Bolivia	boliviano	Bs
Bosnia and Hercegovina	Bosnia and Hercegovina dinar	BiHD
Botswana	pula	P
Brazil	real	R
Bulgaria	lev	Lv
Burundi	Burundi franc	Bufr
Cambodia	riel	CR
Cameroon	CFA franc	CFAfr
Canada	Canadian dollar	C$
Central African Republic	CFA franc	CFAfr
Chad	CFA franc	CFAfr
Chile	Chilean peso	Ps
China	renminbi	Rmb
Colombia	Colombian peso	Ps
Congo	CFA franc	CFAfr
Costa Rica	Costa Rican colón	C
Croatia	kuna	HRK
Cuba	Cuban peso	Ps
Czech Republic	koruna	Kc

Democratic Republic of the Congo	nouveau zaïre	NZ
Denmark	Danish krone	Dkr
Ecuador	sucre	Su
Egypt	Egyptian pound	E£
El Salvador	El Salvador colon	c
Estonia	kroon	EEK
Ethiopia	birr	Birr
Finland	markka	FM
France	franc	FFr
Gabon	CFA franc	CFAfr
Gambia	dalasi	D
Georgia	lari	Lari
Germany	D-mark	DM
Ghana	cedi	C
Greece	drachma	Dr
Guatemala	quetzal	Q
Guinea	Guinean franc	Gnf
Honduras	lempira	La
Hong Kong	Hong Kong dollar	HK$
Hungary	forint	Ft
India	Indian rupee	Rs
Indonesia	rupiah	Rp
Iran	rial	IR
Iraq	Iraqi dinar	ID
Ireland	punt	I£
Israel	new Israeli shekel	NIS
Italy	lira	L
Ivory Coast	CFA franc	CFAfr
Japan	yen	¥
Jordan	Jordanian dinar	JD
Kazakhstan	tenge	Tenge
Kenya	Kenya shilling	KSh
Kuwait	Kuwaiti dinar	KD
Kyrgyz Republic	som	Som
Latvia	lat	LVL
Lebanon	Lebanese pound	L£
Lesotho	loti/maloti (plural)	M
Liberia	Liberian dollar	L$
Libya	Libyan dinar	LD
Lithuania	lit	LTL
Malaysia	Malaysian dollar/ringgit	M$
Mali	CFA franc	CFAfr
Mauritania	ouguiya	UM
Mexico	Mexican peso	Ps

Moldova	Moldovan leu (plural lei)	Lei
Morocco	dirham	Dh
Mozambique	metical	MT
Namibia	Namibia dollar	N$
Netherlands	guilder	G
New Zealand	New Zealand dollar	NZ$
Nicaragua	córdoba	C
Niger	CFA franc	CFAfr
Nigeria	naira	N
North Korea	won	Won
Norway	Norwegian krone	Nkr
Oman	Omani rial	OR
Pakistan	Pakistan rupee	PRs
Panama	balboa	B
Paraguay	guaraní	G
Peru	nuevo sol	Ns
Philippines	Philippine peso	P
Poland	zloty (plural zlotys)	Zl
Portugal	escudo	Esc
Romania	leu	Lei
Russia	rouble	Rb
Rwanda	Rwandan franc	Rwfr
Saudi Arabia	Saudi riyal	SR
Senegal	CFA franc	CFAfr
Sierra Leone	leone	Le
Singapore	Singapore dollar	S$
Slovakia	Slovak koruna	Sk
Slovenia	tolar	SIT
Somalia	Somali shilling	SoSh
South Africa	rand	R
South Korea	won	W
Spain	peseta	Pta
Sri Lanka	Sri Lanka rupee	SLRs
Sudan	Sudanese pound/dinar	S£/SD
Swaziland	lilangeni/emalangeni (plural)	E
Sweden	Swedish krona	Skr
Switzerland	Swiss franc	Swfr
Syria	Syrian pound	S£
Taiwan	New Taiwan dollar	NT$
Tajikistan	Tajik rouble	TR
Tanzania	Tanzanian shilling	TSh
Thailand	baht	Bt
Togo	CFA franc	CFAfr
Tunisia	Tunisian dinar	TD
Turkey	Turkish lira	LT

Turkmenistan	manat	Manat
Uganda	new Ugandan shilling	NUSh
Ukraine	hryvnya	HRN
United Arab Emirates	UAE dirham	Dh
United Kingdom	pound/sterling	£
United States of America	dollar	$
Uruguay	Uruguayan new peso	Ps
Uzbekistan	som	Som
Venezuela	bolívar	Bs
Vietnam	dong	D
Yemen	Yemeni riyal	YR
Zambia	kwacha	ZK
Zimbabwe	Zimbabwe dollar	Z$

World business titles

ABBR.	TERM (COUNTRY)	ENGLISH
(A/B)	*aktiebolaget* (Sweden)	joint stock company
(A en P)	*associación en participación* (Spain)	association in participation
(AG)	*Aktiengesellschaft* (Germany)	joint stock company
(A/S)	*aktieselskabet* (Denmark)	joint stock company
(A/S)	*aktieselskapet* (Norway)	joint stock company
(Br.)	*broderna* (Sweden)	brothers
(BR.)	*broderne* (Denmark/Norway)	brothers
(Ca.)	*compagnia* (Italy)	company
(Cia.)	*companhia* (Portugal)	company
(Cia.)	*compañía* (Spain)	company
(Cie.)	*compagnie* (France)	company
(Com.)	*comanditario* (Spain)	partner (silent)
(Com.)	*comisionista* (Spain)	commission merchant
(C por A)	*compañía por acciónes* (Spain)	stock company
(Eftf.)	*efterfolger* (Norway)	successor
(Eftf.)	*eftertradare* (Sweden)	successor
(Etabs.)	*établissements* (France)	establishments
(Fgo.)	*figlio, figli* (Italy)	son, sons
(F-lli.)	*frateli* (Italy)	brothers
(F-llo.)	*fratello* (Italy)	brother
(Flo.)	*filho* (Portugal)	son
(Fls.)	*fils* (France)	son, sons
(Frs.)	*frères* (France)	brothers
(Gebr.)	*Gebrüder* (Germany)	brothers
(Ges.)	*Gesellschaft* (Germany)	company
(GK)	*Gomei Kaisha* (Japan)	unlimited partnership
(GmbH)	*Gesellschaft mit beschränkter Haftung* (Germany)	limited liability company
(Handelsges.)	*Handelsgesellschaft* (Germany)	trading company
(H/B)	*handelsbolaget* (Sweden)	trading company
(Hereds.)	*herederos* (Spain)	heirs
(Hers.)	*héritiers* (France)	heirs

ABBR.	TERM (COUNTRY)	ENGLISH
(Hers.)	*herdeiros* (Portugal)	heirs
(H.mij.)	*handelmaatschappij* (Holland)	trading company
(Hno.)	*hermano* (Spain)	brother
(Hnos.)	*hermanos* (Spain)	brothers
(Hnos. en Liq.)	*hermanos en liquidación* (Spain)	brothers in liquidation
(Ims.)	*irmaos* (Portugal)	brothers
(K.)	*Kaisha* (Japan)	company
(K.)	*kompaniet* (Denmark)	company
(Ka.)	*Kokeisha* (Japan)	successors
(Kai.)	*Kyodai* (Japan)	brothers
(KB)	*kommanditbolaget* (Sweden)	limited silent partnership
(KG)	*Kommanditgesellschaft* (Germany)	limited silent partnership
(KGK)	*Kabushiki Goshi Kaisha* (Japan)	joint stock limited partnership
(KK)	*Kabushiki Kaisha* (Japan)	joint stock company
(KS)	*kommanditselskabet* (Denmark)	limited silent partnership
(Lda.)	*limitada* (Portugal)	limited
(Ltd.)	limited (U.K./U.S.)	
(Ltda.)	*limitada* (Spain)	limited
(Mij.)	*maatschappij* (Holland)	company
(Mn.)	*maison* (France)	house (or store)
(Mo.)	*Musoko* (Japan)	sons
(Nachf.)	*Nachfolger* (Germany)	successor
(N/V)	*namlooze vennootschap* (Holland)	stock company
(O/Y)	*osakeythic* (Finnish)	stock company
(Pty.)	proprietary (S. Africa/Australia)	corporation
(Pty. Ltd.)	proprietary limited (S. Africa/Australia)	limited liability company
(SA)	*sociedade anonima* (Portugal)	corporation
(SA)	*société anonyme* (France)	corporation
(SA)	*società anonima* (Italy)	corporation
(S.Acc.)	*società accomandita* (Italy)	limited partnership
(SA de CV)	*sociedad anónima de capital* (Spain)	stock company of variable capital
(SARL)	*société à responsabilité limitée* (France)	limited liability company
(S en C)	*sociedad en comandita* (Spain)	limited silent partnership
(S en C)	*sociedad en commandita* (Portugal)	limited silent partnership

ABBR.	TERM (COUNTRY)	ENGLISH
(S en C)	*société en commandite* (France)	limited silent partnership
(S en C por A)	*sociedad en comandita por acciónes* (Spain)	limited partnership by shares
(S en NC)	*sociedad en nombre colectivo* (Spain)	collective partnership
(S en NC)	*société en nom collectif* (France)	joint stock company
(Skn)	*Shoyuken* (Japan)	proprietorship
(Sn.)	*Sohn* (Germany)	son
(Soc.)	*sociedad* (Spain)	partnership or company
(Soc.)	*sociedade* (Portugal)	partnership or company
(Soc.)	*société* (France)	partnership or company
(Soc. anon.)	*sociedad anónima* (Spain)	corporation
(SpA)	*società per azioni* (Italy)	stock company
(S por A)	*sociedad por acciónes* (Spain)	stock company
(SPRL)	*société de personnes à responsibilité limitée* (France)	limited liability company
(SPRL)	*sociedad en participación de responsabilidad limitada* (Spain)	firm in participation with limited liability
(Suc.)	*sucursal* (Spain)	branch
(Succs.)	*successeurs* (France)	successors
(Sucs.)	*sucesores* (Spain)	successors
(Sucs.)	*successores* (Portugal)	successors
(Test. de)	*testamentaria de* (Spain)	estate of
(Ver.)	*vereeniging* (Holland)	association
(Zen.)	*zoonen* (Holland)	sons
(Zn.)	*zoon* (Holland)	son

Examples of the use of time as it differs with culture

Time	Mexico	Turkey	Switzerland	Indonesia
5 minutes early	Much too early		Usual	Appreciable
At appointed time	Too early	Lessers, on time	Right on time	Right on time
5 minutes late			Mumbled apology	
10 minutes late	Very punctual	Lessers, late	Apology	
15 minutes late			Insulting	A little late
20 minutes late			Rude	
30 minutes late	Punctual			
45 minutes late			Very insulting	Apology necessary
1 hour late	Slightly late	Equals, on time	Late	Cancellation of appointment
1 hour and 15 minutes late		Equals, late		

References

Acuff, Frank L. (1993) *How to Negotiate with Anyone Anywhere Around the World*, New York: AMACOM.

Adler, Nancy J. (1986a) *International Dimensions of Organizational Behavior: Negotiating with Foreigners*, Boston, MA: Kent Publishing Co.

Adler, Nancy J. (1986b) "Communicating across cultural barriers," *International Dimensions of Organizational Behavior*, Boston, MA: Kent Publishing Co.

Argyle, Michael (1978) "The laws of looking," *Human Nature*, January.

Axtell, Roger E. (ed.) (1990) *Do's and Taboos Around the World*, New York: John Wiley; originally published by the Benjamin Company for Parker Pen.

Blum, M. D. (1988) "Body language in government," *The Silent Speech of Politicians*, San Diego, CA: Brenner Information Group.

Buck, Peter H. (1963) *Vikings of the Pacific*, London: Cambridge University Press.

Bunton, John (1983) *Building Indonesia: A Market Survey*, Construction Press.

Carlson, Clayton H. (1968) *Palauen Phonology*, Honolulu: University Of Hawaii.

Carnegie, D. (1964) *How to Win Friends and Influence People*, New York: Pocket Books.

CIA (1995) *Official Economic Summaries of the World*, Washington, DC: U.S. Government.

Ciulla, J. B. (1991) "Why is business talking about ethics: reflection on foreign conversations," *California Business Review*, fall.

Cormack, Mark H. (1984) *What They Don't Teach You at Harvard Business School*, New York: Bantam Books.

Craig, Betty (1991) *Don't Slurp Your Soup: A Basic Guide to Business Etiquette*, Minnesota: Brighton Publications Inc.

Engholm, Christopher (1991) *When Business East Meets Business West: The Guide to Practice and Protocol in the Pacific Rim*, New York: John Wiley.

Fisher, Glen (1980) "Cross cultural perspective," *International Negotiation*, Chicago: IL: Intercultural Press Inc.

Graham, John (1985) "The influence of culture on business negotiations," *Journal of International Business Studies* XVI(1), pp. 81–96.

Graham, John L. and Herberger, Roy A., Jr. (1987) "Negotiators: don't shoot from the hip," *Towards Internationalism*, pp. 73-87, Cambridge, MA: Newbury House Publishing.

Hall, Edward T. and Hall, Mildred Reed (1971) "The sounds of silence," *Playboy Magazine*, New York.

Hofstede, Geert (1984) "International differences in work-related values," *Culture's Consequences*, Beverly Hills, CA: Sage Publications.

Jankowic, Elena and Bernstein, Sandra (1986) *Behave Yourself: A Working Guide to Business Etiquette*, New York: Prentice-Hall.

Journal of Commerce (various years) "Trading with" series, New York.

Kung, Emil (1987) *The Secret of Switzerland's Economical Success*, Switzerland: Neue Zurcher Zeitung Verlag.

Levine, Robert (1987) "Waiting is a power game," *Psychology Today*, April, pp. 24–33.

Levine, Robert and Wolf, Ellen (1985) "Social time: the heart beat of culture," *Psychology Today*, March, pp. 28–35.

Morain, Genelle G. (1987) "Kinesics and cross-cultural understanding," *Towards Internationalism*, pp. 117–42, Cambridge, MA: Newbury House Publishing.

Neil, A. B. (1984) *Indonesia in Transition*, London: Oxford University Press.

Nelson, Carl A. (1995) *Import/Export: How to Get Started in International Trade*, 2nd edition, McGraw-Hill.

Nitisastro, Widjojo (1982) *Population Trends in Indonesia*, Ithaca, NY: Cornell University Press.

Oberg, K. (1955) "Culture shock," *Anthropologist*, Brazil: Health, Welfare, and Housing Division, USAID.

OECD (1988) "Switzerland," *Economic Surveys 1985/86*, Paris: United Nations.

OECD (1997) "Turkey," *Economic Surveys*, Paris: United Nations.

Pen, J. (1967) *A Primer on International Trade*, New York: Random House.

Rowland, Diana (1985) *Japanese Business Etiquette*, 2nd edition, New York: Warner Books.

Snowden, Barbara (1986) *The Global Edge: How Your Company Can Win in the International Marketplace*, New York: Simon & Schuster.

Stajkovic, A. D. and Luthens, F. (1997) "Business ethics across cultures: a social cognitive model," *Journal of World Business* 32(1), New York.

Student's Atlas of the World (1984) Maspeth, NY: American Map Corporation, Construction Press.

Swiss Chamber of Commerce (1987) *International Trade and Investment* I(1), Switzerland.

U.S. Department of Commerce (various years) *Country Surveys*, Washington, DC.

United Nations (1988) "Mexico," *Almanac*, New York: United Nations.
United Nations (1988) "Turkey," *Almanac*, New York: United Nations.
Yager, Jan (1991) *Business Protocol: How to Survive and Succeed in Business*, New York: John Wiley.

Index